Body ornaments of Malaita, Solomon Islands

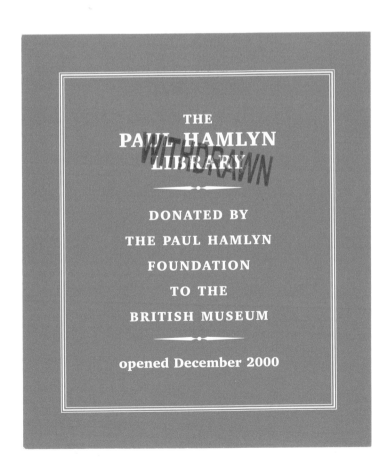

ARTISTIC TRADITIONS IN WORLD CULTURES

Series editor: Jonathan C. H. King

Published with the assistance of The Getty Foundation

Body Ornaments of Malaita, Solomon Islands
Ben Burt, with contributions by David Akin
and support from Michael Kwa'ioloa
ISBN 978-0-7141-2578-7

Nomadic Felts
Stephanie Bunn
ISBN 978-0-7141-2557-2

Tivaivai: The Social Fabric of the Cook Islands
Susanne Küchler and Andrea Eimke
ISBN 978-0-7141-2580-0

This new series looks at art and material culture in rapidly changing societies around the world. Introducing new theoretical perspectives, each title focuses on how objects contribute to social relationships through visual and symbolic values specific to individual peoples.

Ben Burt

Body Ornaments of Malaita, Solomon Islands

With contributions from David Akin
and support from Michael Kwa'ioloa

Drawings by Ben Burt

THE BRITISH MUSEUM PRESS

'Abafola ne'e nau ku saunga'inia fuana
fa'amaurilana na falafala 'i Kwara'ae fa'inia 'i
Malaita. Noa'a nau kusi ngalia ta kabu mani 'ania
folilana.

    Nau ku fata talinga'i ana 'abafola nai'ari fuana
gwaunga'i ngwae 'i na'o kī, ka tasa ana ma'a nau sa
Adriel Rofate'e Toemanu, fa'inia logo fuana talata'i
ngwae ngwae lō ke dao ma'i, ka tasa ana ngela nau
sa Ben Burtte'e.

Sa Ben Burtdoe

Published in 2009 by The British Museum Press
A division of The British Museum Company Ltd
38 Russell Square, London WC1B 3QQ

www.britishmuseum.org

A catalogue record for this book is available from the British Library

ISBN 978-0-7141-2578-7

Editing and project management by Sean Kingston Publishing Services
Typesetting by Sue Bushell

Printed and bound in Hong Kong by Printing Express Ltd

The papers used in this book are natural, renewable and recyclable
products and the manufacturing processes are expected to conform
to the environmental regulations of the country of origin.

Contents

Acknowledgements

Many people have made contributions to this book, from a few words about the ornaments they remembered, possessed or even made, to long interviews and discussions about the culture and history of Kwara'ae and Malaita. Most of these people are Kwara'ae, including my brother and colleague Michael Kwa'ioloa, who has supported my research among his Kwara'ae people for almost thirty years, and my late father Adriel Rofate'e and his family, who began my tuition in Kwara'ae culture from 1979. The greatest single contribution has been made by David Akin, who first arrived on Malaita on the very same day as myself and has since shared the knowledge gained from his research among the neighbouring people of Kwaio. Pierre Maranda has also provided important information from his research in north Malaita. The research in Kwara'ae on which this book is based was approved by the chiefs, the local, provincial and national authorities of Kwara'ae, Malaita and Solomon Islands, and supported by the National Museum of Solomon Islands under its director Lawrence Foana'ota. My colleague Lissant Bolton at the British Museum and editors Teresa Francis and Sean Kingston have helped turn my plans for the book into a reality. Thanks also to my wife Annette Ward for her forbearance.

Grateful thanks to all the following for contributing information or other support for the research:

Abera'u
Abraham Baeanisia
Adriel Rofate'e Toemanu
Aisah Osifera
Alex Rukia
Andrew Gwa'italafa
Arnon Ngwadili
Arumae (1)
Arumae (2)
Barbara Henshall
Betty Afia
Betty Kalianaramo
Betisel Silida'afe
Ben Nongwae
Brian Billy Kali'u'ae
Clement 'Au'au
Clement Maeletege O'ogau
Br. Clifton Henry Diote'e
Sr. Daisy
David Akin
Sir David Attenborough

David Kwa'ite'e
David Rere
Divine Waeti
Sr. Dora
Eric Takila
Ethel Tangoia
Fa'ale'a
Festus Fa'abasua
Filiga Takangwane
Filistas Kokosi
Frank Ete Tu'aisalo
Fr Gabriel Maelasi
Grace Hutton
Graham Baines
Gwaulebe
Hendry Riasi
Hilda Auta
James Abera'u
Jack Mae
Jack Ramosaea
Jephlet Iana

John Gamu
Jimmy Olosua
Johnson Rara
Kay Penstone
Kenneth Roga
Lawrence Foana'ota
Lissant Bolton
Lovea
Maefatafata
Malakai Kailiu
Marcus Bualimae
Mariano Kelesi
Michael Bare
Michael Kwa'ioloa
Michael Ngidu'i
Michael Quinnell
Michael Scott
Moira White
Fr Nelson Safu
Othaniel Aifa'asia
Patterson Suidufu

Paul Oge
Pei-yi Guo
Pierre Maranda
Rhys Richards
Riomea
Samuel Alasa'a
Robert Riria
Samuel Sosoke
Sandra Maxwell
Stephen Binalu
Simon Manifala
Silas Lesimaoma
Silas Sangafanoa
Capt. T.E. Edge-Partington
Rt Revd Terry Brown
Tim Fulbright
Timi Ko'oliu
Tom Russell
Tony Wale
William Kware
Zenas Taoakalo

References and credits

The people listed above include colleagues who have provided unpublished information from their own research. The great majority of this is from Kwaio, all from David Akin and gratefully acknowledged here instead of throughout the text. Other such contributions are those referred to only by surname: as (Pierre) Maranda, (Pei-yi) Guo, (Michael) Scott, (Rhys) Richards, (David) Attenborough, (Graham) Baines, (Tom) Russell, (Tim) Fulbright, (Kay) Penstone and (Kenneth) Roga.

The book's illustrations come from many sources, mostly unpublished. Drawings of artefacts are based on photographs, which are credited to the source of the original images. For artefacts photographed in Malaita this is the name of the photographer, for others it is the name of the museum or other collection holding the artefact or the publication in which it appears. The history of the artefact itself is given separately in its caption, with names of makers or owners where known. When the person's gender is not obvious, the symbol ▲ after the name stands for a man and ● for a woman. Collection catalogue numbers are given where available, with the preface 'BM' for the British Museum and 'SI Museum' for the Solomon Islands National Museum. 'Photo' refers to photographic collections (not necessarily the name of the photographer) as detailed under Photographic Sources.

Chapter 1

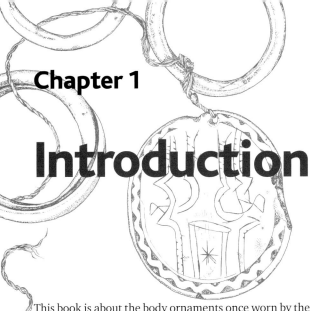

Introduction

This book is about the body ornaments once worn by the Kwara'ae and other peoples of Malaita Island, Solomon Islands. Few such ornaments now remain in Malaita, and the purpose of the book is to describe them for those whose ancestors once owned them, and to explain them for those who can now see them in museums around the world. In bringing together knowledge which the Kwara'ae and their neighbours still retained in the late twentieth century with far-flung objects and images preserved from former times, the book may help us all to appreciate the creativity of the Malaitan people before they exchanged so much of their ancestral culture for that of their European colonizers. To acknowledge the Malaitan perspective, the oraments are illustrated here as part of a broader study of Kwara'ae history and culture. This Introduction outlines the book's approach to the subject.

'Is it art?'

When artefacts such as body ornaments from distinctive local cultures like those of Pacific Islanders are published in books or exhibited in museums and galleries, they are commonly treated as art. This concept, as it has developed within the European tradition during the last few hundred years, makes little sense within a cultural tradition such as Kwara'ae which recognizes no equivalent category. Even within European culture the notion of art is subject to so many different interpretations that it is difficult to use as an analytical concept. Nevertheless, it has helped to define a field of human activity that can be studied comparatively across cultures under the discipline of anthropology. For this purpose art can refer to the human creation of meaningful pattern: physical and mental, visual and aural, as well as intellectual and symbolic, and ultimately cosmological (as suggested by Firth 1992). Such a category, covering most of the cultural activities proclaimed as art by those who regard themselves as artists in the Western sense, and much more besides, brings a certain rigour to the vexed and

tedious question 'Is it art?' Even at this level, looking at artefacts in terms of an essentially European concept begs a lot of questions about how they are regarded in their society of origin, but it does provide a framework within which to examine and describe them.

In treating certain artefact traditions as art, anthropologists have long maintained that they can be analysed as systemic structures, communicating meanings which words cannot adequately convey by using the power of visual symbols to express deep, implicit relationships. This theory allows them, as outsiders, to deduce such meanings from whatever other cultural knowledge local people are able to put into words, but only as understandings which seem to be unconscious or somehow obscured by other levels of meaning. In pioneering this approach for Melanesia in the 1960s, Anthony Forge (1973) demonstrated very plausibly how the Abelam of the Sepik area of Papua New Guinea represent male and female roles as cosmological principles in the paintings and ritual procedures of the men's *tambaran* house, in ways the Abelam themselves appeared unaware of. For Malaita, Daniel de Coppet employed similar structural analysis to describe certain body ornaments from 'Are'are in south Malaita (including the pearlshell crescent pendant and rattan girdle shared by the Kwara'ae) as having open curved or closed circular forms symbolic of the contrasting values of productive social engagement and trapped sterile confinement, respectively. These values he attributed to the opposed but complementary roles of 'peace-master' and 'killer', as they operated within certain cosmological cycles of body, breath and image in 'Are'are society (de Coppet 1995).[1] But however well such structures are demonstrated and even if the reader accepts the particular significances attributed to them, the problem with de Coppet's interpretations is that they would be very difficult for Malaitans to verify, especially if the artefacts do indeed communicate meanings which are beyond words to explain.

A more mundane alternative to such intriguing hypotheses is to look at how participants in the art, those who make, display, view or otherwise use it, assess its value in their own terms. In a study from the Papua New Guinea Highlands, Michael O'Hanlon has focused on the way people judge the appearance of elaborately ornamented dancers as evidence of key moral and political qualities of particular concern in community affairs (O'Hanlon 1989:17–21). Such local criteria may not explain all the structural puzzles which absorb

Plate 1 A north Malaita youth, probably from To'abaita, photographed in the 1900s or 1910s (in the same series as Plates 4 and 22, pages 10 and 28). He wears a single cowrie (*buli*), pattern-bamboos (*fa'i'augwaroa*) and other ornaments in his ears, a small nose-pin (*usuusu*), necklaces of glass beads (*kekefa*) as well as money-beads, and a money-bead bandolier. His *fulu* necklace, of the kind worn by youths and maidens (see page 123) and the pattern-straps (*'abagwaro*) on his arms are of north Malaita style. (Edge-Partington collection, BM Oc,Ca,46.18, photographer unknown)

students of symbolic systems, but they do bring us closer to understanding how people talk about their own cultural traditions which, not being anthropologists, they are less likely to analyse for unconscious meanings.

These contrasting approaches should complement each other, and they share the important requirement that we consider the circumstances in which people participate in their art, that is to say its social context. In the case of body ornaments this means not only how, when and why they are made and worn, but also their other significances and values, whether as exchange valuables, status symbols, ritual objects, or clothing, besides as adornments for the body. Only with this information can we venture to assess how the artistic qualities we perceive in the objects from our own cultural and historical perspective may have been appreciated by the participants in another cultural tradition. Instead of 'Is it art?' we can begin to ask, 'Whatever it is, how does art contribute to what it *does*?'

This is a question addressed by Alfred Gell's theory of art as agency (1998), which treats as art such objects as are attributed the power to act through relationships with and between people. As Lissant Bolton points out (2001), it is when they act, in Gell's terms, through formal qualities created to 'captivate' the observer through mystifying displays of technical virtuosity, that their enhanced power can usefully be distinguished as 'art' from the general properties of material culture. This captivation is ultimately aesthetic, but in a broader sense than that employed in the European tradition of art (and dismissed by Gell). If aesthetic captivation is recognized as operating through the meaningful patterns created not only by visual but also by verbal, musical and bodily actions, it can bring some rigour to the vague European category of 'the arts', which includes everything from literature to dance. If we further extend the notion of meaningful pattern to cognitive and intellectual constructs, as they operate in these culturally shared activities, we have a theory of art which also accounts for the particularly captivating and mystifying properties of symbolic communication. It is the power which these physical and mental patterns lend to the cultural creations which mediate social relationships that makes art a useful analytic category. In these terms, art is not 'art objects' or 'the arts' so much as a pervasive property of cultural production. The artistic processes of creating, perceiving and sharing patterns or structures are ways in which people give cultural and personal meaning to the world of their experience.

Researching Malaita body ornaments

In this book we are dealing with how the people of Kwara'ae and Malaita ornamented their bodies to present themselves to each other and the wider world for the various purposes which might be advanced by the artistic enhancement of personal appearance. The focus is on the artefacts they used as 'body ornaments', which requires some definition in local terms. In the Kwara'ae language, *laungi'a* means ornamented or decorated, and they translate this into Pijin as *flas*, from the English 'flash', meaning smart and showy. So a decorated artefact, house or person is described as *laungi'a*, and the things people use to decorate themselves are *laungi'a nonina*, 'body ornament', or simply *laungi*, 'ornament'.

Some of these things may be described as 'pretty' (*kwanga*) or simply 'looking good' (*lia le'a*), but ornamenting the body was much more than just 'looking good' and most of the artefacts used were more than just ornaments. Depending on the circumstances, the Kwara'ae themselves might treat them as local 'money', as protective charms, heirlooms, status symbols, signs of marriage or maidenhood, or coverings for modesty. It is interesting to note that George Bogesi of Bugotu on Isabel island, in perhaps the only published account on the subject by a Solomon Islander, introduced twelve kinds of ornaments worn by his own people as 'types of Bugotu currency' (1948:228–9). Treating a selection of artefacts as 'body ornaments' is one way of describing how the Kwara'ae regarded them, but it is not the only way of looking at them from a Kwara'ae point of view, any more than 'art' is the only European or anthropological perspective. But it will help explain how and why the Kwara'ae ornamented their bodies, using artefacts with artistic qualities that can also attract outsiders into pursuing insights into their culture and history.

Unfortunately Kwara'ae is by no means the best area of Malaita in which to document body ornaments. Most Kwara'ae abandoned them in favour of foreign clothing several generations ago, and neither symbolic meanings nor artistic judgements have been much in evidence since. The information on Kwara'ae presented here was gathered mostly from recollections of former times, in the course of research since 1979 into other aspects of Kwara'ae culture and history, including conversion from their ancestral religion to Christianity (Burt 1994a), land tenure (Burt 1994b), forest resources (Kwa'ioloa and Burt 2001) and oral history (Burt and Kwa'ioloa 2001). By photographing such ornaments as people still possessed, noting comments on photographs of museum collections and asking for descriptions of ornaments no longer to be seen, an inventory of named ornaments gradually emerged, with accounts of who wore what ornaments, when and why. Some people were able to describe how certain ornaments were once made and others could list things they or their parents had worn when they ornamented themselves for special occasions long ago.

Most of this research is now a generation old and many of the elders who contributed to it have since died and taken much knowledge with them. But their recollections can be compared with the traditions of other parts of Malaita, where body ornaments continued to be made and worn more recently, or were documented much earlier. The most important source is David Akin's research among the Kwaio, immediately to the south, who have retained or revived much that the Kwara'ae have lost. For north Malaita Pierre Maranda has a documented collection from the Lau and their inland neighbours, and for south Malaita there is Ivens' much earlier study of the Sa'a (Ivens 1918, 1927, 1929).[2] There are also many photographs dating back to the late nineteenth and early twentieth centuries which show people of particular places wearing ornaments which can be recognized from the recollections of the late twentieth century. Together these sources helped identify artefacts in museum collections, some of which can stand as illustrations of ornaments which may not otherwise survive.

What the Kwara'ae experience does reveal are the reasons why the transformation of Malaitan society, particularly conversion to Christianity, had such a devastating effect upon their tradition of body ornaments. This itself helps explain the significance of ornaments as society changed in response to colonial hegemony in the course of the twentieth century, and it points the way to research which is more attentive to history and responsive to local concerns. Issues around the role of artefacts in the cultural politics of maintaining and recreating social identities were tackled by the Pacific Arts Association in 1999, including the role of museums (Welsch 2002). A more rigorous and critical approach to the processes of collection, curation and exhibition is now focusing attention on the ongoing transformation of Pacific Islands artefact traditions, on the way the artefacts are interpreted and on the inadequate documentation on which such interpretations are often based. In attempting to salvage the identities of artefacts by field research, often from fading memories of former times, colonial museums are building new relationships with the communities from which their collections derive.

Malaita ornaments and foreign museums

This book comes out of the British Museum at a time when it is reaching out to Melanesia through a major research project into its collections, in collaboration with local communities.[3] The British Museum has a large collection of Solomon Islands artefacts which, like those in so many museums in Britain and other Western countries, are mostly documented only with the names of the foreigners who owned them after they left the islands generations ago. In those times, 'Malaita' or even 'Solomon Islands' were relatively precise provenances, still being mapped and colonized. In many respects the detailed history of such artefacts was of less interest than their contribution to Western popular fantasies of 'others', especially of peoples defined as 'primitive' to contrast with the 'civilization' of Europe, which helped to justify the colonial enterprise.

The British Museum *Handbook to the Ethnographical Collections* illustrates the attitudes prevailing when most of its Solomon Islands artefacts were collected in the late nineteenth and early twentieth centuries. It expects 'ethnographical studies' of exotic cultures to explain 'how our own forefathers passed from savagery to civilization'. They will ease 'the administration of native territories' and reveal 'possible advantages which merchants trading amongst primitive peoples might gain by studying their material wants and their artistic predilections' (Joyce 1910:41–3). Solomon Islanders, and particularly Malaitans ('the island most notorious for the bloodthirstiness of its savages', according to one early colonial observer; Rannie 1912:177), were among those who bore the burden of representing the primitive lower stages of social evolution. This allowed Europeans to imagine themselves as having reached the heights of civilization, from which they could both assert their cultural superiority and question their own values by variously denigrating or romanticizing those they thought of as closer to nature. Among other things, Solomon Islanders were attributed the kind of timeless traditional culture which produces what collectors sensitive

to the derogatory connotations of 'primitive' now call 'tribal', 'ethnographic' or 'ethnic' art. This puts them among 'the people without history' (Wolf 1983), whom too many Westerners still find easier to suspend in the 'ethnographic present' than to describe in terms of the transforming historical relationships through which they and the 'others' have come to know each other.

These attitudes are still revealed in the way Solomon Islands artefacts are treated as art. As David Akin explains, specialists in the subject tend to regard artefacts as 'traditional', implying 'authentic', if they were produced before 'contact' with Europeans, or at least for local purposes, but they lose both authenticity and artistic value when produced for outsiders, as supposedly revealed in the superior quality of old museum collections (Akin 1987). As Akin's own research and cultural development work in Malaita demonstrates, none of these propositions are true, for artefacts such as ornaments have always been sold abroad, were adapted for European markets at the earliest opportunity, and have always varied greatly in artistic and technical quality. Such attitudes to Malaitan artefacts confirm Shelly Errington's account of how the category of art expanded beyond its original application within a European tradition to legitimate the collection and sale of exotic artefacts. If artefacts can be authenticated as having been made for the purposes of unchanging traditional societies, their scarcity, artistic importance and commercial value is ensured by the inevitable disappearance of such conditions under the corrupting influences of modernization and commercialization, which she characterizes in her ironic title as *The Death of Authentic Primitive Art* (Errington 1998).

Museums often tacitly endorse these attitudes when they display or publish such artefacts as art, as if the audience needed a minimum of historical and cultural background to appreciate their significance or value. In fetishizing artefacts in this way they neglect not only contemporary knowledge of their societies of origin but also the resources of photographic archives and libraries, which provide opportunities to enrich cultural and historical understanding. As travel, migration and educational opportunities increasingly allow the distant peoples represented in Western museums to come closer, new challenges arise. These can seem threatening when the politics of emerging identities are involved, when museum collections are claimed back and when cultural 'insiders' turn the tables on the 'outsiders' by inverting colonial patterns of discrimination, but they are a timely reminder that the beneficiaries of colonialism have continuing obligations to those from whom their cultural riches derive. Museums can justly claim to have preserved artefacts which, like Solomon Islands ornaments, were usually freely sold, given or even thrown away by their original owners in pursuit of new ways of life. The question for the early twenty-first century is how can we use them to benefit not only ourselves but also those from whom we obtained them on the unequal terms of colonialism?

Most of the people museum collections are displayed to, as well as those they represent, see artefacts as cultural and educational resources, the former for learning about other people's culture and history, the latter for rediscovering their own. In the Pacific Islands, where both categories include the same people, there is more interest in 'cultural centres' concerned with the reproduction of culture rather than simply the preservation and display of artefacts. At a local level, the Kwaio Cultural Centre on Malaita in the 1980s successfully promoted education in both local and European culture, including the revival and spread of many artefact skills (Akin 1994). The Solomon Islands National Museum has done its best to support such efforts over many years, but with little assistance from the government. At a regional level, the Vanuatu Cultural Centre is a more inspiring example of how relationships between local communities and foreign researchers can be organized so as to benefit both parties and to promote local cultural development (Bolton 2003). Some overseas museums, including the British Museum, have supported such enterprises, and have returned information and images to their home countries for the benefit of national institutions and local people. In doing so they recognize that culture is what people learn and create in society, rather than merely relics preserved to be studied by academics as 'art'.

The issue is not so much where artefacts are held as how they are used and what they can do. Claims for the repatriation of museum collections by Pacific Islanders have not usually been as forceful as those from the colonized peoples who have gained political influence as indigenous minorities in wealthy societies such as New Zealand, Australia and North America. Even so, and contrary to the expectations of Solomon Islanders who sold their body ornaments for tobacco or coins generations ago, artefacts which survive in colonial museums may still inspire the kind of local cultural creativity that Islanders might use to maintain some self-determination in a world ever more subject to the cultural hegemony of the West. This book is intended to assist them.

In Chapter 2 the book considers the disappearance of ornaments from Kwara'ae as part of the history of colonial relationships between Malaitans and Whitemen, as they call Europeans. These began long before their island became part of the British Solomon Islands Protectorate in 1893 and have continued since Solomon Islands became an independent state in 1978. They are relationships of economic, religious and political domination within attempts to impose a Whiteman hegemony, even as Malaitans struggled to retain their political and cultural autonomy, as they have never ceased to do. This is the historical context for Kwara'ae recollections of what body ornaments meant to them when they were still commonly worn, enhancing persons and occasions as symbols of status and power under a traditional social order which was gradually discredited and transformed in the course of the twentieth century.

Describing the ornaments themselves requires an account of how they were made or obtained to wear and how they have been documented and preserved. Chapter 3 considers materials, technologies and trade relationships, which also changed or disappeared during this time. The acquisition of ornaments linked local communities throughout Malaita and Solomon Islands in networks mediated by local 'money' of shell beads and dolphin teeth, themselves used as body ornaments. Whitemen played their part in this trade, particularly by providing foreign goods in exchange for labour and the 'curios' which eventually became museum collections.

Having described this background, Chapter 4 goes on to catalogue the ornaments, illustrating their appearance, describing how they were worn and comparing Kwara'ae traditions with other parts of Malaita and Solomon Islands. This is the most comprensive catalogue of Solomon Islands ornaments yet published, and it features wherever possible objects with known histories and provenances.

Perhaps this reminder of their cultural heritage will encourage Malaitans to reverse some of the decisions made by their ancestors to abandon or destroy such artefacts for reasons which seem less compelling to their descendants, who are now well enough schooled in Whiteman culture to see its limitations as well as its benefits. Of course they may prefer to leave the ornaments of their ancestors in museums or books, or even to forget them altogether. But although such attitudes towards the past change with the circumstances of each generation, in Solomon Islands the conviction remains that the benefits Europeans have gained from the colonial relationship, including possession of their artefacts and cultural knowledge, require some return. This book is offered to the people of Kwara'ae and Malaita in the hope that they will find some use for it as a record of former times and a cultural resource for times to come.

A note on orthography
Malaita orthography follows the conventions of our Kwara'ae language books (Burt and Kwa'ioloa 2001, Kwa'ioloa and Burt 2001), derived from Simons (1977). The sign ' shows a glottal stop. Macrons show long vowels. Double vowels result from compound words. Compound words are hyphenated in English translation. Hence: *fataābu*, compounded of fata = speak and *ābu* = tabu and translated as tabu-speaker.

Notes
1   The terms 'body', 'breath' and 'image' are used here not as in de Coppet's text but as explained in his endnote 1.
2   Because Ivens' work deals also with the small island of Ulawa, which is culturally similar to south Malaita, it is sometimes unclear whether he is, strictly speaking, describing Malaita.
3   Melanesian Art: Objects, Narratives and Indigenous Owners is a research project of the British Museum Department of Africa, Oceania and the Americas with Goldsmith's College that commenced in 2005.

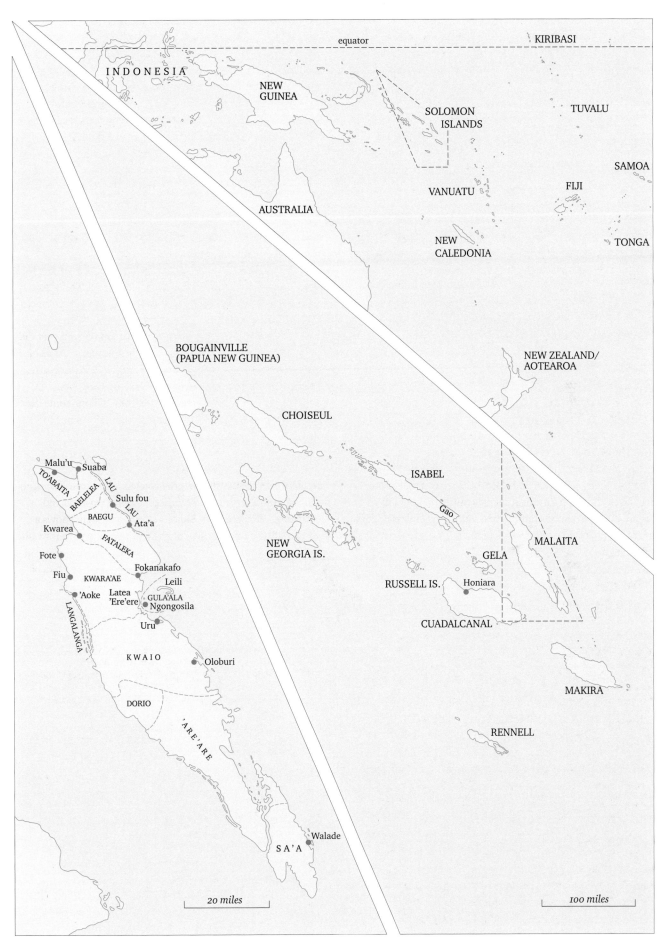

Map The southwest Pacific, the main islands of Solomon Islands, and Malaita with its language groups and places mentioned in the text.

Chapter 2
Wearing and discarding ornaments

Formerly, in 'traditional times' (*kaida'i ana falafala*), Malaitans dressed in very little, but on special occasions they ornamented their bodies with fine and valuable objects. They put on bands and combs patterned with bright red and yellow fibres, rings, pins and pendants of glistening white shell and pearlshell, intricately carved plaques and rings of turtleshell, strings and straps of valuable red, white and black money-beads and dolphin teeth, and coloured and scented leaves. By such means they presented themselves as youths and maidens, husbands and wives, men of possessions, priests, warriors, and worthy heirs to the ancestral ghosts whose festivals they dressed to celebrate.

When the first remembered Europeans arrived in the early 1870s to steal men away for the plantations of Fiji and Queensland, they brought them back with new possessions which quickly began to change Malaitan styles of dress and ornament. Historical accounts and photographs illustrate the development of clothing and the slow demise of old-style ornaments from that time to the present day. As the Kwara'ae reckon it, this is only five or six generations of a history that reaches back twenty-five generations or more to their ancestors' first settlement on the island of Malaita. It has been a time of massive social and cultural transformation, yet in the late twentieth century, when most of this book was researched, it was still possible to see styles of dress and ornament from all periods of this history among relatives and neighbours within the same district of east Kwara'ae. The uneven colonial development of Malaita had created a pluralist society, still united by ties of common descent and identity, but including radicals and conservatives, Christians and ancestor-worshippers, rich and poor, the few who understood the ornaments of former times and the many who could hardly recognize them.

In the 1870s, before these differences arose, Kwara'ae men and children went naked, while women wore no more than waistbands and aprons. When everyone, from the most important man to the humblest maiden, had to spend most of their time labouring in their gardens, building houses, making things, preparing food and raising children and pigs, valuable fragile ornaments were not for everyday wear. People might wear simple earrings and armbands, as old photos show, but other things were stored away safely. Nose-pins and patterned ear-sticks were kept in bamboo tubes with a leaf stopper or bamboo lid, and strings of money-beads, also worn as ornaments, were wrapped in cloth and concealed in the fuel rack over the fire, to stay dry and bright. Men kept important ornaments such as girdles and pendants in their male-only sanctum (*fera*), with weapons and ancestral relics which had to be protected from contact with women, and they might carry valuable pendants and money-bead bands and straps in their personal bags to protect them from playful children and thieves. But day-to-day, as Samuel Alasa'a recalled from his youth at the end of the nineteenth century: 'Women pounded the bark of trees and dressed in it. We men just stayed naked, we didn't dress in anything. If I dressed then it was just tree leaves. I just concealed my front' (Burt and Kwa'ioloa 2001:98).

A man might stick leaves under his belt or girdle for modesty, for ornament or to ward off malicious magic on public occasions, or as a sign of respect when visiting his in-laws. A maiden (*kini sari'i*) wore only a red band-strap (*'aba obi*) from the time her breasts began to grow, and she might continue to wear it after marriage. As a wife (*kini 'afe*), passing from the care of her parents to her husband in return for brideprice, she would receive from her in-laws a great-*susuru* (*gwa'isusuru*) strap of black vine and white beads and a cloth apron to conceal her front.

In the late twentieth century, when the most prosperous Malaitans were clothed like Australians, the few still following their ancestral religion kept to this style of minimal dress in the privacy of their own homes and gardens, mainly in more conservative districts of north Malaita, Kwaio and 'Are'are (see photos in Keesing 1983 and de Coppet and Zemp 1978). Malaitans have now been familiar with these contrasting standards of dress and modesty for several generations, and aware of local alternatives for much longer. As inland peoples (*to'a tolo*) of the forested hills, Kwara'ae and most other Malaitans seldom travelled overseas, except as migrant

Plate 2 A man of Fiu, an early Christian settlement on the coast of west Kwara'ae, photographed by John Watt Beattie in 1906. He wears a big patterned comb (*kafa gwaroa doe*) with a tuft of leaf-shreds and a feather, patterned-bamboos (*fa'i'augwaroa*) and earring-clusters (*barutege*) in his ears and a nose-pin (*usuusu*). His necklace is of Whiteman glass beads (*kekefa ara'ikwao*), with pig teeth (*lifa gwata*) and a tangle-bag (*ngwa'ifirua*) at his back, he has conus (*fa'ikome*) rings on his arms, conus-rattles (*ketekome*) on his legs, and a colourful calico lavalava supported by a Whiteman strap (*'abatarafa*). According to Beattie, he was guarding the community against attack by anti-Christian neigbours. (BM Oc,B114.123)

Plate 3 This photograph, typical of many published by studios in Fiji from the late 1870s onwards, illustrates how the migrant workers took advantage of new cheap materials to make more plentiful and elaborate ornaments than they could have worn at home.

These men all wear glass-bead pattern-straps (*'abagwaro kekefa*), two having north Malaita designs on the upper arms and wrist-bands as worn in south Malaita. They all have glass-bead belts (*fo'o'aba*) with related zigzag and lozenge designs, and glass-bead breast-fastenings (*torisusu*). One has a cowrie-row (*talabuli*) browband and a plume of feathers (*eloelo*), the others separate cowries (*fa'ibuli*) in their hair. Two have turtleshell (*ta'ota'ofunu*) ear pendants and conus-rattles (*ketekome*) at the knees. The club is of the Malaitan *afui* type. (BM Oc,B36.11)

labourers from the 1870s onwards, but their neighbours, the coastal sea peoples (*to'a asi*), were great voyagers who carried ornaments and other valuables, as well as styles of dress, around and between islands. Some seem to have adopted the men's loincloth from elsewhere in Solomon Islands in the mid-nineteenth century, as well as the women's skirt of shredded bark. But even the sea peoples' experience of other cultures could hardly have prepared them for the overseas culture (*falafala 'a'e asi*) and styles of dress brought by the first remembered 'Whitemen' (*Ara'ikwao*), as they came to be called, who arrived off the coasts of Malaita in 1871.

The challenge of foreign ways

The Kwara'ae's first experience of foreign clothing is now recalled in jokes about the naivety of ancestors who tried to eat the boots of Whitemen they had killed, thinking they were part of their bodies. A more plausible story recounted by Andrew Gwa'italafa tells of the first man to return to east Kwara'ae after being stolen away to work overseas: 'When Misuta landed at Kwakwaru, my word, the people were very very surprised. … So the story sped up inland, via the market, of how Misuta had come back wearing a jacket and trousers, talking in a different language and things like that, wearing big boots and everything' (Burt and Kwa'ioloa 2001:87). When the next ship came, Misuta persuaded others to join it voluntarily. So began the change in fashions of dress, as more and more men, and a few women, recruited to work overseas for adventure and the marvellous new goods the Whitemen could supply.

The recruiters themselves provide some of the earliest written accounts of the old ornaments which their business began to displace. Douglas Rannie, a British government agent supervising the recruiting ship *Flora*, described a meeting with east Kwara'ae people in 1886:

> Taking our English-speaking visitors with us the next day we went with the boats as arranged to the Quakwaroo River,[1] and were met by a large crowd of natives—men, women, and children—and received a friendly welcome. None of them boasted of any clothing, but their hair was carefully combed and groomed in most cases, and adorned with handsome combs from which depended bright red tassels of dyed grasses. Many of them also wore gay plumes formed from the many-coloured feathers of various birds; while others wore the long feathers of eagles and the large fish-hawks. Besides shell bangles on their arms the men wore strings of small white cowrie shells bound round their foreheads. All the men were armed with bows and arrows, spears, clubs, and the ubiquitous long-handled tomahawk. (1912:180)

As Rannie described when the ship reached north Malaita, recruits would leave such things behind: 'Before coming on board they denuded themselves of all their arms and ornaments, bracelets, garters, beads, and feathers, and these they were most particular in assigning to absent friends' (1912:186).[2] In their place they received clothing. As a journalist aboard the recruiting ship *Helena* reported in 1892, Queensland ships issued their recruits with 'a yard of calico' to wear as a lavalava, and were obliged by law to provide: 'Males—One flannel shirt, one pair serge trousers, one double blanket. Females—One winsey dress, one flannel petticoat, and one double blanket' (Melvin 1977:57–8).

Photographs, some dating back to the 1870s, show that, once they had arrived in Fiji and Queensland, Malaitans made themselves new ornaments. The men are posed in belts, pattern-straps on the arms and breast-fastening of glass beads, presumably bought with their wages, with cowrie browbands and extra-large turtleshell ear pendants. This fashion for glass-bead ornaments was also taken up in Malaita, where beads were among the goods paid to relatives of the recruits (Rannie 1912:181), and they were later sold by Chinese traders.[3]

The implications of foreign ways became clearer when migrant workers began to come home in the 1890s with not only foreign goods but also a new religion, generally known as 'school' (*sukulu*) after the Christian classes they had attended on the plantations. While most soon abandoned it, some made it their business to challenge the ghosts of the ancestors whose power underlay community health, prosperity, strength and authority under the traditional religion. As dissidents in their home communities, these Christians were supported by visiting Whitemen and women, who began to establish mission stations around the coasts of Malaita in the 1900s. Among other things, their religion required them to cover their nakedness in the fashion of the Whiteman, usually with cotton calico, which gave its name to clothing (*kaliko*) in Solomons Pijin and the languages of Malaita.

In the 1900s the steady return of migrant workers became a flood as Queensland implemented a policy of keeping Australia 'white' by deporting Pacific Islanders, many of whom would have preferred to remain abroad and follow the new lifestyle and religion they had adopted. The Revd Arthur Hopkins of the Anglican Melanesian Mission, its first resident missionary on Malaita (or Mala, as it was often called), witnessed their arrival and commented on how a man would come ashore:

> So he donned all his best clothes, white drill suit, sun helmet, gay socks, probably patent leather shoes, an umbrella, and sometimes even a bicycle, at that time quite useless on Mala. He would also have a box full of all sorts of things. However, the glory was short lived. The contents of the box, even the clothes he was wearing, would be seized and divided among the members of his tribe, which it had taken years of work to earn. (*Southern Cross Log*, Oct. 1940:113)[4]

This distribution of foreign goods was usually more voluntary than Hopkins implied, a way of repaying or creating debts to the relatives whose support the man depended on. But Hopkins illustrates the value placed on clothing as a symbol of the Whiteman's world, a source of wealth and power which has continued to fascinate Malaitans ever since.

This is not to say that all returning migrants were committed to the foreign way of life. While Christian converts and the foreign missionaries who supported them made clothing into a symbol of their religion, ornamented nakedness came to distinguish those who avoided or actively opposed them. In an account of his experiences from 1902 as a missionary in Lau, north Malaita, Hopkins revealed both Malaitan and Whiteman attitudes to local and foreign dress, and the tension between ghost-worshippers and Christians:

> My first contact was naturally with the sea people. … the men wore a waist cloth of calico, a few being in shirt and trousers. I soon

Plate 4 These men, photographed probably in To'abaita, north Malaita, in the 1900s or 1910s (in the same series as Plates 3 and 22, pages viii and 28), would be the kind who so annoyed Revd Hopkins in Lau, displaying their fine ornaments as well as imported axe and gun, lavalavas and vest. They both have serrated-conus (*komegiria*) rings and pattern-bamboo (*fa'i'augwaroa*) ear ornaments, long nose-pins (*usuusu*), conus (*fa'ikome*) rings on their arms, necklaces (*'alu'alu*) of glass beads, girdles (*fo'osae*) of the coiled type, as well as leather straps (*'abatarafa*), one with a whistle hanging from the buckle. The man on the left also seems to have a large conus (*kome*) ring hanging from his ear and an enclosed-strap (*'ababanibani*) glass-bead armband holding his pipe. The other has cowries (*buli*), a hornbill feather and a shell-disk (*sa'ela'o*) on his head, north Malaita-style pattern-straps (*'abagwaro*) on his arms, and a conus-rattle (*ketekome*) on his leg. (Edge-Partington album BM Oc,Ca,46.17)

noticed that there were some big noisy fellows with ornamented combs stuck into their upstanding hair, a long bone [tridacna shell pin] through the nose, a ring hanging over the mouth, pendants in their ears, and many anklets and bracelets of coloured dried grass [orchid stem and coconut cuticle] —looking very like the typical savage of imagination—these men were the flash fellows who had returned from Queensland, and come home to swagger and brag, full of self-importance and jibes against the old tribal constraints. The quiet-faced smiling men in shirt and trousers, with close cut hair and no ornaments, were the Christians who had appealed for means of grace. (*SCL*, Dec. 1939:185)

The first Christians lived in small communities on the coast, constantly harassed by their ghost-worshipping neighbours, but their situation soon changed. By Hopkins' time they were being supported at a distance by watchful government officials based in the colonial capital of Tulagi on nearby Gela, who directed warships around Malaita to retaliate for attacks on Whitemen and their allies. In Kwara'ae there were small Christian 'school' settlements on both east and west coasts by 1910, with a mission station on Ngongosila island off the east coast and a struggling government outpost at 'Aoke in the west. By 1920 the government had gained military and political control of Kwara'ae, undermining the authority of local leaders and their ancestral ghosts. By 1930 followers of the ancestral religion were on the defensive against popular Christian movements which were spreading inland. By 1940 the majority of Kwara'ae were Christians.

Christianity and clothing

Malaitan Christians, influenced by their Whiteman teachers, took up an uncompromising opposition to anything in local culture which seemed to sustain the traditional religion, including practices at odds with Whiteman culture which did not actually concern the ghosts. The South Sea Evangelical Mission (SSEM), which took its inspiration from Australian non-conformist fundamentalists and became the dominant church in Kwara'ae and the largest on Malaita, insisted on 'a clean break from the heathen and their customs and superstitions' (*Not In Vain*, April 1928:7).[5] This included traditional body ornaments and the festive occasions on which they were worn. The mission promoted a policy of 'separation', forming new village communities which could enforce Christian rules by public consensus while breaking ancestral rules to undermine the power of the ghosts or 'devils' and keep the 'heathen' who worshipped them at a distance. This fundamentalist reaction against the ancestral religion and culture was as much a Malaitan as a Whiteman one, mirroring the equally fundamentalist values imposed by the ancestral ghosts through strict rules of tabu and female defilement. Once relationships with the ghosts began to break down, usually when the dead appeared to be failing the living, many Malaitans evidently decided to reject them as completely as they could, which probably accounts for the popularity of the SSEM on most of the island compared with other more liberal churches.

When Kwara'ae people 'went to school' with the fundamentalist mission churches, usually as families or small clan congregations, they were encouraged to desecrate or destroy relics and symbols of their ancestral ghosts, especially their tabu-sanctums (*feraābu*) or shrines and the skulls which were kept there to represent the dead. The converts' Christian sponsors would pray over objects such as ornaments, weapons, dance batons and panpipes to 'normalize' (*fa'amolā*) them so that they ceased to be tabu or sacrosanct (*ābu*) by association with the ghosts. Some of these things were then put away as mementos of former times, seldom to be seen or worn again, or were kept in the church to counteract the influence of the ghosts. More often, in the early years especially, converts disposed of their ornaments by giving or throwing them away, burying them or burning them. When the death of a tabu-speaker (*fataābu*) or priest led his congregation to join the church, they would have the Christians bury him with his ornaments. Some discarded ornaments were sold to visiting Whitemen or given to missionaries and eventually found their way into foreign museums, usually with their history lost.

Andrew Gwa'italafa, whose family had been Christian since his Ubasi clan grandfathers joined the SSEM centre at Nāfinua in east Kwara'ae in the 1910s, helped other relatives to dispose of such things when they joined the church in the 1960s. In 1984 he described the effects of the mission on local culture:

People destroyed their tabu-places, burned all their tabu-sanctums, took all the bones so that in some tabu-places you can hardly see any bones or any relics of the past, the things they put on the body such as for dancing, pattern-straps ['*abagwaro* armstraps] and things like that. They said, 'You shouldn't take things like that into the mission. When you come out to join us, destroy them, burn everything which you used for the ghosts, such as pattern-straps and clash-rattles [*rākete* leg rattles], everything. If anyone wants to join the mission, don't take the wooden bowls [for sacrificial meals], don't practise anything which you did while you lived as pagans.' So we threw out everything and ruled that no-one could wear anything which they used from the past. So that's why our tradition, many children at present are starting to forget how to … plait, do all kinds of things like arts, and anything which we did formerly. … it's as if all our traditions which you saw then are no more. Some people forgot them for good because the church started to emphasize, 'Don't you bring any relics of anything.' There were only a few people who kept them and you can see they still have some, because some people who were still pagan didn't want to join the mission. … for example a few people kept a few crescents [*dafe* pendants], but only people who converted about ten years ago or twenty years ago, only they keep a few traditional things.

Although some people, like Gwa'italafa, regret the damage done in these rituals of conversion, they were regarded as a necessary precaution in the fundamentalist churches, which held that objects such as ornaments would attract the ghosts, 'as ants smell blood' as one man put it. This was a self-fulfilling belief which might lead people to experience dreams or possession from ghosts tempting them into worshipping the ancestors once again. Even so, the minority Anglican Church in Kwara'ae, under the more tolerant leadership of missionaries who had a more positive interest in local culture, seems to have avoided this problem. Anglicans, and an even smaller minority of Catholics, have managed to put local arts such as body ornaments to the service of the church, rather than consigning them to the ghosts. But despite these churches and those who held to the traditional religion, it is clear that for most of the twentieth century most Kwara'ae have been prepared to discard their tradition of body

Plate 5 This stereograph photo, labelled 'A missionary and her escort. Mala.' in Thomas Edge-Partington's album, was taken by George Rose in 1907 on the coast of northwest Kwara'ae or west Fataleka. The 'escort' is as well dressed in Whiteman clothes as a local Christian could hope to be, while the missionary wears more than a local Christian woman could ever aspire to. The others, identified in another photo as 'Bushmen', that is inlanders, seem to be ornamented for visiting with various conus (*kome*) rings, and with cowries (*buli*) and shell-disks (*sa'ela'o*) on the head. Two wear girdles (*fo'osae*), apparently of the coiled type, one wears northern-style pattern-straps (*'abagwaro*) on his arms and one wears a nose-pin (*usuusu*). (BM Oc,Ca,44.198)

Plate 6 A display of colonial dress and ornament in 1927 at Tulagi, capital of the British Solomon Islands Protectorate on Gela, for a visit by the High Commissioner for the Western Pacific. The Whitemen wear their full dress tropical uniforms, very different from those of the native police or 'soldiers', whose rifles enabled them to impose British rule on Malaita at this time. (Wilson photo, BM Oc,A56.2)

ornaments for the sake of a new religion that promised to help them deal with changing times more effectively than their ancestral ghosts.

The missionaries were equally concerned to ensure that their converts were properly clothed, as V.M. Sullivan explained, writing of the SSEM churches in the 1930s:

> The ordinary garment, if such it may be called, is a lavalava, which consists of a piece of calico worn around the waist and reaching to the knee. It is suitable to the climate, is inexpensive, and easy to obtain. I might say that the native dress is 'undress,' and one of our problems in this connection was how to provide this one garment for those who had broken away from the heathen and joined the Christian community. The Christians were inclined to look to the mission to provide this, but it was rightly thought that the Church should be responsible for providing these first garments from the offerings. This money is dispersed by the elders, and calico purchased for the newcomers; but any calico needed after that is provided by the man himself. (*NIV*, Apr. 1933:6)

The European prejudice against what the Revd Hopkins called 'the typical savage of imagination', underlying the dress codes of the missionaries, was shared, more or less, by other colonial agents: government officers, businessmen and educators. While the missionaries promoted clothes, the Royal Solomon Islands Police Force set the style for men with smart lavalavas, cummerbunds and leather belts with brass buckles and ammunition pouches. Their Whiteman masters wore shirts, shorts and socks, or trousers, like the owners and overseers of the plantations. On ceremonial occasions government officials dressed all in white with sun-hat, jacket and tie. The Whitemen were very conscious of the

status this conferred and concerned that local people should not emulate them. As Charles Woodford, first Resident Commissioner of the British Solomon Islands Protectorate, maintained:

> The cotton waist-cloth, the *sarong* of the Malay, the Fijian *sulu* and the Samoan lavalava, is the proper garment for a native to wear, and in such a climate as the Solomons a man wants nothing else. … In the case of a woman, a loose cotton blouse, hanging to the waist outside the waist-cloth, might be worn if it were considered necessary. (Woodford 1922:75–6)

Woodford's justification was hygiene and health, because clothing was seldom washed, but his own dress code suggests other motives as well. The visiting photographer J.W. Beattie described him at a church convention on Gela in 1906; 'The Governor arrived in full uniform—white duck, fine helmet with enamelled coat of arms, and dress sword—very imposing' (Beattie 1906:41). Malaitans could hardly be indifferent to these symbols of hierarchy and power and, whether they rejected or imitated the Whitman style, they were all affected by it.

The prejudice against nakedness is evident in the condescending accounts of even the relatively liberal Anglican missionaries. Florence Coombe, visiting Lau in the 1900s, described, 'A little crowd of women (poor, poor things!) with the scantiest possible approach to decency, but a plethora of ornaments' (*SCL*, Aug. 1908:304). In the 1930s Mrs Mason in the hills of Kwara'ae wrote of 'the headman, who had a ferocious expression, a button in the tip of his nose, and was fully clothed in a battered hat and a bib for a loin-cloth' (*SCL*, Oct. 1934:150).

Plate 7 This man and wife were photographed by Martin Johnson in the Kwara'ae inland in 1917. The man wears only his calico (*kaliko*), tied around the waist to hang down in front, with a Whiteman hat. The wife wears the great-*susuru* (*gwa'isusuru*) beaded strap and cloth ('*abalaua*), and her ornaments include a small crescent (*dafe*), a necklace ('*alu'alu*) of money-beads with conus (*kome*) rings, several other conus rings on a cloth around the neck and a longer string of probably glass beads. She has a piece of calico around her head, bands (*obi*) of rattan on her arms and some kind of ear ornaments, difficult to distinguish in the photograph. (Johnson photo 250788)

Plate 8 One of a series of photographs taken by Revd David Lloyd Francis of the Melanesian Mission in 1932 or 1933 in the hills above Fauābu Hospital, on the west Kwara'ae-Fataleka border. The wives wear their everyday dress of cloth aprons and the men wear calico tied to hang down in front, or as a lavalava. One man wears turtleshells (*ta'ota'ofunu*) in his ears and a conus (*fa'ikome*) ring on his arm, and another has a big shell-disk (*sa'ela'o doe*) and a big patterned comb (*kafa gwaroa doe*) in his hair. A child seems to be wearing a shell-disk-rattle (*ketesa'ela'o*). (BM Oc,A5.22)

Malaitans, with their own interpretation of the conventions of clothing, often dressed in ways which appeared incongruous to Whitemen, whose accounts imply that, in any case, apparent attempts to emulate them would be met with condescension or ridicule. Ernie Philp, a labour recruiter in the southeast Solomons in 1912–13, was less hostile than many in his descriptions:

> We have a great dandy among our crew now—a Malaita boy named Bobbie. He wears more than twice as many clothes as I do. He boasts ponderous turtle-shell earrings, and his belt is garnished with quite an array of pouches, keys and whistle etc. But the summit of coloured dandyism is reached by him! He wears a small wristlet watch, and when he goes ashore he carries a small brief bag—with tobacco. (Herr 1978:102)

Perhaps such men, following their own styles of dress despite the disapproval of government and the mockery of other Whitemen, were making a gesture of resistance to their colonial masters.

Reasserting tradition

The political and cultural domination of the Whitemen was not accepted uncritically, and their authority was eventually challenged by a growing resentment against the racism inherent in the culture of colonial government, missions and business. In the 1940s the Japanese and American invasions of the Second World War eclipsed the authority of the British administration and prompted a Malaita-wide movement for independent self-government, Māsina Rul (known as Māsing Rul in Kwara'ae). The movement took control of the whole island until the British suppressed it in the late 1940s and early 1950s and set up an island-wide Malaita Council. During Māsina Rul, if not before, Malaitans began to debate the possibilities of a cultural tradition (Kwara'ae *falafala*) which was compatible with Christianity but free of foreign control. According to the history widely accepted in Kwara'ae, when their ancestors first settled Malaita they followed the Jewish religion of the Old Testament, before falling into ancestor-worship and pig-sacrifice. In accordance with this history, Christianity came to be seen as fulfilling tradition rather than destroying it, although opinions varied as to what this might mean.

During the 1950s and 1960s, still pursuing the ideals of independence voiced during Māsina Rul, members of the SSEM formed the independent South Sea Evangelical Church (SSEC), or defected to other fundamentalist churches such as the Jehovah's Witnesses or Baptists. They continued to maintain their uncompromising opposition to culture identified with the ancestral religion, but this was increasingly challenged by a movement to re-establish tradition or *kastom* (from English 'custom') under the leadership of clan heads as 'chiefs'. In Kwara'ae the movement included members of all churches and of the ancestral religion in what eventually became known at the Kwara'ae House of Chiefs. Its main concern has been the re-establishment of traditional law and land claims, under local control, but some leaders have also raised other questions about local culture. The Revd Arnon Ngwadili, a prominent chief and leader in the SSEC in west Kwara'ae, returned from church training overseas in the early 1970s convinced that Christian values need not be European ones, and persuaded by Papua New Guinea and Maori Christians that God approved of local culture, including body ornaments. At a great meeting of Kwara'ae chiefs at 'Aimela in west Kwara'ae in 1976, chiefs of various Christian denominations appeared in ornaments and there were performances of the old festival dances. Some fundamentalists continued to question whether such things were really 'Christian', and their leaders continued to ban such dances when they could. But as Christianity has established itself in Malaitan culture over several generations, SSEC congregations in the 1990s eventually gained the confidence

Plate 9 A singing band from Na'oasi in east Kwara'ae giving a night-time performance of Christian choruses in 1983. (Burt photo)

to incorporate ancestral traditions of music, dance and body ornament into Christian worship without fear of backsliding into heathenism.

For all its achievements during the second half of the twentieth century, the *kastom* movement did little to halt the decline in local styles of body ornaments, and Christianity was only the most obvious of the colonial influences leading to their disappearance. The Second World War brought Malaitans unprecedented quantities of clothing, provided by American servicemen, and this was put to the service of tradition by dressing the Māsina Rul 'duties' or police in military uniforms. The economic development which followed from the 1960s increasingly introduced the fashions followed in Australia and Southeast Asia, from whence clothing was imported. As colonial administrators prepared to relinquish power in the lead-up to Solomon Islands national independence in 1978, the local elite they trained to succeed them maintained their style of dress. Even after independence, when barriers between Whitemen and Islanders were officially abolished, ordinary people were kept out of the clubs and hotel bars of Honiara by dress codes requiring shirts and shoes.

The more old-fashioned people, particularly those who continued to worship the ghosts, usually had less stake in the colonial economy, less reason to wear clothes, and less money to buy them. Even so, from the early twentieth century they were influenced by the fashions of their Christian relatives and neighbours, and by the Whitemen before that. Everyone became more sensitive about modesty, with inland men wearing loincloths of imported cloth for visiting as early as the 1910s, if not before, as old photographs show. Even when men could get a larger piece of calico they often preferred to wear a strip tied around the waist with the ends hanging down in front, rather than as a wrap-around lavalava. This was the style still followed for everyday dress by Timi Ko'oliu, last senior tabu-speaker of Kwara'ae, until his death in 1984, although he would hang a better piece of cloth over the front of his girdle when dressed for visiting. Even in his time those ancestor-worshippers who preferred the lavalava wore it much shorter than most Christians, in what was recognized as a 'traditional' or 'pagan' style. Being less able to afford larger pieces of calico, they would have kept such clothes as they had for special occasions.

Kwara'ae women living under the ancestral religion in the late twentieth century were still obliged to retain the old style of band-strap (*'abaobi*) or beaded great-*susuru* (*gwa'isusuru*) strap and apron at home, to avoid offending the ancestral ghosts or becoming too cosmopolitan for their men-folk. Several generations ago wives replaced their local cloth aprons with calico, which was better looking, more practical and comfortable. Women would carry a skirt in their bag to put on while visiting Christian relatives or going to market (as some still do in Kwaio). As old photographs show, such a skirt, sewn as a tube and gathered at the waist, unlike the men's lavalava, was usually all that Christian women wore

Plate 10 Leading figures at the 'Aimela chiefs' meeting in February 1976 posing for an official photograph. The Revd Arnon Ngwadili is on the right of the front row, wearing a bag (*ngwa'i*) ornamented with leaves, and second on the left of that row is Adriel Rofate'e, leading Paramount Chief of east Kwara'ae, wearing the big shell-disk (*sa'ela'o doe*) pendant of the tabu-speakers of 'Aimomoko (see page 99). Four of the others are wearing ten-string (*tafuli'ae*) moneys, including Selwyn Ngwadili, who also has a necklace (*'alu'alu*) with dolphin teeth, pattern-straps (*'abagwaro*) on the arms and a deflector (*alafolo*) club, and Selwyn Kwaifi'i, wearing a fish-teeth-cluster (*barulifai'a*) as a browband. Three have rattan girdles (*fo'osae*) with their calico hanging down in front in the old style, including Aisah Osifera of 'Aimomoko, next to Ngwadili. (Laka photo 12A)

Plate 11 A To'abaita dancer for an Anglican church festival at Malu'u in 2005. The money-bead brow-binding (*fo'odara*) is a new style and the breast-fastening (*torisusu*) bandoliers are now general to Malaita. The string of large dolphin-teeth, broad pattern-straps (*'abagwaro*) on the arms, rattan girdle (*fo'osae*), leather strap (*'abatarafa*) and conus-rattles (*ketekome*) on the legs are all older styles in north Malaita, but he has none of the ear and nose ornaments common in former times. (Brown photo)

Plate 12 A Kwara'ae wedding photograph from about 1994. The 'new wife' wears a fish-teeth-cluster (*barulifaī'a*) as a brow-binding (*fo'odara*), a breast-fastening (*torisusu*) and a necklace of dolphin teeth, and pattern-straps (*'abagwaro*) of the Kwara'ae 'arrows' design on the arms. (Kwa'ioloa photo)

until after the Second World War, when dresses and blouses or other upper garments became more available. As ancestor-worshippers became an ever-smaller minority in the second half of the twentieth century, women became increasingly shy of nakedness, adding to other inconveniences as an incentive to convert to Christianity. In the late twentieth century few younger women would go bare-breasted and the bra came into use for the kind of traditional dress worn by Christians for events such as weddings.

By this time everyday dress had little distinctive local style, with only conservative elderly men continuing to wear the lavalava rather than shirts and shorts or trousers, and a few women wearing their skirts without tops around the home. Only the patterns on some T-shirts printed in Honiara were distinctive of Solomon Islands, including some local Malaitan designs. In his candid autobiography, Michael Kwa'ioloa describes how he would dress up as an unmarried youth in the 1970s, for the same reasons that his fathers and grandfathers would once have put on their finest ornaments:

> I had long hair when I was young and I usually wore sunglasses and I always wore bellbottoms and I really liked the kind of shirt

that had cords across the chest. Sometimes I'd double up with both a tee shirt and a jacket. With all this I'd wear a wristwatch and I liked to carry a camera and use perfumes. I adopted European culture, because I'd been to school and seen all these things. When I was born again I dressed up even more to go to service. (Kwa'ioloa and Burt 1997:74–5)

Local styles of ornaments were now worn mainly for self-conscious displays of traditional values or *kastom*. Women might dress for their marriage in breast-fastening (*torisusu*) or ten-string (*tafuli'ae*) moneys, with brow-binding (*fo'odara*) and pattern-straps (*'abagwaro*) on the arms, worn with skirt and bra, as well as changing into a white wedding dress for the church service. For dance performances, men would dress in some old ornaments and as many imitation ones, such as shell-disks and crescents of painted board, with either lavalavas or loincloths (*kabilato*) of local cloth (*'abalaua*), a new form of traditional clothing. In contrast to former times, the effect often seems intended to be crude and rough rather than beautiful and valuable, reflecting colonial prejudices about local culture. Perhaps the most creative and artistic ornaments are those made by the sea people of Langalanga. Developing the old brow-bindings and breast-fastenings of money-beads, they make all kinds of net-patterned sashes, collars, belts and even hats, but fringed with worthless *mumu* seeds instead of valuable dolphin teeth, as in the past. For the new elite of Honiara, who tend to regard the lavalava as traditional dress and the loincloth as indecently revealing, such ornaments may stand as symbols of national identity, but not as best dress for themselves. Most Malaitans for most occasions, and particularly for Sunday service, prefer the smartest Western clothes they can afford, with white uniforms and coloured sashes for the church singing-bands with which the more fundamentalist churches have replaced the old-fashioned festival dances.

When ornaments were worn, and why

When Malaitans ornamented their bodies in local style, they did so to look good and show off. Youths were ornamented to attract maidens and maidens' ornaments showed they were eligible for marriage. Wives and husbands were ornamented less elaborately as serious and responsible adults, while on public occasions important men and their families wore ornaments that proclaimed their wealth and prestige. Some say that tabu-speakers and warriors wore particular kinds of ornaments, others distinguish only between ornaments appropriate to men and women, but in general people were ornamented to enhance their status as well as their appearance, as the occasion allowed. Ornaments marked important social events and celebrations, and for everyday work only a few simple things were worn, such as armbands, earrings and basic necklaces. Fine ornaments were most inappropriate in times of mourning, when the bereaved showed their grief by denying themselves the good things of life, including making themselves look good. Wearing ornaments then was offensive and might be taken as a sign of being pleased with the death, or even an admission of having caused it, perhaps through sorcery.

In Kwara'ae the great occasions for displays of ornaments were sacrificial festivals (*maoma*), when men of a clan came together to honour their ancestral ghosts, entertain their relatives and neighbours, and raise their own name through a generous distribution of food and display of wealth. Michael Kwa'ioloa described how his relatives in 'Ere'ere in east Kwara'ae appeared in his youth, in the late 1960s:

> Once I went up to the pagans and saw how they held a festival and a panpipe dance, eh, if you saw it you'd be impressed and a bit overawed. Just to describe it; the sun is beating down and everyone gathers together to hold a big feast of festival pigs shared out for everybody and they're enjoying themselves and wearing traditional ornaments, eh, it looks really nice. The women put on plaited bands [*gwa'iobi* armbands], the men put on pattern-straps ['*abagwaro* armstraps], girdles [*fo'osae*], crescents [*dafe* pendants], they hold angle-clubs [*subi*] and deflector-clubs [*alafolo*], put traditional combs in their hair and also put nice-smelling traditional leaves, euodia [*ri'i*], on their combs, also put on shell-disks [*sa'ela'o*]. It all looks really nice, this traditional costume. But I don't see anyone doing this nowadays. (Kwa'ioloa and Burt 1997:158)[6]

Most Kwara'ae people of Kwa'ioloa's generation, born after the Second World War, have never witnessed such events, and it is also a long time since Whitemen have been able to

attend them, as the ancestor-worshippers have been reduced to those most fiercely opposed to colonialism (including anthropology). However in 1946, a few years before Kwa'ioloa was born, the missionary Robert Vance of the SSEM did describe such a festival, in Kwara'ae or north Malaita[7]:

> The young men have their machetes or clubs, and a handful of ornamented spears, and wear new yellow and red plaited earsticks or other ornaments through the lobes of their ears. The older folk have shell rings in their ears, and perhaps a nine-inch shell 'bone' [tridacna pin] through the septum of the nose. The younger men and women have hibiscus in their hair, and ginger plant twigs in belt and armlets; [the men] also a comb that looks like a miniature garden fork upright in their fuzzy mop of hair.
> The women and girls take up positions round the sacred [dance] ground [*fulisango*]. The older men and the conveners of the feast are busy fixing up the final arrangements for the roasting of the pigs and taro, the division of the feast, and the redistribution of the shell money in proper proportion according to the prestige and precedence of those who have come. The witch doctor [tabu-speaker or priest, *fataābu*] has to be identified with the sacrifice, take the portion for a whole burnt offering into the most holy place [tabu-sanctum, *feraābu*], give praise and thanks to the spirits, receive the firstfruits, and again identify himself with the sacrifice before distribution is made to the worshippers.
> The hired dancers are now ready to perform. They form up in two ranks away from the arena. Two men with large branches screen the head of the column as it prances forward towards the ground. As they reach the edge of the ground these branches are suddenly whisked away to reveal the ornamented dancers in all their glory. The spectators watch carefully the intricate movements of the stamp dance and appreciate fully the detail hidden to the foreigner. The different movements take up to fifteen minutes each. After four or five of these movements the dance is finished. The dancers' pig and betel nut reward is brought out with great hilarity and skylarking. (*NIV*, Dec. 1946:11)

Although sacrificial festivals were the most important gatherings for which the Kwara'ae made a special effort to ornament themselves, there were other occasions for local leaders to gain fame (*taloa*) by generous distributions of food, and for both hosts and guests to show themselves off. These included pudding-feasts (*siufa, sau'a*) with great quantities of

Plate 13 This photograph, apparently taken in Fiji at the end of the nineteenth century, may be the earliest image of the Malaitan *sango* dance performed at festivals. The wealth of these migrant workers in manufactured goods is shown in their matching sulus or lavalavas, and in the umbrellas and clothes of their audience. The dancers carry hornbill batons (*taba*) and some wear the kind of glass-bead ornaments shown in the portraits of Malaitans in Fiji, including a breast-fastening (*torisusu*) with a Christian cross. (Brodziak postcard, Burt)

Plate 14 These men, ornamented in Kwara'ae style, were photographed and filmed by Edward Salisbury in 1921, at a dance on the coast of Langalanga. They all wear hornbill or other feathers in combs and, of the twelve, two have cowries (*buli*) in their hair, and most seem to have earrings (*tege*) with shell rings or patterned-bamboos (*fa'i'au gwaroa*) in their ears. Ten have nose-pins (*usuusu*), four have fish-teeth-cluster straps (*barulifaī'a*) at the neck, two have shell-disk-rattles (*ketesa'ela'o*) and one a pearlshell crescent (*dafe*). Five have pattern-straps ('*abagwaro*) of the Kwara'ae 'arrows' design, four have conus (*fa'i kome*) rings on the arms, of the narrow type. One wears a belt (*fo'o'aba*), probably of glass beads, the others Whiteman straps ('*abatarafa*) and all have calico (*kaleko*) worn as lavalavas. Several have shell-rattles (*ketela'o*) of white money-beads at the knees, and most have bands (*obi*) of rattan at the wrists and ankles. The man with the gun seems to have shell-disks (*sa'ela'o*) on his wrist. (Corbis photo agency)

Solomon Islanders Dance

Plate 15 Dancers at the 'Aimela meeting in 1976 performing a *sango* dance. The Anglicans and Catholics of west Kwara'ae continued to perform the old festival dances for such occasions, but with fewer of the old-style ornaments. Almost all these men wear girdles (*fo'osae*), apart from one who has a bead belt (*fo'o'aba*); several have Kwara'ae-style pattern-straps ('*abagwaro*) on the arms; there are some cowrie (*buli*) head ornaments; and some strings of dolphin teeth and shell-rattles (*ketela'o*) below the knee. But there are none of the more valuable shell ornaments, only imitations of painted board. They carry batons (*taba*) in the shape of hornbills and staffs with cordyline (*sango*) leaves, and have crash-rattles (*keterā*) on their ankles. (Laka photo 19A)

Plate 16 A *sango* festival dance staged by Anglicans and ancestor-worshippers in east Kwara'ae in 1979. David Rere, at the front with Nguta, wears a wooden crescent (*dafe*) (see page 113) and one pattern-strap ('*abagwaro*) on the arm (the other was being remade at the time, see page 46). The dancers carry hornbill batons (*taba*) and cordyline (*sango*) leaves and wear rattles on their legs, keeping time with the music of the panpipers who play behind, ornamented in leaves. (Burt photo)

taro and nut (*ngali* / *Canarium*) or coconut pounded in bowls, funeral normalization (*mola'a*) feasts to end the mourning period, and marriage feasts (*tolonga*) where the wife's family made a return in food for the brideprice they had received for her. There were inauguration feasts for major projects such as a patterned sanctum (*fera gwaroa*), with an expensive facade of carved posts and beams and plaited walling, and until the 1910s there were reward (*fo'oa*) presentations and feasts for killings. For Christians of the Anglican and Catholic churches there were church festivals such as Christmas, Easter, Whitsun and patron saints' days when traditional ornaments could be worn and dances performed. Anglicans might also wear ornaments for Sunday church services, just as other Christians put on their best clothes.

While feasts and festivals were the big events for dressing up, people would wear ornaments for other social occasions too. Youths and maidens ornamented themselves to impress and attract each other for visiting, for supervised courting and even for illicit meetings in the forest. They would wear whatever they owned or could borrow, with colourful and scented leaves and, no doubt, love magic as well. Historical tales describe maidens being impressed by appearance: 'Oh, you're a nice [looking] boy, where are you from?' (while the youths respond to the challenge of courting forbidden maidens). Once men and women were married, they were expected to be more sober in dress, bearing as they did the responsibilities of family life and now strictly forbidden from even attending at formal courting. Women, who took a lesser part in public life, had fewer occasions to ornament themselves. For going to market men might wear ornaments and, formerly, carry weapons to stand guard against attack, while the women were carrying and exchanging the produce of the sea and inland: fish for vegetables, and sometimes shell goods for ornaments of forest materials. Men's business took them on visits for meetings and gatherings, for which they might ornament themselves in at least a modest way. In 1910 the anthropologist Albert Lewis, staying in the government residence at 'Aoke and hoping to purchase 'curios', was rather disappointed by a party from the Kwara'ae inland, which none the less allowed him to describe the characteristic ornaments of the area:

> One day about 80 bush people came up to see the house. Many of them had not seen a white man before. At home the men go naked, but here most of them had a strip of cloth on, wrapped around the waist and drawn between the legs. They had almost nothing with them—a few combs, ear sticks, belts, and shell ornaments being all of interest. The combs and ear sticks were nicely ornamented with colored fibre woven in patterns, also the belts (of rattan) in places. The shell ornament most valued was circular, about 2—2½ in. in diameter, with black incised lines representing birds, etc. One to several were worn on a string around the neck. All these are made by the bush people, and that is about all of interest which they have. (Welsch 1998, vol. 1:363–4)[8]

Beyond their appearance, what made certain ornaments attractive for display was their value, which Kwara'ae elders familiar with ornaments could readily cite in terms of the local shell-bead money (*mani*). The Kwara'ae use this money to pay for goods such as pigs and gardens of food and present

it to mediate relationships such as brideprice for marriages and restitution or compensation presentations to make good for offences, but formerly it could also be exchanged for many goods now bought for cash. The values attributed to ornaments can only be very notional, taking no account of the variable quality of either the ornaments or the money, or of the variable exchange rates between local money and cash, also used to measure the value of ornaments. However, they do give an impression of the exchange values of ornaments in relation to each other and to certain other social values.

The most valuable shell ornaments, including the cowrie-row (*talabuli*) browband, pendants such as shell-disk-rattles (*ketesa'ela'o*), big shell-disks (*sa'ela'o doe*) and crescents (*dafe*), and pattern-straps (*'abagwaro*) of money-beads for the arms, were reckoned as equivalent to the highest northern money denomination, a fathom-long ten-string (*tafuli'ae*). Large denominations like ten-strings were and still are worn as ornaments on important occasions (as at the 1976 'Aimela chiefs' meeting, see Plate 10, page 16), and the kinds of beads used for them could be made into other ornaments. Dolphin teeth ('fish teeth', *lifa ī'a*), used as small change before cash became dominant, were also made into ornaments, and a fish-teeth-cluster (*barulifaī'a*) strap might be worth several ten-strings, depending on the number of teeth. Lesser ornaments, such as patterned combs (*kafa gwaroa*), single cowrie (*buli*) shells, patterned-bamboo (*fa'i'au gwaroa*), bamboo-tree (*'ai'au*) and turtleshell (*ta'ota'ofunu*) ear ornaments, nose-pins (*usuusu*) and single small shell-disks (*sa'ela'o*) were commonly valued at a *la'usu'u* arm-length string of northern red money-beads, or various lesser denominations of southern white money (such as *gwau'aba*, *fa'afa'a* or *lima'ae*).[9]

As valuables with recognized exchange values in local money or cash, ornaments could themselves be acceptable contributions to the kind of payments made in money. In Malaita, as elsewhere in Solomon Islands, the prestigious, versatile and durable goods preferred for certain exchanges as local 'money' were generally derived from ornaments, including items actually made to wear.[10] Writers of the first half of the twentieth century habitually list cash values for such things, implying that, even though cash was not a generally acceptable substitute for local exchanges, it was commonly exchanged for things that were (see Bogesi 1948:228–9, Belshaw 1950:172, Hogbin 1964:48). It would take a thesis on colonial economics to assess the variable and changing exchange-value of cash in Malaita, and the value of local money gives a better impression of the value of ornaments to Malaitans themselves. In Kwara'ae, formerly the brideprice negotiated to repay a woman's family for giving her to her husband might amount to twenty or thirty ten-strings or more, but even the limit of five ten-strings observed by most Christians usually requires families to borrow contributions from relatives. Hence a man dressed in a full set of ornaments might bear the equivalent of a small brideprice on his body, sufficient to add a productive woman to his family. Such a display was worthy of a wealthy 'man of possessions' (*ngwae to'orū*) who used his plentiful gardens, pigs and money to become 'big' or 'important' (*doe, 'inoto'a*)

Plate 17 This photograph is one of a series taken by John Beattie in 1906 in an Anglican coastal settlement at Kwarea, on the west-coast border between Kwara'ae and Fataleka (the same area as the photo of Fauābu by David Lloyd Francis, see Plate 8, page 14). The men are standing outside their church after a service and, according to Beattie, include 'the chief and a noted warrior now a man of peace' (1906:45). These are presumably the man with the hat and the tall man on his left, who has the tip of his nose pierced for a stud (*'otu*), as worn by those who had killed.

However it is not they, but the younger men who have apparently ornamented themselves for church. The man on the extreme right is wearing a cowrie (*buli*) in his hair, sawn-conus (*komefuria*) rings at the top of his ears, clusters of conus (*kome*) rings hanging from earrings (*tege*) on his earlobes, a fish-teeth-cluster (*barulifaī'a*) strap around the neck, pattern-strap (*'abagwaro*) money-bead armstraps of the broad north Malaita type, conus-rattles (*ketekome*) below the knees, and plaited bands (*obi*) on his ankles. His calico is supported by a leather belt or strap (*'abatarafa*). Further along is a man with a large nose-conus (*komerakana*) ring, a fish-teeth-cluster and a fine crescent (*dafe*) pendant at the neck. One boy wears a small crescent and another man with a crescent also has a long comb (*kafa*) in his hair. Others are wearing perhaps their best Whiteman clothes, vests and a jacket, or have pieces of calico around the neck and shoulders. (Beattie photo 537, BM Oc,B114.87)

by helping his relatives and neighbours, or even 'famous' (*talo'a*) by staging great feasts and festivals.

Body ornaments were among the ways that the important men of Kwara'ae displayed their wealth and power on such occasions. A feast-giver might commission others to make ornaments for him and his family to wear, and use the occasion to show off prized belongings, from rare birds to persons. A ghost might choose a favoured son to make tabu (*o'abua*) for a festival, staying secluded in the sanctum from the time of the preliminary sacrifices until the great public occasion of the feasting and dancing. He would then be dressed in the finest ornaments and brought out to be shown off and envied by all the guests, raising the name of the man who could afford to keep, feed and ornament him. A man of possessions might have his wife dressed in valuable ornaments for a festival, hidden and then shown off to the assembled people to proclaim the importance of her husband

and his clan, and an adopted son or stranger might be publicly displayed in the same way as a valuable addition to his new community (see Robbins and Akin 1999:28–32; Graeber 1996).

Although women took part in such displays, which acknowledged their work in producing the wealth of food and pigs, it was men who took the most prominent public roles, including the dancing. On some occasions at least, women seem to have been ornamented to show off their men-folk as much as themselves. The time a woman was most fully ornamented was for her marriage when, after the brideprice presentation, she was dressed in money and valuable ornaments as gifts from her own family and sent to live with her husband. She would wear one or two high-value moneys such as ten-strings, perhaps with pattern-straps (*'abagwaro*) on her arms and a browband (*fo'odara*) of money-beads and dolphin teeth or a fish-teeth-cluster (*barulifaī'a*) (as in Plate 12, page 17). Betisel Silda'afe recalled how, in the 1930s or 1940s, a maiden from a wealthy family might wear three fish-teeth-clusters, around her neck and head and over the top of the head, earring-clusters (*barutege*) in her ears, a woven money-bead belt (*fo'o'aba*) as a sash over the shoulder and under the arm, a money-bead breast-fastening (*torisusu*), and a maiden's-cincture (*susuru sari'i*) belt of money-beads. Altogether these were probably worth more than the brideprice given for a lesser maiden. After marriage she would wear such ornaments only for feasts and festivals.

Men and women, tabu-speakers and warriors

Malaitans ornamented themselves not only for the occasion but also according to their status in society, especially as men or women. In Kwara'ae there were some essentially masculine or feminine ornaments, such as the man's girdle (*fo'osae*) and turtleshell (*ta'ota'ofunu*) ear ornaments, and the woman's red band-strap (*'abaobi*) and beaded great-cincture (*gwa'isusuru*) straps. There were some particularly associated with men, such as frigate-bird shell-disks (*sa'ela'o*) and crescents (*dafe*), of which women sometimes wore smaller versions, and others associated with women, such as cross-design women's shell-disks (*sa'ela'o kini*). Certain valuable and prestigious men's ornaments, such as pattern-straps (*'abagwaro*) for the arms, might be worn by women when they were the focus of important occasions, as at their marriage. Many other things were worn by men and women, including valuable fish-teeth-cluster (*barulifaī'a*) straps, nose-pins (*usuusu*), most ear ornaments and breast-fastening (*torisusu*) bandoliers. However, the men's ornaments were often larger and more valuable, as with conus (*fa'ikome*) arm-rings and belts of money-beads and glass beads (distinguished by name, *fo'o'aba* and *susuru*, rather than by form).

Equally important, there were strict rules on men and women wearing particular ornaments belonging to each other. Under the ancestral religion, women's contribution to society in reproducing the living was held in delicate balance with the power of the ghosts of the dead, controlled mainly by men to ensure health and prosperity, wealth, influence and military might. This balance required precautions to protect the ghosts and the men who dealt with them from defilement by women, particularly from their monthly periods and childbirth, when they had to live apart in a seclusion house (*bisi*). Among other things, rules about defilement affected what women could wear and meant that ornaments belonging to senior men were tabu to them, and sometimes even to men who were less strict in observing these rules. Even a wife's own cloth apron was tabu to wear during her period, lest it become too defiled to wear in the home, and she would wear a 'shut' leaf (*bono*, a kind of wild taro) instead. Likewise, a female tabu-speaker (*fataābu kini*), usually the wife of a male one, would have to change her apron for a 'worship' leaf (*folota*) when she entered the tabu-sanctum to deal with the female ghosts during a festival. Although women could deal with ghosts on their own account, their defiling power was opposed particularly to the most powerful male roles of tabu-speaker and warrior, representing the contrasting but complementary masculine values of peaceful and violent

Plate 18 Women's everyday dress in 'Ere'ere, east Kwara'ae, under the ancestral religion, in 1979. Musuba'eko, daughter of the tabu-speaker Timi Ko'oliu, wears an apron of calico supported by the wife's great-cincture (*gwa'isusuru*), and her 'sister' Le'akini wears the maiden's band-strap (*'abaobi*) of red rattan-strip. (Burt photo)

authority. It was dangerously tabu for such men to wear ornaments belonging to women, and likewise tabu for women to wear their ornaments, particularly those which had been dedicated to ghosts.

A tabu-speaker (*fataābu*) was the religious leader of his local clan, dealing with the ghosts of their ancestors as their priest. Ideally he would be heir to a firstborn line of fathers and sons descended from the ancestors who claimed their land and established their tabu-sanctums (*feraābu*) as shrines, where their ghosts were represented by skulls, bones and other relics. Men descended from men of the clan were its senior members, but ghosts were also concerned with their daughters and sisters and their descendants, particularly those living nearby. The tabu-speaker was a moral leader of this local congregation, upholding the rules of tabu which honoured ghosts, men and women by keeping them separate according to their status. By divining, praying and sacrificing pigs to the ghosts to secure their support and appease their anger, he ensured the well-being of their descendants in every way, from good harvests and protection against enemies to saving them from sickness and death. It was the tabu-speaker who organized the periodic sacrificial festivals for the rebuilding of the tabu-sanctum which housed the relics of the ghosts. Those who represented the ghosts of the most ancient tabu-sanctums, ancestors of many dispersed local clans, could involve these clans in great festivals where a hundred or more pigs were sacrificed, bringing fame and political influence.

Tabu-speakers, backed by the awesome power of the ghosts, represented the values of quiet stability, hard work and harmony among the living and the dead which brought prosperity to Kwara'ae society. Some compare them to Christian pastors or say they were the only true leaders or chiefs of former times, when the Kwara'ae lived under theocratic government. They had to keep strict rules separating themselves from women and from men who did not themselves keep such rules, in order to become acceptable mediators with the ancestral ghosts. Ornaments associated with a tabu-speaker represented this esteemed status and were tabu from being worn by a man who himself was particularly tabu, including his body and particularly his head. Some of them might be inherited, often over many generations, from the very ghosts he now prayed and sacrificed to. Some such heirlooms were so tabu that they were rarely worn at all but kept in the tabu-sanctum with other relics of the ghosts.[11]

Those Kwara'ae who recall the ways of communities following the ancestral religion say that when a family came visiting only their tabu-speaker would be wearing ornaments such as turtleshell (ta'ota'ofunu) ear ornaments, crescent (dafe) or shell-disk (sa'ela'o) pendants and pattern-straps ('abagwaro) on the arms, although his son, who was likely to be his trainee successor, might dress in his ornaments. If these things were indeed tabu for others to wear, it is probably because they were dedicated to or inherited from particular ancestral ghosts. Such were the big shell-disks (sa'ela'o doe) once belonging to the tabu-speakers of the ancient tabu-sanctums of 'Aimomoko and Mānadari (see pages 99 and 100), and the turtle-design (funifunu) and crescent (dafe) of Timi Ko'oliu, the last senior tabu-speaker of Kwara'ae (see pages 74 and 111). But it is also said that most families would only have one full set of ornaments, which were worn by their firstborn or leading man (fa'ina'ona'o, ngwae etaeta) for special occasions. If ordinary men were not as finely ornamented as their tabu-speaker, this was probably because he inherited the valuable heirlooms as head of the family, while they could not afford to acquire such things on their own account. The dead were sometimes buried in their ornaments, and objects such as conus (fa'ikome) arm-rings sometimes turn up when graves are disturbed.

In contrast to the tabu-speaker, the warrior (ramo) represented violent and aggressive masculinity, disruptive and opposed to the qualities of peaceful co-operation necessary for prosperity. While tabu-speakers are compared to pastors, warriors are said to have been the police of former times, enforcing the law (taki) to uphold tabu and punish disrespect (maladalafa), although they were also regarded ambivalently as dangerous and unruly.[12] A warrior would kill for restitution or vengeance on behalf of his clan community and to collect rewards from others who were unwilling to kill for themselves or preferred the prestige of paying someone else to do so. He would have spiritual support from an ancestral warrior ghost,

requiring him to avoid women whose defiling qualities would feminize and quieten or pacify him, and warriors were most powerful while they remained unmarried. Some are said to have spent all their lives as warriors, becoming warrior ghosts in their turn, but most men would have taken up the role at a certain stage of their lives, whether from bravado or from the need to defend themselves. Even famous warriors might eventually marry and settle down, and some later became tabu-speakers.[13]

Warriors presented a macho image which youths still aspire to, although now more in imitation of American film stars than the warriors of old. The ornaments most commonly associated with them were the 'man-grabber' conus (fa'ilolongwae, fa'ikome) arm-ring of tridacna shell, used to break an enemy's ribs, and the girdle (fo'osae), dedicated to a warrior ghost to give strength and protection. The girdle, bound tightly around the waist, helped sustain a man during the fasting required for the ghost's support, and some say it was worn only for fighting and kept in the sanctum the rest of the time. Others say girdles were worn for visiting, like other ornaments, as shown in photos from the early twentieth century and in the fashion of some senior men in the late twentieth century. In former times, when men went everywhere armed, girdles, like weapons, would have served for masculine display as well as for fighting, and Kwara'ae historians describe men putting on girdles to go visiting or courting, taking them off on return home. The ornament most exclusively identified with the role of warrior is the 'stopper' ('afudu'udu'u) nose-stud, commonly said to have been worn only by a man who had killed someone. The lesser-known 'man-eater' (fafangalalo) nose-stud carried a similar message. Warlike deeds were also publicized by trophy objects attached to a man's bag. Other ornaments associated with warriors include cowries (buli) and hornbill feathers worn in the hair, and the shell-disk-rattle (ketesa'ela'o), but other men (or even boys, as in Plate 8, page 14) also wore these.

Some say that men, and especially warriors, would dress in a full set of ornaments when setting out for a fight, even on a secret raid, while others say a warrior would wear only his girdle and conus arm-rings. Elders recall ornaments making men look intimidating and say they distinguished raiders from their unprepared enemies in the confusion of combat. There is a certain romanticism about the warriors of former times which may have coloured popular recollections. Even so, when men sacrificed a pig for the support of the ghosts before setting out to fight, making them particularly tabu for any contact with women, their weapons and ornaments also became tabu and remained so even after the men were normalized again by a further sacrifice.

The greatest opportunity for display as a warrior was the collection of a reward (fo'oa) offered by someone who wanted a killing to pay back for an offence. When the offender or someone from his community had been killed, the reward would be presented at a public ceremony from a raised platform, where strings of money were hung from a crossbar and large trussed-up pigs, heaps of garden food and quantities

Plate 19 Two of the four remaining tabu-speakers in east Kwara'ae in 1979, posing in their heirloom ornaments at a meeting. Timi Ko'oliu wore his turtle-design (*funifunu*, see page 74) and single turtleshell (*ta'ota'ofunu*, see page 76) ear ornament, a crescent (*dafe*, see page 111), red-stained bands (*obi*) of rattan on his arms, and a girdle (*fo'osae*) with a strip of calico. Maerora wore a very fine crescent (see page 111), pattern-straps ('*abagwaro*) on the arms and a police-style leather strap ('*abatarafa*) which supports a blue lavalava, the colour preferred by the ancestor-worshippers. They both have shell-rattle (*ketela'o*) strings of white *galu* beads below the knee. (Burt photo)

of betelnut were laid out below. Sometimes, as histories tell, a marriageable maiden or a piece of land might be included. The killer, with his band in all their ornaments as a guard, would take slow rhythmic steps up to the platform, holding their bows in outstretched hands and waving them from one side to the other as they uttered a gasping 'heee' with each step. The presenter would hang the money around the killer's body and his band would carry off the pigs and food for a feast at their home.[14] Aisah Osifera of 'Aimomoko described the last reward collection in Kwara'ae, which he witnessed in 1919:

> When they came up for the reward, they danced and came up and reached for the moneys. ... They ornamented their bags, they held their bows, and they held the things called red cordylines, they picked them and held them as well as their bows, and they stepped up for the reward. As they did this it was really like a dance, and they reached out for the moneys on the platform, they climbed up by a ladder and they reached for it and came down. To look at, rewards really looked like dances. They looked really good, because they were ornamented with pattern-straps, crescents, and shell-disks. (Burt and Kwa'ioloa 2001:71)[15]

The ornaments now associated with tabu-speakers and warriors may have been regarded as appropriate to their roles, but they do not seem to have served as symbols to identify the roles themselves. Writers who represent Malaitan ornaments as if they were badges of office may have misread the ambiguous comments of informants who, for their own reasons, shared their desire to formalize the status of their leaders, perhaps in European terms.[16] In some parts of Malaita leadership did indeed entail much clearer distinctions of rank and office than among inland peoples like the Kwara'ae, whose attitude gave one early colonial official to comment that 'The District [of Malaita] seems to be inhabited solely by chiefs' (Burt 1994a:67). Among the sea people of Lau in northeast Malaita, with a tradition of Polynesian immigration from Ontong Java, and the Sa'a of south Malaita, with overseas links to the aristocratic traditions of Arosi, west Makira, only those who inherited aristocratic rank could gain support and recognition as important men or chiefs through the organization of feasts. But although the Lau regarded whole great-shell (*gwa'ila'o*) pendants and local *dala* shell-disks as aristocrats' ornaments, and the Sa'a were familiar with the Arosi practice of restricting certain ornaments to aristocrats, even they wore the most valuable ornaments not as badges of rank but as symbols of the wealth which rank could confer (Maranda, Ivens 1927:chs 5 and 6, 465). For inland people like the Kwara'ae, inherited rank was more a historical ideal than a present reality. The title 'lord' (*aofia*), associated with the prestigious great-shell pendant, was inherited by the feast-giving chiefs of Lau, but in Kwara'ae in the later twentieth century it was more a claim to precedence as 'paramount chief' in the chiefs' organization (see Burt 1994a:75, 272).

For most of Malaita, a man's heirloom ornaments might show his seniority within a more or less important clan, but it was the value of the ornaments which he and his family wore that showed him to be an important man. Kwara'ae tabu-speakers could gain wealth from fees and contributions to sacrifices, and fame from organizing sacrificial festivals, and warriors could receive and distribute wealth from rewards for killings. Not all became wealthy men of possessions, but they wore their ornaments as symbols of wealth and prestige. Claims to exclusive use of ornaments had to be defended, as when a Kwaio clan proclaimed copyright over a certain design of rattan band (*obi*) for the arm (see page 128), and the people of Dai island, north Malaita, claimed exclusive rights over a certain design of bag (Maranda). Such claims invited challenges and, as in the Dai case, could lead to violent feuds.

Plate 20 This man may have been a tabu-speaker or a warrior, from Kwara'ae or north Malaita. He wears a big patterned comb (*kafa gwaroa doe*) and two cowries (*buli*) in his hair, a big shell-disk (*sa'ela'o doe*) on his head, patterned-bamboos (*fa'i'augwaroa*) and earring-clusters (*barutege*) in his ears, a scorpion (*fafari*) ornament in his nose and a string of human teeth (*ūma ana lifa ngwae*) around his neck. On his arms are a plain dark fibre ring (*sangisangi*) and a patterned one, probably an enclosed-strap (*'ababanibani*) of glass beads, two sets of conus arm-rings (*fa'ikome*, of the third type described on page 138) and plaited rattan bands (*obi*) at the wrists. His leather strap (*'abatarafa*) has pouches and a sheath-knife. His serrated-clothing (*tagiri*) lavalava with its jagged edge was a fashion in north Malaita before the Second World War.

Who he was we do not know. Like ornaments in museums, old photographs from the Solomons often bear no information apart from the colonial visitor who owned them, in this case Alexander Wilson, Government Surveyor and Commissioner of Lands for the British Solomon Islands Protectorate during the 1920s and 1930s. (BM Oc,A56.30)

Plate 21 This delegation of chiefs from Rakwane in the Fataleka inland came down to Fokanakafo on the east coast in 1949 to meet a touring government party. This was during the Māsina Rul period and these men, who had declined to join the movement, seem to have ornamented themselves to proclaim their own status and their respect for the colonial government.

Their ornaments give an interesting glimpse of how the chiefs of their near neighbours in Kwara'ae might have appeared, a generation before their first formal portrait in 1976 (see Plate 10, page 16). Among the six of them there are five fish-teeth-cluster (*barulifaī'a*) straps worn around mariners' hats (relics of the German colonial presence west of Solomon Islands until the First World War; Russell), another five such straps worn around the neck, and four great-shell (*gwa'ila'o*) disks (contradicting the common opinion that this was only worn by a great 'lord' or *aofia*). One man has a shell-disk-rattle (*ketesa'ela'o*) around the neck, one a scorpion (*fafari*) nose-pendant, and one a stopper (*du'udu'u*) nose-stud. The man on the right wears one money-bead and one dolphin-teeth bandolier and the man next to him wears the money-bead-net sash fringed with human teeth (Kwaio and 'Are'are *'umaaru*), as well as a fish-teeth-cluster (*barulifaī'a*) at the neck. Some wear lavalavas, some have their calico tied in front in the older style, and one also wears a piece of calico over his shoulder. The tall man with the girdle (*fo'osae*) also wears as a bandolier a belt of shell beads and dolphin teeth from Isabel or New Georgia (as in Plate 38, page 55), illustrating the point that unusual ornaments might be traded from afar (see page 52). (Russell photo 10)

The glamour of power and the power of ornaments

The beauty of Malaitan body ornaments, their striking shapes, shiny surfaces and bright colours, enhanced by the bodies of their wearers, long ago gained the admiration of foreign visitors and collectors, museum curators and even missionaries. The people who made and used these things must have enjoyed their appearance too, so why were they so willing to dispose of them or destroy them under the influence of these foreigners?

The value of this artistic tradition evidently depended on more than visual appearance. Body ornaments also reflected the glamour of wealth, power and prestige of those who could best afford to wear them, contributing a powerful artistic quality to the dominant values of Malaitan society. They helped youths and maidens to attract one another, married men and women to appear as respectable members of the community and leaders to become impressive figures of authority. But when colonial trade, religion and government shifted the balance of economic, spiritual and political power towards the colonial Whitemen and those who mediated or shared their influence, much of this glamour was lost from the art of body ornaments. Their symbolic value under the old social order made body ornaments inappropriate to the new order of colonial and global society.

Kwara'ae elders describe people dressed in ornaments in former times as 'looking very good' (*lia le'a liu*), 'looking right' (*lia 'olo'olo*) or 'perfect' (*sali*), their oiled bodies and ornaments 'gleaming and colourful' (*lia mamarigwa'ila'a*). They made a festival 'look beautiful' (*lia kwanga liu*) and everyone happy, including the ancestral ghosts in whose honour it was held. People enjoyed seeing the festival-giver's wealth displayed in his and his family's ornaments as signs of the prosperity he was sharing with them. But the effect went deeper than this. 'Looking good' is a rather commonplace expression, suitable for a good-looking youth or maiden, but a person dressed in ornaments also 'looked important' (*lia 'inoto'a*), or even 'very good and important' (*le'a 'inoto'a liu*), meaning significant and impressive. For the wearer himself, the ornaments 'made him (feel) important' (*fa'a'inoto'a*), strong (*fa'angasi'a*) and confident (*fa'amamana*), or even warlike (*ramo'a*), if he was preparing to fight. As in spiritual matters, effectiveness (*mamana*) is a matter of emotion as well as action.

Elders recall how, in their youth, they found such sights so impressive as to be intimidating and awesome, making them tremble or start (*lebe*) with surprise and fear. Aisah Osifera recalled attending the last great festivals at the ancient tabu-sanctum of Siale in the 1930s:

'Let's go and see Siale.' Because they made the place like a town, they'd go not to eat but just to look; 'Oh my word! It's no lie!' I saw it myself. Many men came. Sometimes I was frightened to approach them, frightened by the senior men with their crescents [*dafe*], spears and clubs. Eh, it was strange, the men looked different. (Burt and Kwa'ioloa 2001:28)[17]

Looking 'different' or strange (*lia matamata*) is a common description for such sights, implying unusual and special. Such was the impression created by politically influential senior men and by warriors when they ornamented themselves in preparation to fight. Ornaments contributed to the aggressive, intimidating display conventionally staged by men on public occasions.

When people came together for feasts, festivals and presentations there was always an element of competitive display and challenge between hosts and guests, good humoured perhaps, but reflecting political tensions between clans which could lead to sorcery or even open fighting. For such occasions men would not only dress in their finest ornaments, with magical protection, but also add the leaves of decorative shrubs and trees, forest trees and ferns, to give a wild and exciting effect. As a party of guests crashed out of the forest into the clearing they would shout and make a great noise to show their enjoyment of the occasion, but also to challenge and startle their hosts as they gave and received presentations of food or strings of money. Malakai Kailiu, who witnessed such events in his youth, drew on the experience in his history of how a famous warrior arrived with food for a competitive feast in Latea in east Kwara'ae:

[Kali] called up lots of men of the inland and they shouldered the pudding, then they warded off ghosts and went. Later on many men and many women heard that pudding coming as they shouted with it, and they began to be afraid; 'Oh, it's a band, they're coming to kill us today.' They said 'No, stand still. What can it be?' They listened and said 'That's Kali, it's his pudding coming.' Well, that man Kali brought the pudding and shouted, trees were breaking, the people were frightened, they arrived with the pudding and put it down.

The Revd H.S. Hipkin of the Melanesian Mission described a similar scene at a brideprice presentation for a maiden from Lama in central Kwara'ae in the mid 1930s:

After five hours' loud-voiced bartering, men adorned with leaves came through the bush from all directions carrying strings of money on long poles, dancing and screaming in an alarming manner, until finally about 100 strings of red and white shell rings [beads] accumulated on the stand [hung on a beam] erected for the purpose. … The whole thing is a game which gives pleasure and creates mirth. (*SCL*, June 1936:90)

Such experiences, enhanced by the display of ornaments, are now receding into folklore as the old people who witnessed the feasts and festivals, feuds and rewards disappear one by one. For many Kwara'ae today the old body ornaments are a rather ambivalent symbol of former times; a tradition they take a certain pride in but know little about and do not much care to bring into the present. One reason for this is that the glamour of ornaments has a spiritual as well as a social power, which is hard to reconcile with the Christianity and global culture which has permeated the Pacific Islands during the twentieth century. For some, ornaments represent the ancestral religion, as the dominant fundamentalist churches have in effect given them to Satan and the ghosts now associated with him by declaring these things to be heathen and unacceptable to God. Samuel Alasa'a, who grew up in the traditional religion, used the imagery of the old-time warrior to describe its patron: 'Satan girded on his patterned girdle, grasped his bundle of arrows, put on his new bag, stepped out on the hill and a gong cried out' (Burt and Kwa'ioloa 2001:124). The visual and emotional impact of ornamented persons was evocative of spiritual and magical power, making them apt symbols of ancestral ghosts, both to Christians and to their opponents, like those who confronted Revd Arthur Hopkins in the 1900s.

In Kwara'ae, emotional experiences induced by prayer and concentration are crucial to the invocation of spiritual power

Plate 22 Irobaoa of Suaba, on the coast of north Malaita, posed as a wealthy chief of the sea people (mentioned by Ivens 1930:55, 69) for this portrait, and a closeup, in around 1910 (in the same series as Plates 1 and 4, pages viii and 10). He wears a fine set of valuable north Malaita ornaments.

On his head Irobaoa has a mass of split-bright-strips (*'abafilutafi*) of palm-leaf, probably stained red and fixed to a comb, two cowries (*fa'ibuli*) and a large turtle-pattern (*funifunu*, or *dala*) ornament, probably especially valuable for having been traded from western Solomons (to judge by the design). He has earrings (*tege*) of turtleshell, one with a conus (*kome*) ring, and a fine scorpion (*fafari*) nose-pendant. His necklace is of hundreds of the most valuable *robo* dolphin teeth.

The enclosed-strap (*'ababanibani*) bands on his arms and his belt (*fo'o'aba*) are of glass beads (the belt would normally be tied at the front, as it is in the close-up). He also has conus (*fa'ikome*) arm-rings, conus-rattles (*ketekome*) at the knees and rattan bands (*obi*) at the ankles. He wears his calico in a characteristic Malaitan style, and holds a deflector (*'alafolo*) club.

Irobaoa's daughter wears a valuable fence (*biru*) of dolphin teeth around her neck and a maiden's *susuru* belt, probably of glass beads, holding her leaf apron. (Photographer unknown, Edge-Partington collection, BM Oc,Ca46/20)

through trance and possession by spiritual beings, whether ghosts or God in the form of the Holy Spirit. When people encounter ghosts (or 'satans' as Alasa'a's generation called them in Pijin), as even good Christians may do in dreams and visions, they tend to see them as people in traditional 'heathen' dress. Michael Kwa'ioloa, Alasa'a's son, described such an experience in his autobiography:

> As I slept I dreamed that my [dead] mother had come once again. I saw her stand facing me and I saw a very old man come and stand beside her, but he wasn't looking at me, he was looking at a thicket of bamboos down the hill. He was carrying a big angle-club on his arm and I could see he had a pattern-strap [*'abagwaro* armstrap] and I could see the tip of a crescent [*dafe* pendant] and the end of a nose-pin [*usuusu*] sticking out, and he was wearing a girdle [*fo'osae*]. … Then my mother said 'Look at him, it's your ancestor standing here. If it wasn't for mother he'd kill you. Get up and go while you're still alive.' … I was in those pagan districts where my ancestors are, where they still offer sacrifices to the ghosts. (Kwa'ioloa and Burt 1997:64)[18]

Andrew Gwa'italafa recalled his mother explaining how a certain crocodile, the creature worshipped by her clan at Kwarea in west Fataleka, was identified as the ghost of her father Fane'oro'oro after he died in the 1940s:

> Because Fane'oro'oro used to wear a crescent [*dafe* pendant] and pattern-straps [*'abagwaro*] and a stud [*'otu*] in his nose. Well, because the real man Fane'oro'oro, his sons and others still worshipped him [after he died]. That's why, when they called for him to come up from out of the water and he wanted to show himself, they could see the marks on his two arms and on his nose, where the stud had been, and where he had lost one hand, and it always showed out.

As symbols and relics of ancestors, old ornaments are still likely to evoke dreams from ghosts, who are always ready to offer their power to those who will worship them. That many important ornaments were tabu or sacrosanct, to be protected from unauthorized persons and especially from women, as possessions of tabu-speakers and warriors or heirlooms from the ghosts, confirms this identification with the old religion. Indeed, some ornaments were actually dedicated to ancestral ghosts to gain their spiritual support (as were weapons). A man might name an important ornament such as a crescent (*dafe*) or great-shell (*gwa'ila'o*) pendant for an ancestral ghost so that it would cool harmful magic (*'ainifalia*) at public gatherings and turn it back upon the attacker. He might dedicate his girdle to a ghost who would give him power for fighting, tying to it a packaged relic such as a piece of bone and praying to the ghost as he put it on, or he might attach a charm to an ornamental comb for protection against sorcery. Some of the leaves worn as ornaments also had magical powers for protection from magic and sorcery. Men wore *Litsea* (*sarufi*) tree leaves covering their fronts on public occasions, to block and turn back harmful magic; and decorated their bags with *Euodia* (*ri'i*) to attract women; while colourful crotons (*'ala'ala*) and cordylines (*dili*), planted and picked for various magical and ritual purposes, were also favourite leaves for sticking under armbands and girdles. There were also men who could apply 'attraction' (*'ilu*) to a person or an object such as an ornamented bag by a sprinkling of coconut water, to make a girl fall in love with a man (sometimes with uncontrollable and disastrous results, as old histories tell). A team of dancers would be given such an 'attraction blessing' (*'ilungwalungwalu*) before performing for a festival, with a prayer for the spectators to be 'startled' (*lebe*) at how good they look and sound. Women dared not look at them during their first dance for fear of falling madly in love.

Beyond these spiritual and magical associations, the powerful effect of an ornamented person upon others reflected the power of money, itself a form of ornament, to mediate the important relationships in Kwara'ae society. The Kwara'ae emphasize the importance of their local shell-bead money in creating and restoring relationships in its use for marriage payments (*daura'ia*), presentations in restitution (*fa'aābua*) for grievances, and compensation (*to'ato'a, toli'abua*) for death and bloodshed. Men, and to a lesser extent women, became community leaders by helping their relatives and neighbours to make such payments, and they raised their names by using the influence so gained to organize great community projects like feasts and festivals. In developing the prosperity and solidarity of their own communities, such leaders also defended them against others by providing rewards (*fo'oa*), again including money, for killing in restitution and vengeance. Control of the money which mediated this political power was concealed for most of the time in the debts and obligations which people owed to their elders and leaders, as the money itself was concealed in secret caches in their houses. Money was usually displayed to public gaze only when presented to others, hung on a beam as it was contributed and then redistributed piece by piece. It was on such occasions that it might be worn, draped around the body as a symbol of wealth and influence. These displays were brief but crucial demonstrations of how money served its purpose in mediating relationships of power in being given and repaid.

On the other hand, purchasing ornaments with money was an investment in prestige which endured over generations. The ornaments of an important man, tabu by their intimate association with his person, eventually became symbols of social identity for his heirs. Ornaments like big shell-disks, crescent pendants and pattern-strap armstraps, although notionally valued as equivalent to a ten-string money, became valued even more as heirlooms, symbolic of descent from the ancestors from whom people also inherited their claims to land and spiritual support. It is for this reason that the lineage of ornaments is so well remembered by their owners over many generations (as in some examples illustrated in Chapter 4). As heirlooms these ornaments could no longer be exchanged like the money which may once have purchased them, as impersonal units of value. Instead they were worn as symbols of everything which money represented and more, inviting others to acknowledge its power in the person of the wearers, far outlasting the wealth which created it. If they were exchanged, it was as prestigous gifts confirming clan membership and identity.

The visual effect of body ornaments, when their bright colours and intricate patterns were displayed to best effect against the dark body, is only part of the explanation for their power in Kwara'ae society. Participants in this artistic tradition,

Plate 23 'Tausfera', a senior man of 'Aoke island, Langalanga, photographed in 1907 by George Rose and identified by District Officer Thomas Edge-Partington.[19] He wears a big patterned comb (*kafa gwaroa doe*) and cowries (*buli*) in his hair, various indistinguishable ear ornaments and a scorpion (*farifari*) nose-pendant. The large pig teeth (*lifa gwata*) at his neck hang from necklaces ('*alu 'alu*) of large glass beads (*kekefa*). He has a band (*obi*) of plaited vine-strip on one arm and an enclosed-strap ('*ababanibani*) of glass beads and a conus (*fa'i kome*) ring on the other, a calico loincloth (*kabilato*) with leather strap ('*abatarafa*), and what may be strips of calico below the knees. (Edge-Partington collection, BM Oc,Ca47.74)

the viewers as well as the wearers of the ornaments, would respond at the same time to the wealth and influence, the inherited identity and personal status, which these glamorous artefacts displayed on certain social occasions. If and when ornaments were disposed of, this represented a renunciation of this complex of traditional values, as when joining the Christian church. The Whiteman response confirmed these values in its cruder and less positive interpretations of the attractive 'curios' which created the also glamorous 'savage of imagination', as Revd Hopkins so aptly described him.

From either perspective, body ornaments were so intimately involved in Kwara'ae economic, political and religious culture that they were bound to fall from favour when their society was transformed by colonialism. From the first, Malaitan Christians who turned their backs on the competitive status-seeking of men of possessions, on the demands of ghosts for sacrifices mediated by the tabu-speakers, and on the coercive aggression of the warriors, inevitably found themselves questioning the visual symbols of

the traditional social order which these men represented. The Whitemen provided an alternative in the clothing promoted by employers and Christian missions, symbolic of the new cultural and political realities of the colonial order. This clothing took on a glamour of its own from the early years of labour migration in the nineteenth century, as trappings of the powerful and exciting world beyond the Solomons which was imposing itself so forcefully upon the people of Malaita.

The capitalist world order to which the Kwara'ae were introduced from this time makes few allowances for the local cultures of small corners of the world, dominated as it is by the economic, political and religious interests of people far away who have never heard of Solomon Islands, let alone Malaita. For all their determined resistance to foreign domination, the Kwara'ae and most of their neighbours have gradually forsaken the artistic power of their traditional body ornaments for the ubiquitous global culture of the Whiteman.

Notes

1 This was, presumably, the inlet leading to the present-day village of Nāfinua. Kwakwaru, a coastal area just to the north, was a general name for the district later known as Kwai.

2 A practice also noted by the labour recruiter Ernie Philp at Sio in north Malaita in 1913 (Herr 1978:175).

3 Almost all extant nineteenth-century photographs of Solomon Islanders in glass-bead ornaments, if they have provenances, are from Fiji, but an example in the State Library of Queensland State ('South Sea Islanders dressed in traditional costume, Mackay, Queensland, ca. 1890', Image No 13355) shows that similar styles were worn there too.

4 *The Southern Cross Log* is the newsletter of the Melanesian Mission, cited hereafter as *SCL*.

5 *Not In Vain* is the newsletter of the South Sea Evangelical Mission, cited hereafter as *NIV*.

6 This translation is slightly different from that previously published.

7 Although the author does not mention which language group or even island he is describing, this can be deduced from the description and the use of the Kwara'ae / Fataleka / Baegu term *akalo* for ghost elsewhere in the passage.

8 The photographs Lewis took on this occasion (Welsch 1998, vol.2:221) have unfortunately disappeared from his collection in the Field Museum of Natural History in Chicago.

9 These valuations were also recognized in Lau, and no doubt elsewhere in north Malaita, apart from some differences from the smaller Kwara'ae money denominations (Maranda).

10 For instance, the arm-rings, nose-pins and money-bead belts listed by Bogesi among the 'currency' used on Isabel (1948:228).

11 In Kwaio priests keep necklaces of ancestral relics (called *furu'ai*, *kwalofuru* or *matala*) including ornaments, some of which they display publicly for particular rituals, others which can never be seen by anyone but themselves. These are particularly important in rituals to magically attract wealth.

12 Hence the Pijin translations for *ramo*: *larakin* and *kaoboe* (cowboy).

13 As described also for Kwaio by Keesing (1985).

14 The shell-inlaid stone-and-pearl (*fou'atoleeleo*) baton worn by the killer or his representative at such ceremonies in Kwaio and areas to the south (as illustrated in de Coppet and Zemp 1978: 105–6 and described in Akin 1982) was not used in Kwara'ae and few people had even heard of it (see page 158).

15 This translation is slightly different from that previously published.

16 For instance, Harold Ross's description of a Baegu portrait as showing 'the ceremonial dress of a war leader (*ramo*)' (1973:21) could equally be a tabu-speaker or a man of possessions in Kwara'ae, and de Coppet's symbolic schema for 'Are'are ornaments in terms of 'killers' and 'peace masters' contradicts the evidence from other parts of Malaita, as mentioned in the Introduction (1995:238–9).

17 This translation is slightly different from that previously published.

18 This translation is slightly different from that previously published.

19 The Rose Stereograph card 12,273 is labelled 'THE CHIEF of one of the Fortified Islands in the LANGA LANGA LAGOON, MALAITA, SOLOMON ISLANDS', whereas Edge-Partington, who presumably knew the man personally, labelled a print in his album as 'Tausfera of Auke Id. Mala.'

Plate 24 Eleson La'ake of Kafomaro stood out in the crowd at a feast at 'Afi'o in west Kwara'ae in 1984, as the only person ornamented in local style. He carried a *tari'olo* club and tangled-bag (*ngwa'ifiura*) and wore plastic split-bright-strips (*'abafilutali*) on his comb and a plastic nose-pin (*usuusu*). His ornaments were of glass beads, second best to the money-bead ornaments he would have worn to take part in the festival dances, planned but abandoned due to the opposition of local church leaders. (Burt photo)

Chapter 3

Making, selling and documenting ornaments

To appreciate the many kinds of body ornaments worn and discarded by the people of Malaita, it helps to understand how they were made and traded, then collected and documented by the Whitemen who have preserved so many more of them than Malaitans now possess. Ornaments were valuable, made to be sold as well as to wear, often requiring scarce materials, special skills and hard work to make. They were valued by Whitemen too, as 'curios' or mementos of exotic peoples and places. Their arrival created a new market for ornaments, a minor sideline in the exchange of local labour and raw materials for foreign manufactured goods. As time went on, this curio trade played an important part in depleting Malaita of ornaments, while also encouraging their production, influencing their style and preserving them for posterity.

Making ornaments

The materials used for ornaments – money-beads, shell, teeth, turtleshell and strips from vines and trees for twine, bindings and coloured patterning – derived from both the sea (*asi*) and the inland (*tolo*). In most of Malaita these were the domains of different peoples, who exchanged goods with one another under conditions of political tension which, formerly, made it difficult for each to gain direct access to the other's resources. Inland people like the Kwara'ae could produce the forest materials, but the most valuable ornaments were made from the more durable products of the sea.

The techniques involved were not difficult for a people who all learnt the manual skills required for their own basic material needs. Anyone could try their hand (as shown by the many ornaments made by people who were evidently not very good at it), but such skills were usually passed down in a few families. The best results required tuition and practice, as the Kwaio Cultural Centre demonstrated when it promoted the revival of ornamental crafts in the early 1980s. Novices

learned by observation as much as instruction, and although experts would demonstrate valuable knowledge and skill for their own children, they expected others to repay them in some way. Their pupils in their turn hoped to earn money from their new skills.

Most ornaments were made by men, particularly those which men wore, including the valuable shell ornaments; but women made the waist straps they wore and both women and men made patterned bands and straps. Some individuals specialized in making ornaments for sale and became well known for it, like Laete'esafi of 'Ai'eda and Sulafanamae of Tofu, east Kwaio, whose work appears a number of times in this book. Inland people would still depend on farming for a living, but for the sea people of Malaita ornamental valuables were an important part of the inland trade that enabled them to live and prosper on offshore islands without sufficient land to grow their own foods. Besides supplying fish, the west coast Langalanga made shell money-beads and the east coast Lau hunted dolphins for their teeth and took fees from Langalanga shell-gatherers. These valuables, which they exchanged with their inland neighbours and traded by sea around Malaita and beyond, served as money in the sense that they were widely acceptable in exchange for a range of things which were less easily exchanged for each other. The Lau and Langalanga, prospering from this trade in moneys and other products of the sea, preferred to buy most of their ornaments from inland rather than develop the skills to make them for themselves (Paravicini 1931:157, Maranda).

The inland people exchanged their garden foods and pigs with their sea neigbours not only for fish and money but also for the raw shell and turtleshell to make ornaments and some kinds of money themselves. They were also the best placed to make the objects of forest materials, patterned in yellow, red and black, which were characteristic of Malaita. But, unable to travel much by sea except as migrant workers from the late nineteenth century, the inland people participated in long-distance trade mainly through their sea neighbours. The sea people also had the advantage when trade with Whiteman ships began to introduce new foreign (*faka* or ship) ornamental materials, particularly glass beads and cloth, as well as new technologies and designs. These were quickly adapted to enhance Malaitan body ornaments even as the ornaments were declining under the impact of colonialism.

Plate 25 The people of Langalanga have long been demonstrating their money-making to foreign visitors. In 1933 Toshio Asaeda photographed the people of 'Aoke island for the American Museum of Natural History. These women are drilling the money-beads. (National Museum, Osaka no. X0076781)

Most techniques and materials were used for a variety of different ornaments, so they are best described in general terms. We begin with the money-beads which are such an important feature of Malaitan body ornaments, before considering other work in shell, then vine and other forest materials, and some of the techniques for making these things into body ornaments.

Money-beads / *Maga mani kī*

Beads (*maga*, which also means seed), made from shell and strung into local money, can also be made up into body ornaments, and some moneys can also be worn to ornament the body. The Kwara'ae seldom make such money themselves, but buy it from neighbouring peoples and say that originally they paid for things, including brideprice, with vines of flowers, valuable objects such as weapons and ornaments, or dolphin teeth. The value of money-beads depends both on the type of shell and on the labour required to work them. Most valuable are beads of the scarcest red shell, ground small and smooth, which takes more work and incurs more breakages.

The main suppliers of money-beads for Malaita as a whole are the west-coast sea people of Langalanga, from the island of 'Aoke in the north (after which the neighbouring capital of Malaita was named) to Bina in the south. They are said to have learnt to make money-beads from a Guadalcanal woman who came to Malaita to marry a Kwara'ae man and moved to Langalanga.[1] The Kwaio and other inland peoples of central and south Malaita also make their own kinds of money. Anyone can make money if they can obtain the materials, like

people in Lau who began to make money of the Langalanga kind in the 1980s (Woodhead and Maranda 1987).

The manufacture of money in Langalanga has long fascinated visiting Whitemen, who have been writing about it since the early twentieth century. The best sources, Charles Woodford, the first British Resident Commissioner (1908a), and J. F. Bartle (1952), are in general agreement with recent Langalanga accounts, although technology and trade patterns have changed somewhat since the Second World War.

Most of the work making these money-beads is done by women, especially maidens who have fewer domestic duties and may devote a full day to the work. They begin by chipping the shell into rough beads, formerly using a specially shaped long hammer and anvil of 'hammer stone' (*fau li 'ui*), a smooth black volcanic rock, more recently with an iron hammer-head. The beads are ground flat by embedding them in a 'wooden face' (*mā'ai*) of *rarala* wood and grinding them on stone with an abrasive powder (*taradi*), made by burning a type of coarse flint. Each bead is then drilled, supported in a coconut shell 'drill-rest' (*teo li futa*). Formerly the drill was a wooden pump-drill with a turtle-bone flywheel, propelled by cords running from the top of the shaft to the ends of a crossbar. The cords are wound around the drill shaft and as the crossbar is pushed down they unwind, spinning the shaft and then winding up again in the opposite direction by the action of the flywheel. The drill-bit was made from flint (*naki*) of a particular kind, sharper than that available locally, pressure-flaked from a core with a *keke* clam-shell (Kwara'ae *ba'uba'u*) from the mangroves. Such drills were still in routine

Plate 26 Asaeda's 1933 photographs of 'Aoke show all the stages of money-making. Of the two women, one chips shell into disks with a hammer-stone while the other grinds them flat on a stone, embedded in the face of a wooden block. (National Museum, Osaka no. X0076775)

Plate 27 The man smooths a string of beads with a grinding stone. (National Museum, Osaka no. X0076782)

use after the Second World War, but were eventually replaced by imported drills like the wheel-brace. After the 1960s the special skill for making flint bits with minimum wastage of the scarce flint was lost, but the old drills are still used for tourist demonstrations.

Once the beads are shaped and drilled, it is men's work to grind the edges smooth. Formerly the rough beads were threaded on a length of *lili* vine, which grows in the creeks and has to be specially stripped and prepared, but since the early 1970s this has been replaced by heavy-duty plastic line. The length of beads is laid along a groove in a long wooden plank and ground with a grooved stone to smooth the edges. Formerly this was done with a local 'grinding-stone' (*fau li ara*, a kind of white limestone) and black sand, but since the 1970s imported whetstones have been used. When made up into strings for exchange, the beads were strung on twine made from the bark of certain vines or trees (see below, page 42), which has also been replaced by plastic string.

Types of beads / *Malita'i magarū kī*
The Langalanga make different kinds of beads for different markets, including several kinds used in Kwara'ae. The Kwara'ae themselves admit they know less about money-beads than those who make them, and would defer to the Langalanga sources from whom the following derives.[2]

Galu, which the Langalanga usually call *galia*, are white beads made from a type of cockle found in the mud

(Langalanga, *kakadu*, single shell, *rakwasi*; *Arca granosa*; Woodford 1908a:82). The Kwara'ae call varieties of this shell *gwarigwari* and *uriuri* (meaning they find it by treading with the feet). Shells were bought from Tarapaina in 'Are'are, south Malaita, and from Gela.

Safi are brown-red beads made from *kē*, a type of mussel found in pockets in the rock on the reefs. The shell is grey and the blanks for beads are turned red by placing them on a heated river pebble (*fau li para*).

Romu are brighter red beads made from *romu*, a type of clam found many fathoms down on the face of the reef (*Chama pacifica*; Woodford 1908a:82). *Romu* is particularly valuable not only because of its colour but also for its scarcity and the difficulty of obtaining the shell. Formerly Langalanga men dived for *romu* shells under the direction of their tabu-speaker with the support of their shark-ghosts, and since becoming Christians they have found it more difficult to dive deep enough. They also dived for it or bought it in various places around Malaita, including Tarapaina in the south and Mānaoba in the north and, until a ban in the 1970s, also from Gela. Ordinary or second-grade *romu* beads are made from the 'left hand side' of the shell (near the hinge), where the colour is paler, white and pink, although the blanks for the beads may be be heated on stone to turn them a deeper brown-red, as with *safi*. Since the Second World War *safi* has replaced this kind of *romu* in money.

Fira'i are the first-grade type of *romu*, made from the deep crimson-red 'right hand side' of the *romu* shell (at the lip), and are most valuable of all as very few beads can be made from each shell.[3]

Kurila, which the Kwara'ae also call *gorila*, are black beads made from a type of large oyster which is found in the sand in shallow water.

Fulu are black beads made from the seeds of the *fulu* shrub (Gesneriaceae, resembling a pandanus), which grows inland. A smaller kind of *fulu* is made from the seeds of a similar shrub called *tasisi* (Cyperaceae), which grows in the mangroves. The ends of the seed are cut off using a special 'fulu stone' (*fau li fulu*) and when the kernel is removed this leaves a disk with a hole in the middle. Although not regarded as money-beads themselves, *fulu* are used to decorate both northern and southern kinds of money.

'Alu'alu are white beads made from *iriiri* clam-shell, which is easier to work than the cockle (*gwarigwari*) used for money-beads, but is not of a quality suitable for money. They are used for ornaments such as necklaces (also called *'alu'alu*). Necklaces are also made from other shells such as 'joined' (*adoma*), a black mangrove clam-shell which produces purple beads.

Mani kwao or **white money** is a Kwara'ae description of a kind of small grey-white beads made from the tips of several kinds of conical winkle (*karango*) shells collected from the beach. In the 1930s the Kwara'ae were reported to be making these beads themselves (D.O. Malaita 1935), but more recently they have obtained them from the Langalanga and the Kwaio, whose names for the beads are *kofu* and *māmalakwa*i, and from the smaller community of sea people off the coast of east Kwara'ae.

The making of these beads in Kwaio is described by David Akin (1993:879–80).[4] The whorl of each shell is broken off, formerly with a stone tool, now with wire-cutters. Formerly the tip was pierced by setting several at once into a piece of soft wood and grinding them down on a stone until they could be pierced with a hardwood stick, but more recently they are simply pierced with a steel needle. The resulting rough beads are threaded on several splinters of a smashed bamboo, the intact base of which is used as a handle while they are ground and polished all at once on a stone with water, or on a whetstone, in such a way that the beads rotate and become round. When finished they are usually threaded on shreds of bark such as *sula* and *malao* (*Trichospermum*), being too small for the twine used for most Langalanga beads.

'Afi'afi, also called *utafunu*, is a particularly fine kind of the white money (*kofu*) beads made in Kwaio, ground smaller and double the value. It is used for certain kinds of moneys in Kwaio and 'Are'are and for ornaments requiring fine beads.

Soela are flat white beads made in Langalanga by grinding down a type of small cone-shell, with a large hole formed from the cavity of the shell. They look like tiny rings and hence may be referred to as conus (*kome*, see below, page 40) and are used for ornaments such as the circle-fence (*barafā*) and earring-cluster (*barutege*). *Soela* may also be identified, or confused, with *galu* money-beads, but although the circle-fence is used as money in north Malaita, *soela* are not used for either the northern or southern kinds of money. They were also made for ornaments in Guadalcanal and western Solomons.

Dodo are small flat conus (*kome*) rings, named for the way food is pressed into flat disks when packed (*dodoa*) into a bamboo flask. They are used to ornament *bani'au* money denominations by threading several on each string of beads. They are not regarded as money in themselves and were also used on certain ornaments. In Kwaio similar beads are also made of blackened coconut-shell (*sonabo'o*, *sona* being Kwaio for *dodo*).

Dolphin teeth / *Lifa kirio kī*

Dolphin teeth, more commonly but less precisely called *lifa ī'a* or fish teeth, are also used as money in Malaita, particularly by the sea people who catch the dolphins, and like shell beads they are also used for body ornaments.

At one time or another all the sea peoples around Malaita caught dolphins.[5] The practice lapsed in many places during the 1920s, partly due to doubts about the loss of necessary spiritual support after conversion to Christianity. However, Anglicans in Sa'a were demonstrating the power of God to secure a good catch as early as 1900 (Wilson 1932:200) and Christians in certain communities revived dolphin catching in the late 1940s, responding to shortage of dolphin teeth and encouraged by cultural revival under Māsina Rul (Hill 1989). The main sources of dolphin teeth during the twentieth century have been Bita'ama in To'abaita, Lau lagoon, and the Lau people of west Sa'a, for each of which dolphin catching has been described in some detail (by Ivens 1902 and 1930: Ch.9, Hopkins 1930:18, Dawbin 1966, Takekewa 1996). Others included Kwarea in the northwest, occasionally the sea neighbours of the Kwara'ae on Kwai, Ngongosila, Leili and Uru islands in the east, and the Langalanga, who gave it up after the Second World War (Guo). Dolphin teeth were also much used on Makira, where the dolphin catchers of Anuta in Arosi were said to be the main source for that island in the early twentieth century (Dickinson 1927:59). There is also a tradition that dolphins were once caught in the Maringe area of Isabel (Naramana 1987:41).

Catching dolphins is a task for a whole community. In the season, schools of dolphins are located far out at sea and driven ashore in an operation requiring skilful co-ordination

Figure 1 Examples of money-beads (*maga mani*), of varying size and quality.

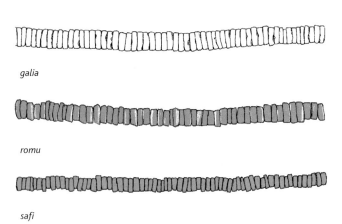

galia

romu

safi

kurila with *galu* and *safi* in a ten-string (*tafuli'ae*) money

fulu with *galu* and *safi* in a ten-string (*tafuli'ae*) money

kofu

of a fleet of canoes, with spiritual support, formerly from ancestral ghosts and associated sharks. A community might catch about 800 dolphins a year, averaging 100 per drive, each one reckoned to provide about 120 teeth, besides large quantities of meat (Takekewa 1996). The subsequent work of drilling a hole near the base of each tooth to string them was a major task occupying the whole community (Wilson 1932:204).

The money trade
The valuables of shell, teeth and other materials which Islanders regard as local 'money' were once traded through networks linking districts and islands, directly or indirectly, throughout most of what is now Solomon Islands. Even the making of money-beads involved an extensive trade network around Malaita and beyond, for although all kinds of shells are available in Langalanga, they have not always been sufficient to meet demand. Alternative sources, where the Langalanga could either buy, or pay to dive for, shell by special arrangement with local communities, include west 'Are'are in south Malaita, north Malaita and Lau Lagoon, and Gela (Bartle 1952, Connell 1977, Belshaw 1950:174). Formerly the tools also required specialized materials from elsewhere. Some came from the Kwara'ae inland, such as flint for the abrasive *taradi* powder, hammer-stones, flint for drill bits, grinding-stones and a black mud used with it (BSIP n.d.). Other materials came from further abroad: hammer-stones also from north Malaita (Bartle 1952:380) or even from the Weather Coast of Guadalcanal, and flint for drill-bits from Tarapaina and sometimes Ulawa (Woodford 1926). The Langalanga people of Manaafe had a special trading relationship with Tarapaina, voyaging to each other's homes to exchange materials for money, which they traded onwards. Various people specialized in preparing drill-shafts, grinding-stones, *lili* vine and twine, all in return for payment, although by the late twentieth century most of these things had been replaced by industrially produced foreign imports. There were also centres of money-bead production at the Malaitan settlement of Marau in east Guadalcanal and at Hounihu in Arosi, southeast Makira, both of which were sources for the white cockle and red clam-shells. The Makira industry declined with conversion to Christianity before the Second World War but later revived, and in the late twentieth century money-beads were being made at Su'uwaiwora in the southeast and Su'unamuga in the southwest (Belshaw 1950:173, 179, Scott).

The Langalanga made and exported different kinds of money according to the local preferences of their trading partners in Malaita and the neighbouring islands. In the late nineteenth century they were voyaging regularly to Gela and Isabel to exchange money for large quantities of food (Penny 1887:86). These islands linked Malaita indirectly into the money system to the west, based on tridacna arm-rings made in New Georgia, and by the mid twentieth century the people of Bogotu in eastern Isabel were using red money-beads and dolphin teeth from Malaita and New Georgia arm-rings in place of their older local moneys such as ornaments of cuscus

teeth and fine white beads (Bogese 1948:228–9). At this time the Langalanga were making different kinds of money for Gela and Savo and for Guadalcanal (red for the coastal people to use, white for them to trade on inland; Hogbin 1964:48), as well as ten-strings (*tafuli'ae*) for Kwara'ae and north Malaita, double-length ten-strings (*bate e tekwa*) for Lau, and *safi* in single strings and four- and ten-string units for 'Are'are, Sa'a and the 'Are'are people of Marau on Guadalcanal (Malaita Council 1955). South Malaita and Marau were also part of a trading circuit including west Makira (Naitoro 1993:26–8).

In the first half of the twentieth century dolphin teeth from north Malaita were also widely traded throughout most of Solomon Islands, as well as sometimes from Makira to Guadalcanal (Ivens 1930:170, Hogbin 1964:50). By the late nineteenth century Whiteman traders, travelling the islands in their small ships, were also participating in the money trade in the course of other business, such as labour recruiting (Wawn 1893:406). In the 1890s they were trading dolphin teeth to Makira, dog's teeth probably to Guadalcanal, tridacna arm-rings from New Georgia to Makira and Guadalcanal, and red money-beads all the way to New Guinea to exchange for gold dust (Woodford 1897:15). By the 1880s traders were importing dogs from Australia for their teeth (Woodford 1890:54), and by the 1920s they were importing dolphin teeth from Micronesia to take advantage of a decline in the local supply (Ivens 1930:170).

For most of the twentieth century, if not before, the Langalanga were the main source of money-beads in Solomon Islands as a whole, although the trade fluctuated according to economic circumstances. There was a serious decline in production in the 1930s, perhaps associated with the depression of the plantation economy, and a boom in the 1960s and 1970s to supply Bougainvilleans enriched by copper mining (D.O. Report 1935, Cooper 1971, Connell 1977). With the development of Solomon Islands' capital Honiara in the second half of the twentieth century, much of the trade within Solomon Islands shifted to the Central Market there.

Shell and winkle-shells / *La'o ma karango*
Shell provided material not only for money-beads but also for ornaments such as rings and disks. *La'o* is a general name for shell, but even ornaments referred to as 'shell' are usually made from particular kinds of shell, including both clam-shells and winkle-shells (*karango*).[6]

Shell was worked by chipping, grinding on stone with sand, drilling with a pump drill as used for money-beads, sawing with vine-strip and sand, and incising with flint, teeth or steel. Although sea people like the Langalanga specialized in working shell, they also traded it inland, enabling people like the Kwara'ae to make shell ornaments themselves. As with money, the labour required to work shell, if not the material itself, gave such ornaments a high exchange value.

Kome or **conus** (textile cone-shell / *Conus imperialis*) was used to make rings by cutting a cross-section of the cylindrical shell so that its cavity forms the hole. Kwaio recall that formerly the cut shell was pushed onto the end of a stick and its tip ground on stone to form the hole, which was then ground smooth by rubbing with a long stone. The shell is particularly strong and hard to work, so this reaming might be done in the course of other activities such as travelling.

Conus (*kome*) is also a general term for shell rings, including large ones for the arms, made from tridacna and trochus as well as conus, medium-sized *'aimamu* rings worn as pendants, small *dodo* rings strung on *bani'au* money, and even small white *soela* beads worn on earrings. Rings of conus are distinguished by traces of the spiral interior of the shell and sometimes also by brown flecks from the stripes on its outer surface. The end of the shell can also be made into a disk, which became fashionable for pendants in the 1980s and was previously used by sea people of Malaita and the southeast Solomons as decorative inlay on wooden objects such as canoes and bowls.

While the Kwara'ae no doubt made conus rings, like the Kwaio, they were probably more a speciality of the sea people. In 1910 the Langalanga were reported to 'Make shell rings about 2in. diameter (for ears)' (Welsch 1998:364) and in the 1940s it was recalled that they had formerly exchanged 'ear rings of clamshell' for cockle shells for money-beads from Gela (Belshaw 1950:174), so conus rings were evidently part of the Langalanga money trade.

'*Ima* or **tridacna** (giant clam / *Tridacna gigas*, also called *unu*) provided a dense white shell for making various kinds of ornaments, including incised shell-disk (*sa'ela'o*) pendants, conus (*kome*) rings for the arms, and pins (*usuusu*) and studs (*otu*) for the nose. The tridacna used included both fresh shell from the sea and fossilized shell found inland, and both sea and inland people worked it. Inland people made shell-disks from *laufi*, a type of tridacna with a wide flat lip, obtained from the sea people, and nose-pins (*usuusu*) from the hinge of the shell.

In east Kwaio, where such ornaments continue to be made, the tridacna is ground on a flat rock in a stream. For shell-disks the surface is incised (*rokoa*) with designs, formerly using flint or the tooth of a large rat (*kwete / Mus rex*, now extinct on Malaita), gradually replaced since the end of the nineteenth century by steel tools. Blacking is rubbed into the designs to show against the white shell.

The making of conus arm-rings (*fa'ikome*) of tridacna ceased long ago, but was described for the Sa'a of south Malaita by Ivens in the 1920s. They would break a piece of shell from the hinge, grind it flat with flint and coral, pierce it by pecking with a flint hammer and form the hole by working with flints set in a wooden handle (Ivens 1927:392). A similar techique was observed in Arosi, west Makira, in the 1840s (Verguet 1885:203), and in east Makira in the 1930s conus rings were still being made by grinding the hole with a long stone file (Conru 2002:243). However, some conus rings in Kwara'ae show on the inside marks of having been sawn all the way round with a flexible vine-strip, a variation on a technique observed in New Georgia by B. T. Somerville in the 1890s:

A suitable piece of a large clam shell … is chosen, and roughly broken round to what is to be about the size of the outside diameter. This is then taken and ground down with sand and water till its outer edge is nearly circular, and free of irregularities. … a series of closely adjoining holes is bored, making a circle around the centre an inch or so in diameter. A piece of wiry creeper is next taken, introduced into one of these holes, and, by using it like a fretsaw, in conjunction with sand and water, (preferably fresh), the complete centre block is cut out.

The ring is now placed on a stick of hard wood or stone … and the central hole is gradually ground out large and larger, still with sand and water … The completed rough article is then smoothed and polished with fine sand and a piece of bamboo. (Somerville 1897: 364–5)

In 1908–9 A. M. Hocart observed this method used on Simbo, New Georgia. The shell blank was bound between tongs of split stick while the centre was sawn out, producing a cylinder which was jammed onto a pole to hold it fast while it was sawn into two rings (Russell 1972:24). In Choiseul local tools were being used to make such shell rings as late as the 1920s, but there the tridacna was chipped and ground into a longer cylinder and bored with a hard black stone. After being ground smooth inside and out, it too was held on a pole to be sawn into three or four rings, the vine being wound around it and pulled back and forth with water and sand (Piko 1976:101–2). A broad conus arm-ring of clam-shell obtained in 1865 in Ulawa (BM Oc,6406) which has been partly sawn through suggests that this method was also used in southeast Solomons.

By the late nineteenth century imported tools were also in use. In Savo in the early 1880s a rough hoop-iron saw was being used to cut out the centre of the ring (Guppy 1887:132). In New Georgia, by the 1900s, the blank was cut from the shell with a strip of hoop iron, a hole was bored in it with an iron-tipped pump-drill, the centre of the ring was cut out with a weighted bow-saw strung with iron wire, using abrasive sand, and the surface was polished with file and grindstone. Even so, the process was said to be 'long and laborious' (Welsch 1998:362, Russell 1972:24, Woodford 1905:39). No doubt people continued to experiment with new technologies until they ceased making tridacna rings altogether; when Langalanga people revived the making of rings of western Solomons style for foreign markets in the late twentieth century they used industrial tools.

Siare or **trochus** (*Trochus niloticus*, also called *'imae* or 'low-tide' for its collection on the reef) was also used for arm-rings, cut from a narrow cross-section of the conical shell. The material is pearly, white on the outer edge only, sometimes with flecks of red from the shell's surface, giving a quite different appearance to tridacna. Solomon Islanders have also long exported trochus for mother-of-pearl buttons.

'*Umari* or **pearlshell** (*Pinctada*) was used for crescent (*dafe*) and great-shell (*gwa'ila'o*) pendants. The silvery-coloured 'dark pearlshell' (*'umari bulu*, 'blacklip') used for vegetable knives is available locally, but the larger yellow-tinted 'important pearlshell' (*'umari 'inoto'a*, also called *'umari kwao* or 'white pearlshell' and 'goldlip'), which lives in a more specialized habitat of deep, clear water and strong currents, was imported. In the 1920s the people of Sa'a, and presumably elsewhere, regarded the important pearlshell as a recent introduction from Gela, supplied along the coast of Malaita by the Langalanga in the course of their money trade. The shells originated mainly from resident Whiteman traders, who were importing them from beyond the Solomons from at least 1880 (Guppy 1887:131, Ivens 1927:393–5) and employing Japanese to dive for them at Kia in western Isabel in the 1900s (Baines).

Buli or **cowrie** (in full, *karango buli* or cowrie-winkle; egg cowrie / *Ovula ovum*) of pure white was bored with a hole at the ends to be worn as a head ornament. In Kwaio, and no doubt elsewhere, the cowries were obtained by driving a pounded *doodongala* (*Pipturis argenteus*) stick into the mud of the mangroves, which attracted them so they could be gathered. Although requiring little work, they had a high value as ornaments.

Golo or **annulus** (golden ringer cowrie/*Monetaria annulus*) is a small cowrie-shell sometimes strung into ornaments and, in the late twentieth century, made into household ornaments. Unlike the white cowrie (*buli*), annulus shells and the ornaments made from them had little exchange value.

Other materials / *Tirūla'ukī*

Ulifunu or **turtleshell** (lit. turtle-skin / bark) was used for earrings (*tege*) and several other kinds of ear ornaments, the turtle-design (*funifunu*) head ornament and other small objects such as spacers for strings of money-beads. The sea people of Lau and Kwai caught turtles with nets which were particularly tabu and required special precautions to make and use. These were set outside the reef and men would dive and knock stones together to drive turtles from the reef and then tie them into the net; a difficult and dangerous exercise (Ivens 1930:176–7). Several kinds of turtle are caught for food but the hard turtleshell for artefacts comes only from the 'carapace turtle' (*funu bala* / hawksbill).[7]

In Kwaio, as presumably elsewhere, turtleshell was cut with a bamboo knife (*'aba nini*) which heated and softened the material by friction, although a bow-saw strung with fine wire such as guitar-string is now the usual method, working in the same way. In Lau, large circular holes such as the centres for earrings (*tege*) and finger-rings, are made by burning with a heated iron rod (formerly presumably a burning stick). The hole is smoothed using a pointed conical winkle-shell (*gwaliu*) with an abrasive ridged surface, found in the mangroves, which is inserted into the hold and turned back and forth to grind away the turtleshell. The outer edge of the ring is then cut with the wire saw and smoothed and shaped by grinding on a stone, held by a stick passing through the hole, maybe several at a time. For certain ornaments such as wide earrings, turtleshell (*ta'ota'o*) ear pendants and money-bead spacers, the turtleshell was softened by boiling in water in a bamboo flask and bent, retaining the shape when it cooled.

Techniques for making the fine and complex fretwork designs on turtle-designs (*funifunu*) in former times have not been documented for Malaita and seem to have been lost long ago. The two Kwara'ae examples (see pages 74 and 75) appear to have been cut with some kind of blade, as in Bougainville, where a shell blade and later a knife are said to have been used (Blackwood 1935:422). However, in the western Solomons the work was done by drilling holes and cutting between them with a bow-saw strung with a twisted shred of bamboo or other vine-strip (Roga, Salisbury 1928, Duff 1947). In the 1980s, when the making of turtle-designs was revived in Honiara by Jack Saemala of Langalanga and Marion Clark, a Whiteman running an artefact shop, they devised new methods of cutting the turtleshell using industrial tools.

Lifasakwalo or **bat teeth**, the canine teeth of certain bats, were used on ornaments such as bamboo-tree (*'ai'au*), as well as an alternative to dolphin teeth (*lifa kirio*) on other ear ornaments, although they were not used as money.

Mumu or **tight-lip** is a shiny brown seed with a mouth-like slit which is used as a fringe on ornaments of money-beads and shell, as well as for rattles (*kete*).

Kekefa or **(glass) beads** (in full *kekefa ara'ikao* or whiteman beads) are named for the seeds of the coix (*sila* / Job's tears) plant originally used as low-value beads (*kekefa*) for ornaments. Glass beads imported from Europe became popular in many colonial areas around the world in the nineteenth century, as cheap and colourful alternatives to local beads. Peoples of North and South America, sub-Saharan Africa, Southeast Asia and the Pacific Islands all adapted them to local styles of body ornament and clothing, often using very similar techniques. Malaitans discovered glass beads as migrant workers on the plantations of Fiji and Queensland from the 1870s. The early photographs of Malaitans in Fiji in the late nineteenth century show men dressed in ornaments of glass beads resembling the money-bead straps they would have worn at home.

As already mentioned, glass beads were included in payments to the relatives of labour recruits and were later sold by the Chinese merchants, who have dominated the local retail trade since the early colonial period, first as touring traders, later as storekeepers. They came in various sizes and many colours, once distinguished by local names. *Kekefa* is a general name but probably applies particularly to a large kind, similar in size to money-beads, which could be used for similar purposes, such as women's great-*susuru* (*gwa'isusuru*) belts. *Buruburu* is a name for the large round glass beads formerly used for necklaces and the strings for crescent (*dafe*) pendants (hence called *kekefa dafe* or crescent beads in Lau).

Plastic beads are also made in Kwaio from the coloured insulation of electrical wire, to add colour to ornaments of money-beads such as *'afi'afi*.

Vine-strip and twine / 'Abakwalo ma dadalo

As the sea people dominated the production of money-beads, dolphin teeth and shell, so inland people like the Kwara'ae produced materials and ornaments from forest plant fibres. Most ornaments required vine or string (both *kwalo* in Kwara'ae, *rop* in Pijin), which could be made from a wide range of forest plants, selected for strength or appearance. Some vines were used entire but with others the skin was peeled off to provide 'vine-strip' (*'aba kwalo*), which could also be made from the skin or bark of certain trees. The vine-strip might be split into 'shreds' (*sisilirū*) using a sharp flake struck from a piece of flint. Shreds might be plaited (*faosia / folia*) into bands or straps, made into braid (*gwa'inili*), used as coloured vine (*kwalo dae'e*) for patterning (*gwaroa*), or twisted into twine (*dadalo*). Even finer 'threads' (*fisifisirū*) were used for fine bindings.

For twine, especially if it was to be fine and flexible, the shreds might be softened by pulling to and fro around a pole, by pulling through a tightly clamped pair of bamboo tongs, or by scraping with a clam-shell. For the best twine some kinds of vine-strip were cooked on the fire in a bamboo flask of water, or boiled in a saucepan, then left in the water for several days until they began to rot. Once prepared and dried, a pair of shreds was twisted into twine by rolling along the thigh with the palm of the hand. Although important for threading money-beads and ornaments, such twine was formerly used in greatest quantity by the sea people for fishing nets and lines.

The vine-strips used for ornaments included:

Kwalo salu or **Araceae vine** climbs trees and produces hanging root-tendrils. Both the main stalk, when soft, and the tendril can be peeled to make a very strong twine or braid.

Kwalo 'adi'o or **Vitaceae vine** winds around trees. The skin is removed and the light-coloured inner part of the vine is used entire, without further treatment, for binding things like girdles (*fo'osae*) and bound-combs (*gau'adi'o*).

Kwalo 'abe or **Anodendron vine** winds around trees in certain places in the lowlands. The skin is peeled off into vine-strips which can be dried, stained red and dried again for making orchid-pattern (*gwaroa'adi'adi*) armbands. To make twine the vine-strips are cooked, left in the water for two or three days and then scraped with a clam-shell to produce clean, flexible shreds. When dry, these are rolled into twine which is fine and very strong, suitable for threading money-beads and binding. The body of the vine, with the skin removed, can also be dried and used entire or twisted into twine.

Susuru or **cincture** (*Ficus tinctoria*) is a vine which grows on rotten wood and winds around trees. The vine is black and is used entire, maybe pared into several strips but not scraped or rolled into twine. It was used especially for the women's straps, especially the great-cincture (*gwa'isusuru*), which seems to be the source of its name.

Sula and **malao** are two similar medium-sized trees (both *Trichospermum*) which are common in newly regrown forest. The bark of the young tree is peeled off, the outer skin removed from the vine-strip and the inner part dried and shredded for making into twine or braid. The small shreds can be used without further work for threading lengths of money-beads, especially the small Kwaio white money. To make the vine-strip soft and flexible it may be cooked and the sticky sap scraped off before it is dried and shredded. *Sula* and *malao* are also the most common vine-strips for plaited bags.

Taketake niu or **coconut cuticle** is peeled from the new-leaf shoot, cooked and left in the water until it stinks, then stained with red dye (*dilo*) (see page 44). It was used mostly as one-sided shreds for decorative patterning, combined with yellow orchid (*'adi*) stem.

'Adi or **orchid** of two kinds (*Cadetia* and *Diplocanlobium*) grows at the top of trees and provides bright yellow stems used for decorative patterning, usually combined with red coconut cuticle. One kind, with a longer, smaller stem, was

Plate 28 Adriel Rofate'e of Faureba beginning to plait a bag from sula vine-strip in 1979. (Burt photo)

simply dried and flattened to provide a less flexible two-sided vine-strip for coarser work, including patterned girdles (*fo'osae gwaroa*). The other, with a larger, shorter stem, had the outer skin peeled off to provide a one-sided strip which was split into shreds for the finest work, as for patterned combs (*kafa gwaroa*).

Fisifisina niu or **coconut thread** is coconut-husk fibre used for fine bindings on things such as patterned combs (*kafa gwaroa*).

Luluka or ***Gleichenia*** is a kind of branching fern with a dark brown stem, not very common, which grows in the lowland. The skin is peeled and the vine-strips cooked and left in the water until they stink, then the shreds were used for binding things like bound-combs (*gau'adi'o*) and girdles (*fo'osae*), and plaited into orchid-pattern (*gwaroa'adi'adi*) armbands.

Ongaonga (unidentified) is a black-stemmed vine which is split into vine-strips, shaved and cooked, then left in the water for ten days before using. It was plaited into orchid-pattern (*gwaroa'adi'adi*) armbands and used to bind girdles (*fo'osae*).

Bunabuna or ***Cyclosorus*** is a small tree or shrub which grows in wilderness. Its main stem is cooked, left in the water for several days, then scraped to remove the skin and dried. It is then made into a twine which is fine and very strong, formerly used for plaiting orchid-pattern (*gwaroa'adi'adi*) armbands and binding girdles (*fo'osae*), and for the black bands on nose-pins (*usuusu*).

Kalitau or **rattan** (lit. 'winds-far', *Calamus*) is split into vine-strips with the curved skin on one side, the other shaved smooth, and plaited into bands (*obi*) for the arms and legs.

Obi or **band** is a large kind of rattan, named for its use to make bands (*obi*), but also used for the larger strips required for men's girdles (*fo'osae*) and women's band-strap (*'abaobi*) belts.

Dae or ***Gnetum*** is a medium-sized tree, the skin of which can be twisted into very strong twine suitable for money-bead ornaments such as pattern-straps (*'abagwaro*) for the arms.

Filu tali or **split bright** is a palm tree (fan palm, *Licuala lauterbachii*) with leaves which can be dried in the sun and split to provide bright white ornamental strips for decorating bags, or shredded and stained red to make streamers for decorating combs worn in the hair.

Fa'u or **pandanus** was probably used in former times as vine-strip for plaiting and braiding red-stained straps and bands, as in other parts of Malaita and Solomon Islands.

'Abanaelon or **nylon-strip** is a general name for plastic string or line. This has been substituted for local vine-strip and twine in the late twentieth century, being stronger,

more durable and, in some opinions, better looking, as well as taking no labour to prepare. Money-beads, including denominations like the ten-string (*tafuli'ae*), and ornaments such as necklaces (*'alu'alu*) and pattern-strap (*'abagwaro*) armstraps, are now commonly strung on commercial plastic string, on twine made from shreds from plastic sacking, or on nylon line, long in general use for fishing line and nets. Nylon line and coloured plastic cord has been used to bind combs, girdles (*fo'osae*) and bands (*obi*) for the arms (see Plate 39, page 56), and there have even been experiments with red and yellow plastic shreds for making patterned-bamboo (*fa'i'augwaroa*) ornaments for the ears. In Kwaio a certain kind of black plastic fishing line has proved a good substitute for *susuru* vine for making the wife's great-*susuru* (*gwa'isusuru*) belt. Plastic has also largely replaced the turtleshell (*bala*) spacers on money-bead denominations.

'Abalaua or **cloth**, meaning 'flat and flexible', also called *'abaifi*, meaning 'hammered-flat', was made from the bark of fig trees, either 'smooth' tree (*sala* / *Ficus nodosa, F. variagata*)

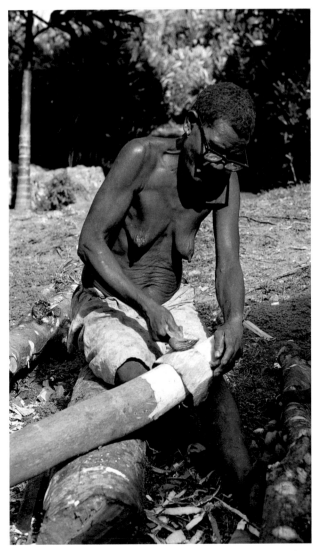

Plate 29 Christina Maeunuunu making cloth at Taba'akwaru in east Kwara'ae, in 1984, hammering the inner bark of smooth (*sala*) tree-trunk with a cockle-shell. (Burt photo)

or *bubulia* (*Ficus austrina, F. hombroniana, F. pachystemon, F. smithii*). It was formerly used for the wife's apron and more recently for the man's loincloth (*kabilato*), a new form of traditional dress in Kwara'ae. Other uses for this local cloth include baby-slings and wrapping local money to store in the fuel rack over the fire, where the smoke and oils in the cloth keep the money-beads shiny and bright.

Kwara'ae cloth is very basic compared with other kinds of Pacific Islands barkcloth. A piece of the young tree is cut, the hard outer bark is scraped off to the length of the cloth and the inner bark is hammered, still on the wood, with a ribbed cockle-shell (*gwarigwari*, as used for white money-beads) or a stone hammer. As the bark softens and expands it forms a loose tube around the wood, which can be cut open to form a strip of cloth (or used as a tube for wrapping money). The cloth dries stiff but can be softened by soaking it in fresh or salt water for four or five days, then rubbing and wringing it and drying it in the sun. It is a natural brown colour, but for a wife's apron it was sometimes stained black with wild banana (*sasao*) sap.

Staining / *Atongi'anga*
Some materials were stained red or black by various methods.

Dilo or **dye** (Indian Mulberry / *Morinda salomonensis / M. citrifolia*) is a medium-sized tree which grows by the sea in regrown forest. It produces a bright red stain for vine-strips such as coconut cuticle (*taketake niu*) and rattan (*kalitau* and *obi*). A paste made by scraping the bark of the root is put into a bamboo flask with water and the material to be stained and cooked on the fire to turn it red. The process is not always successful and other plants and procedures may be used to ensure good results. A similar tree, *kikiri* (*Morinda citrifolia / M. umbellata*) was used in the same way.

Bunabuna or **Cyclosorus** (*Cyclosorus inivisus*), a small tree used for twine, also produces a red stain for use on vine-strips such as *Anodendron* vine (*kwalo 'abe*) and tree bark, for making things such as *sangisangi* armbands and twine. The leaf was pounded with water in a bowl, this was cooked in a bamboo flask and then tipped back into a bowl with the material to be stained.

Akwasi or **with-ease** (*Rhus taitensis*) is a small tree with shoots that produce a sap used as blacking for vine-strip such as *dae* (*Gnetum*), for incised designs, and also for the teeth.

Sasao or **wild banana** sap was used to stain things black, including the wife's cloth apron and the brown *Gleichenia* (*luluka*) vine-strip of orchid-pattern (*gwaro'adi'adi*) armbands. It is also used by thieves and raiders to stain their faces to avoid being recognized.

Saia or **putty** (puttynut, *Parinari glaberrima*) is a medium-sized tree of the lowland bearing a round fruit which can be pounded or scraped to make a sticky adhesive paste, mixed with charcoal to blacken it, and left to dry hard. It was used to strengthen certain kinds of patterned comb and as blacking on certain shell ornaments, including the borders for great-shell (*gwa'ila'o*) pendants, the incised designs on shell-disks (*sa'ela'o*) and the tips of nose-pins (*usuusu*). Other uses included inlaying shell on ornamented wooden objects and caulking canoes.

Rokoa or **incised** designs on objects of tridacna (*'ima*) such as shell-disks (*sa'ela'o*) were stained by rubbing blacking of various kinds into the lines. The Lau use powdered *areko* (*Strychnos*) vine charcoal soaked overnight in sea water (Maranda). The Kwaio use either putty (*saia*) mixed with soot, or *akwasi* (*Rhus taitensis*) tree sap or the blue juice of the *alamaakwanga* berry (Kwaio language).

Patterning with vine-shred / *Gwaro'anga 'ania sisilirū*
Vine-strip patterning was applied to a wide range of ornaments and other artefacts, using shreds of yellow orchid-vine (*kwalo 'adi*) and red-stained coconut cuticle (*taketake niu*), often combined with dark *Gleichenia* (*luluka*) or *ongaonga* vine-strip to give a three-colour effect of yellow, red and black. The techniques and finished effect of this fine plaiting and weaving (*foli'anga*) on ornaments have much in common with the patterned bamboo-strip walling used on patterned sanctums (*fera gwaroa*) and churches (see Kwa'ioloa and Burt 2001:71, 73). The skills were passed down in only a few families and the men who are still sometimes commissioned to make patterned walling include the heirs to those who formerly made patterned ornaments too. However, in Kwaio, where such ornaments are still made, patterned bands and ear-sticks are among the few ornaments commonly made by women.

Patterned-bamboo (*fa'i'augwaroa*) ear-sticks and other solid objects such as girdles (*fo'osae*) (as well as spears, bows and houseposts) have vine-strip patterning woven around them. The warp shreds, usually of yellow orchid (*'adi*), lie along the length of the object and the wefts threads, usually of red coconut cuticle (*taketake niu*), wind around them.

Orchid-pattern (*gwaroa'adi'adi*) armbands and other plaited straps and bands have the patterns embroidered in yellow orchid, usually combined with red coconut cuticle, onto a background plaited in plain weave or twill[8] from dark *Gleichenia* (*luluka*) or *ongaonga* vine-strip. Following the plaited shreds of the band, the stitches of the pattern usually lie diagonally to the edge, giving an effect like a woven money-bead strap but with greater flexibility, allowing an enormous variety of designs.

In another less common technique, simple patterns were plaited into the band or strap itself and then outlined in embroidery to give bold rectangular designs. In some cases the background plaiting is of red-stained vine-strip with the patterning in yellow and black.

Patterned combs (*kafa gwaoa*) were the most complex patterned ornaments, and the patterning is integral to the structure of the comb, binding together separate sticks of wood. The sticks were carved from black tree-fern (*kwa'e / Cyathea*) or 'set-solid' palm (*bōfau / Ptychosperma / Strongylocaryum*), which has particularly hard wood, and were bound together with *Gleichenia* (*luluka*) fibre as well as with the patterning of yellow orchid (*'adi*) and red coconut cuticle (*taketake niu*). Small combs are flat while most large ones are curved to the shape of the head.

By the late twentieth century the few Kwara'ae who still remembered how to make patterned combs were mostly old men with failing eyesight, but in a few areas of Malaita the making of the small kind continues in the twenty-first century.

The large patterned combs (*kafa gwaroa doe*) must have been far more difficult to make because, being curved to fit the shape of the head, each of the sticks is not only tapered up to the neck but also chamfered and bound to form the curve. These combs have space for more elaborate patterns, especially on the body. The pattern is normally on the convex front only, the red coconut cuticle shreds on the body being turned back on themselves on the reverse and trapped between the sticks. Instead of a crosspiece below the patterned area, the comb is held together by a strong curved binding of brown vine-strip, possibly of Vitaceae vine (*kwalo salu*) or *Gleichenia* (*luluka*), consolidated with putty (*saia, Panari*).

Plate 30 Fo'olamo of Kafu'ailari, east Kwaio, working on the neck of a small patterned comb of 'split-comb' (*faafari*) design, in 1996. (Akin photo)

David Akin describes how small patterned combs are still made in east Kwaio:

The structure of the comb is of the black core wood of tree ferns called *ona* (*Cyathea lunulata*). The *ona* strips are straightened by heating them over coals and bending. Each strip must then be shaved down until paper thin. It must be thinnest where the comb's neck tapers and thickest at the teeth. When the wood strips have been prepared they are bound together at the middle with fiber from the inside of a coconut husk, around the crossbar of the same wood, called *maa'eona*. The top of the comb is then temporarily tied together to keep it stable during the neck's plaiting.

Next the comb's neck is plaited with yellow *'adi* orchid vine. The prepared, split and thinned orchid vine is yellow on one side, and white on the other. This means that when the neck is plaited, the *'adi* must be twisted so that both sides of the comb will be yellow. The twist is trapped between the wood strips in the neck. To thread the *'adi* between the wooden strips, a sharpened flying fox bone, or a flattened nail, is inserted to hold the strips apart. When the needle is removed the twist in the vine is trapped between the wood strips and cannot unwind. About half of the time of making a comb is spent plaiting the yellow neck.

There are many different neck designs of varying difficulty. The hardest are diamond shapes, called *lodo'efuu*, representing a kind of seed. Another design $+\,+\,+$ is called *buruburu* or stars, while zigzag patterns $\wedge\!\wedge\!\wedge\!\wedge$ are named after fruit bats (*late'esakwa'o*) or boa constrictors (*fi'ona*).

When the neck is finished, the comb's midsection or belly (*ogona*) is plaited with the waxy skin from a coconut palm (*taka*) (and occasionally other materials dyed orange or black). This skin is first dyed red. Several different designs are plaited on comb center sections. One popular design—individual segments of yellow inverted Y shapes—was invented in the 1940s by Sulafanamae of Tofu for decorating combs he sold to American troops while working in the Solomon Islands Labour Corps on Guadalcanal during World War II. An older design is a vertical zigzag pattern called *susudau'ai*. *Susu* means plait and *dau'ai* is a kind of edible caterpillar. There are many less common patterns, most of which have no names.

When the middle section is complete, the comb's end is trimmed and permanently bound. It is now ready to wear.

Weaving straps of beads / *Faosilana 'abarū 'ania magarū kī*

Money-beads, glass beads and dolphin teeth were made into woven straps for head, arm and waist ornaments, generally using a simple stick-loom. Most were patterned, the principal colours being the red of *firai* or *safi* beads, the white of *galu* and the black of *fulu*, but glass beads also introduced blue, among a wide range of other colours. The designs reflect a number of different weaving techniques.[9]

Mani faosia or **woven money-beads**, such as pattern-straps (*'abagwaro*) for the arms and belts (*fo'o'aba*), are made on a stick-loom, which holds the two warp threads forming the long sides of the strap. The other warps hang loose, since each bead has to be threaded on both a warp and a weft thread where they cross, so that the beads lie diagonally to the edge. The pattern follows changes in direction of the diagonal from one row to another along the length and lends itself to zigzag and lozenge designs, while lines across the strap have a stepped edge.

In a slightly different technique, perhaps used occasionally on Malaita but more typical of Shortland Islands (e.g. BM Oc,1905.256), the threads are plaited to lie diagonally to the edge (instead of forming distinct warp and weft sets), so that the beads lie parallel to the edge, each row overlapping the next like bricks in a wall. The pattern then follows the diagonal threads or the lines of beads along the length of the strap.

The best money-bead straps are made with old beads, including the brighter red *firai* beads of *romu* shell, which have been worn down through long use and re-ground to make them especially smooth and fine, and hence also more valuable. In recent times poorer quality beads have been used, including more brown-red *safi* beads. Although the money-beads were made by the sea people, inland people like the Kwara'ae made the pattern-straps, which the sea people might buy from them.

Plate 31 David Rari of Sakwalo, east Kwara'ae, beginning to remake a pair of worn pattern-straps in 1979. These particular pattern-straps were said to be about eleven generations old, which would date them to the beginning of the eighteenth century, but if this is so they must have been remade many times since. (Burt photo)

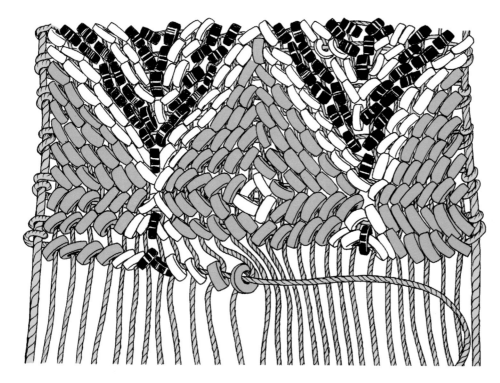

Figure 2 The construction of a pattern-strap (*'abagwaro*) of money-beads. 200%

Plate 32 A woman of northeast
Kwaio finishing work on a great-
susuru (*gwa'isusuru*) strap in 1996.
(Akin photo)

Gwa'isusuru or **great-cincture**, worn by wives, has wefts of black *susuru* vine, entire (not shredded or twined) twining in pairs around warps of strong twine. White beads are strung on the warps in blocks between the twined sections, forming simple black and white patterns.[10] Although some old great-*susuru* straps have white *galu* money-beads, glass beads seem to have been preferred since at least the early twentieth century.

In the Uru area of Kwaio these are still made, using a stick-loom which holds all the warps in place along a long flat piece of wood, spaced by tying to a crosspiece at each end. Presumably the beads would be strung on the warps before the twining began.

Kekefa faosia or **woven glass beads** have the beads (*kekefa*) threaded on pairs of fine wefts which lie one to each side of coarser warps threads running between each row of beads. These were also made on a stick-loom holding all the warps in place.

With this technique, the beads all lie in the same direction, forming a grid of straight lines across and along the strap. This makes diagonal lines steeper than on money-bead straps, with a stepped edge of about 45 degrees, which gives the same design a quite different appearance.

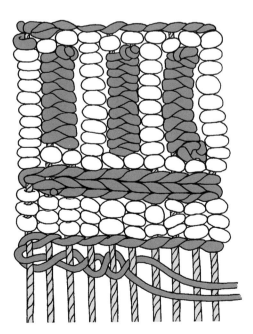

Figure 3 The construction of a great-*susuru* (*gwa'isusuru*) strap.
200%

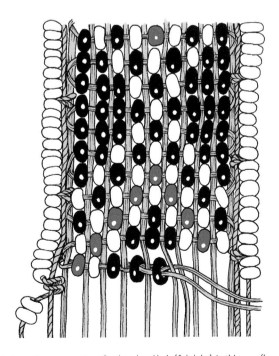

Figure 4 The construction of a glass-bead belt (*fo'o'aba*). In this case (based on Figure 217, page 148), the warps and wefts are of untwined shreds except for the twined warps at the sides, which give strength.
200%

Barulifaī'a or **fish-teeth-clusters** of dolphin teeth are made by threading the teeth on the warps between pairs of twined wefts, as in the great-*susuru* (*gwa'isusuru*) strap, and using a similar stick-loom. Extra warps and wefts space out the teeth and can be increased to make a larger strap from a smaller number of teeth. Each tooth is secured by a weft which encircles it and twines around another weft which passes around the warps.

On the best straps the teeth are drilled at a certain distance from the tip to appear the same length at the front of the band, facing the same way and decreasing in size from the centre to the ends. There are usually beaded sections at the ends and sometimes in the middle, woven like the glass-bead straps.

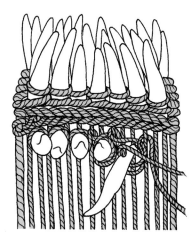

Figure 5 The construction of a fish-teeth-cluster (*barulifaī'a*) strap. 200%

'Ababanibani or **enclosed-straps** of glass beads for the upper arm, actually circular bands, were made by a technique more like the shell-bead armbands of Vanuatu, and possibly introduced from there. A coil of coarse twine is bound, each coil to the next, by a winding length of fine twine, which threads through a bead each time it passes around the outside of the band. The beads thus lie parallel to the edge, each row overlapping the next, favouring patterns of rows and diagonals rather than columns across the band.

Figure 6 The construction of an enclosed-strap (*'ababanibani*). 200%

Patterning and drawing

The designs of ornaments reflect the materials and techniques by which they are made, particularly when they are 'patterned' (*gwaroa*) with geometric designs. Patterning covers various ornamental techniques, including carving and incising, but for body ornaments it is usually produced by weaving and plaiting (*faosia*) or embroidery, mainly using beads (*magarū*) or shreds (*sisilirū*) of vine-strip (*'abakwalo*). The designs often seem to derive from these techniques, on ornaments as on other artefacts such as house walling. They allow for lines along and across the patterned area but especially favour diagonals to produce 'frigate-bird' (*gaula*) shapes /\/\, named for the appearance of the bird in flight. 'Rows of frigate-birds' (*tala 'i gaula*) /\/\/\/\ form the basis for many further designs, not only woven and plaited but also 'drawn' (*kerekerea*, also meaning 'written'), whether incised, carved or painted, on shell, turtleshell, wood or other materials. They can be drawn along lines to form 'hill-shapes' (*ma'e ua*) /\/\/\/\ or more pointed 'arrow-shapes' (*ma'e sima*) /\/\/\. When such rows are paired with the points facing inwards and alternating, another row of frigate-birds is formed by the space between. WWWW When the points face each other, 'fish-shapes' (*ma'e ī'a*) ◆◇◆◇◆◇ or ◆◆◆◆◆ are formed instead. On the borders of shell-disks (*sa'ela'o*), where facing rows of hills or arrows are often reduced to pointed nicks along a line, the fish-shapes become ovals or circles described as 'cowrie-shapes' (*ma'e buli*) or 'egg-shapes' (*ma'e fakela*).

Other pattern designs include 'star' (*fa'i bulubulu*) + (not to be confused with the crucifix or 'sign of the cross', *rarafolo*), 'sun' (*sina*, of three or more crossed lines) ✳ and 'flower' (*takarū*) ❀ of ovals around a central point (referring particularly to a hibiscus, *tatali*). 'Nuts' or 'nut kernels' (*fa'i ngali, sa'e ngali*) ⬭⬭⬭⬭⬭ are a rounded variant of the fish-shape ⬭. There are also 'cloud-shapes' (*ma'e salo*) or 'wave-shapes' (*ma'e nafo*) (((((, 'row of sticks' (*tala 'i 'ai*) | | | | | and 'tree-snake-shape' (*ma'e tafo*) ⊓_⊓_⊓_⊓, named for the wriggly track this snake leaves on the ground.

Such names seem to identify the form of designs rather than to give them any particular symbolic meaning. Whether designs are incised on weapons, painted on dance batons, woven into money-bead straps or worked in coloured strips on combs and arm-bands, their names such are of less interest than how good they look. While some names like 'frigate-bird' and 'nut' are widespread (also used in north Malaita), others vary between Malaitan languages and even individuals (as with some Kwaio names for comb designs; above, page 45). The popularity since the nineteenth and early twentieth century of foreign designs such as Union Jack flags (see pages 147 and 155) and playing cards (Paravicini 1931:150) seems to confirm that the appeal of patterns and motifs owed less to any symbolic meanings than to their ornamental effect.

Even so, some designs are evidently images as well as patterns. Coiled *Dennstaedtia*-fern crowns (*gwa'i 'unu'unu*, said to look like eyes), human figures, canoes and fish appear on ornaments of shell and turtleshell, and most common of all is the frigate-bird, as a creature rather than as a pattern design. Whether such images necessarily had much more symbolic meaning than the named designs is another matter. Among the sea people of Malaita and southeast Solomon Islands, frigate-birds and fish, particularly sharks and bonitos, were prominent images, painted, inlaid or carved on canoes, fishing floats, food bowls, skull coffins, house posts, beams and festival platforms. For these people, sharks were ancestral protectors, bonito were prestigious food and the focus of male initiation ceremonies, and frigate-birds guide and assist in fishing. However, they had little of this significance for the inland people. For the Kwara'ae the frigate-bird is merely a sign of bad weather when it flies inland, while the eagle was respected and even worshipped as the symbolic bird. Likewise, sharks (ba'eko) have their equivalents in venomous snakes, the 'inland sharks' (ba'eko tolo) associated with omens and sorcery, as crocodiles do in monitor lizards, said to be born from the same clutch of eggs.

Nonetheless, frigate-birds were the most common image on Kwara'ae and other inland ornaments, especially on shell-disks and crescents. Elders in Kwara'ae and other inland areas of Malaita have no explanation for this (Akin, Ross 1981:23), and the fact that some frigate-bird designs are so stylized that local people have difficulty in recognizing them as birds (as on the shell-disk-rattles pages 104 and 105) also implies that their purpose was more ornamental than symbolic. Snakes, eagles, hornbills, lizards and human figures were sometimes painted or carved on house posts and beams, food bowls, staffs and other things, but they seldom appear on ornaments. Living creatures, especially hornbills,[II] are most common on flat wooden dance-batons (taba).

Patterning and drawing depend on colour, black on white shell, white, red and black in woven money-beads, and yellow, red and black on plaited vine-strip, with the yellow equivalent to white. Woven glass beads, despite a wider range of available colours, also show a preference for the same basic combination of red, white and blue (equivalent to black; both bora in Kwara'ae).

In general, patterning seems to demonstrate the 'technology of enchantment' described by Gell (1998), bemusing the viewer by its complexity, as conveyed by the Kwara'ae term 'eye-narrowing' (sisimā) for the dazzling effect of patterned walling. It enhanced the glamour of wealth and power which gave ornaments their value in Malaitan society. This is not to say that their makers always realized the potential of the styles they were following. Drawn designs in particular, less constrained by technical processes than geometric patterns, were often interpreted so freely that many appear more individual than conventional in style. With an equal variation in craft quality from accomplished to crude, this gives the impression that anyone who could grasp basic motifs like two or three frigate-birds and pairs of frigate-bird lines felt free to render them in their own way.

Selling and documenting ornaments

The appearance of Malaitan body ornaments has always attracted Whiteman visitors, who have collected them as fast as Malaitans discarded them. Records of Whiteman visits, from casual encounters to long-term residence and research, preserve much information since lost to local people and help to set the traditions of Kwara'ae and Malaita in the wider context of the history and culture of Solomon Islands. As a background to the catalogue of ornaments which follows in Chapter 4, an account of these sources will help explain the colonial legacy which has preserved Malaitan body ornaments even as it has undermined the tradition which produced them.

The curio and art market

From as early as 1850, when ships called at a few favoured anchorages such as Port Adam in south Malaita, the Whitemen traded for ornaments and other artefacts as exotic 'curios', and Malaitans often chose selectively from the equally exotic artefacts offered in return (Vigors 1850:213, Wood 1875:137). The thousands of Malaitan body ornaments exported since that time and kept by museums around the world were mostly sold to seamen, labour recruiters, traders, colonial officers, missionaries, tourists, visiting professionals, anthropologists and collectors. Their journals make frequent reference to curios being offered for sale by sea people coming out to visiting ships. Revd Arthur Hopkins of the Melanesian Mission recalled his first meeting with the sea people of Lau in 1902:

> The men carried with them for sale all sorts of things, clubs, old spears, and badly made new ones, shell ornaments, porpoise teeth, turtle shell. What they wanted was tobacco … (Hopkins n.d.:13)

Hermann Norden, travelling on a recruiting ship in 1926, described the curio trade on the east coast of 'Are'are:

> The men in the canoes at once learned that ours was no serious recruiting cruise, and they adjusted themselves to the idea of a tourist abroad. I bought shell bracelets and lips [goldlip crescents] from their bodies; the curious combs they wore in their hair, and ear and nose ornaments and dilly bags galore. When they had stripped the treasures they were wearing they went back to look for other curios which might tempt. … they would not take trade goods in payment. They wanted silver and insisted on having it.

Perhaps these people were having trouble obtaining cash to pay the newly introduced government tax. Later, at a sea settlement on the west coast of 'Are'are or Sa'a, the visitors

> … spread the news that trade goods would be exchanged for ornaments, so old and young came, heavy with their decorations of mother-of-pearl, trochus and tortoise shell. These things were the personal treasures of the people who traded them; nothing is made to sell. Here they made no suggestions of receiving money; gladly they gave their armlets and anklets, [gold]lip crescents and nose ornaments for calico and tobacco. (Norden 1927:80–1, 92–3)

Norden was wrong to think that 'nothing is made to sell', for local trade had already adapted to the export market, as Revd Walter Ivens noted of the Lau in the 1920s:

> The shore man … does not make the plaited earsticks and decorated combs which he sells to the white men, but gets them all by barter from the hills. (Ivens 1930:34)

In the late nineteenth and early twentieth centuries various colonial residents and visitors made collections of such curios which they eventually sold on to other collectors or donated to museums in their home countries (e.g. Rannie 1912:184, Melvin 1977:26, 34, Herr 1978:9, 167–8, 171, 195). The Melanesian Mission in particular accumulated quantities of ornaments and other curios as personal gifts to missionaries and as offerings from local congregations to be sold in support of the church (SCL 1905:9, 1906:39, 1911:252, 245). Most of these eventually also found their way into museums in New Zealand and Britain.

In the 1940s the curio market expanded rapidly when the Second World War brought thousands of American troops to Guadalcanal. Malaitans and other Solomon Islanders responded by producing artefacts for sale in such quantities that the colonial authorities felt obliged to regulate and administer the trade (Akin 1988). When this market disappeared another developed in the new Solomon Islands capital, founded at Honiara after the War, as the colonial authorities began to promote and conserve local 'arts and crafts'. During the 1950s this led to the development of what eventually became the Solomon Islands National Museum, after Independence in 1978.[12] During the 1960s new woodcarving traditions were developed by Solomon Islands plantation workers, who found markets for these and other arts and crafts in Honiara among foreign residents and occasional tourists, including visiting tour ships. In the 1970s several craft shops opened there, promoting the sale of Malaitan ornaments among other artefacts. National independence in 1978 inspired a revival of interest in making characteristically Solomon Islands artefacts for sale, with some consulting museum collections and using new technologies such as electric tools (Clark and Kelesi 1982:1).

During the 1980s the craft shops provided outlets for high quality Malaitan ornaments, among a wide range of artefacts such as wooden sculptures and bowls, baskets and bags, from various parts of Solomon Islands, some in old local styles and others adapted to the tastes and expectations of foreign residents and tourists. An illustrated catalogue published by the Ministry of Trade provides an overview of the artefacts on general sale at this time (Austin 1986). It includes money-bead breast-fastening (*torisusu*) bandoliers and necklaces with conus-disk pendants from Langalanga, incised shell-disk (*sa'ela'o*) pendants from Kwaio and north Malaita, *dala* (so-called *kapkap*) disks from Langalanga makers in Honiara, turtleshell and dolphin-teeth ear ornaments from Langalanga and Lau, and patterned combs, bands and ear-sticks from Kwaio. New styles of Malaita ornaments made for the foreign market included incised designs added to pearlshell crescents, nets of money-beads with seed fringes as collars and as borders for pendants, and head-bands modelled on patterned arm-bands.

In the late twentieth century some of these things, particularly money-bead ornaments, were also worn as symbols of Malaita or even Solomon Islands identity, along with imitation shell-disks and pearlshell crescents of painted board, not suitable for sale. But the finest ornaments of shell and red and yellow vine-strip patterning were seldom bought by Solomon Islanders to wear, going rather to the foreign tourist or art market, except in the areas where they were made. With a growing awareness of the international trade in antiques, some makers also developed ways of aging new shell objects, making them difficult for foreign collectors to distinguish from the old ornaments they coveted. At the same time new materials were being adopted, particularly plastic as a substitute for local vine-strip twine. Ornaments made for local use, including old heirlooms, continued to be sold and exported, having become international commodities, featured in the sales catalogues of prestigious auction houses in Europe and America.

Insofar as the study of Malaitan body ornaments has to draw upon exports as well as things retained or remembered by local people, it is important to consider the implications of the export trade. As O'Hanlon (2000) demonstrates, Whiteman collections reflect the interests of the sellers in providing certain artefacts for their own purposes, including controlling the market itself, as well as the concern of the buyers to represent local culture, whether through souvenir curios or systematic research. The sellers are most in control of the market when, as for many Malaitan ornaments in museum collections, collectors are passing through rather than resident. The effect would be that artefacts most attractive to Whitemen, of which more would have been made for export, may have become more common in Whiteman collections and scarcer in Malaita. This might have affected, for instance, the styles of some common exports such as incised shell-disks and patterned combs, the rarity of valuable ornaments such as turtle-designs prized by Whitemen, and the proliferation of simple but characteristic ornaments such as money-bead and dolphin-teeth necklaces. Such things could have been adapted to the preferences of the buyers in ways they were unaware of. If detected, these would have been treated as inauthentic tourist art, which typically requires a century or so of historic patina to gain commercial or academic value.

A more dispassionate anthropological approach recognizes production for export as the development of the artistic tradition in response to new opportunities. Even a study concerned with the local use of body ornaments must recognize that the tradition has long operated within a colonial and global commodity market.

Identifying body ornaments

Most of the curios which found their way into museums and private collections in Whiteman countries around the world say less than they might about the traditions from which they derive. Very few of the older ornaments are identified more precisely than being from 'Malaita' or even 'Solomon Islands' and although names and dates sometimes indicate the Whitemen who owned them, this seldom helps to identify their origins or cultural background. Whitemen gave and exchanged curios much as islanders did ornaments, and by the time they were catalogued their identity was usually a matter of deduction or even speculation. (Hence a Malaita angle-club (*subi*) in Chicago's Field Museum catalogued as an 'Australian canoe paddle', and a Malaita glass-bead belt (*fo'o'aba*) retrieved from a British Museum collection of African 'duplicates'.)

The British Museum is fortunate to possess a number of fine old Malaita ornaments collected by people who knew at least which island they had come from. Some of those identified as 'Malaita' in this book once belonged to the researchers and authors Revd Robert H. Codrington, working in the Melanesian Mission school on Norfolk Island from the 1860s to 1890s, and Charles Woodford, who was in Solomon Islands between 1886 and 1914, first as a naturalist and then as first Resident Commissioner of the British Protectorate. One of the few early collections which has some more local identifications was given by Mary Edge-Partington, widow of District Officer Thomas Edge-Partington, who was with him on Malaita from 1913 to 1915. While she collected local curios herself (Herr 1978:195), her husband also sent some to his father James Edge-Partington, the famous collector and associate of the British Museum, many of which are now in the Auckland Museum. By contrast, the artefacts left by Revd Walter Ivens, a major contributor to Malaitan ethnography, are better documented in his books than in the British Museum's records, where they are attributed simply to 'Mala or Ulawa'.

Without the knowledge of those Malaitans who still possessed or remembered their ornaments, most such museum collections would remain little more than curios for Whitemen, or perhaps symbols for Solomon Islanders of some vague notion of *kastom*. What we now know about Kwara'ae body ornaments is salvaged from a century and more of cultural challenges which have largely consigned them to 'former times' (*kaida'i ma'i na'o*), along with the ancestral religion and inter-clan feuding. By the late twentieth century there were few Kwara'ae alive who could recall the time before this artistic tradition was challenged by Christianity, or had heard the stories of the first arrival of the Whitemen from those who actually witnessed it a generation before that. Their recollections of traditional dress and body ornaments, as documented during the last 20 years of the twentieth century, mostly describe followers of the ancestral religion who were resisting the colonial culture which was transforming their society. The few ornaments still kept in Kwara'ae by that time provide important confirmation of this oral record, but fortunately we can also draw on evidence from other parts of Malaita where the tradition was documented earlier, or maintained later.

The earliest and best published account of Malaitan ornaments is scattered through Walter Iven's books on the Sa'a of south Malaita and the related island of Ulawa, researched in the 1920s following his work there as an Anglican missionary from 1896, before the Sa'a tradition was seriously challenged by Christianity (Ivens 1927, 1929). For north Malaita the most important source is Pierre Maranda, who has shared his research among the sea people of Lau from the late 1960s. His is the best documented collection from the northern part of the island, sea and inland, and includes many ornaments disposed of as people became Christians. But the best source from anywhere in Malaita is David Akin's research in the culturally conservative inland of east Kwaio, where he

and Kate Gillogly assisted the 1980s ornamental craft revival, from whence he has assembled a major collection from the makers themselves.

Apart from this research, the best information on how ornaments were worn in former times comes from the photographs of Malaitans in libraries and archives, including a large collection of prints and copies in the British Museum. (These and other sources mentioned below are listed under Photographic Sources, page 166). The earliest photographs, usually identified only as 'Solomon Islanders', show Malaitan migrant workers in Fiji in the 1870s and 1880s, ornamented to pose for studio photographs. Few photographers dared to venture ashore on Malaita before the twentieth century, although Richard Parkinson published a remarkable photograph from east Malaita in the early 1890s of what looks like a feuding party from the inland, with many weapons but few ornaments (Meyer and Parkinson 1894: vol. 2, pl. 45).

By the 1900s, as Whitemen began to feel more secure on Malaita, missionaries of the SSEM, particularly Northcote Deck, were taking photos of both clothed Christians and

Plate 33 This man was photographed aboard the British warship HMS *Royalist* in the early 1890s, at Port Adam, a Lau settlement in Sa'a, south Malaita. The pearly-row (*Sa'a tala 'reoreo*) of pearlshell plates around his nose is a former fashion sometimes described but seldom photographed (see pages 92 and 96). He also wears a comb (*kafa*) and cowries (*buli*) in his hair, patterned-bamboos (*fa'i 'au gwaroa*) in his ears and a nose-pin (*usuusu*). He has a pig-tooth (*lifa gwata*) pendant, four wide conus (*kome*) rings and bands (*obi*) of red-stained rattan on his wrists. His belt appears to be of calico, but is reminiscent of the wide glass-bead belts (*fo'o'aba*) worn in those times. (BM Oc,B38.7)

ornamented potential converts, although few of the latter have clear local identifications. In 1906 the photographer John Watt Beattie of Hobart joined the Melanesian Mission's ship *Southern Cross* on a tour which visited the coasts around Malaita (including west but not east Kwara'ae) and made a fine pictorial record which he documented in a journal and a published catalogue (Beattie 1906, Beattie n.d.). Next year, in 1907, George Rose sailed from Langalanga north along the west coast of Malaita taking photographs which he published in his vast series *The Rose Stereographs*. Perhaps the best extant collection of such photographs was made by Thomas W. Edge-Partington, who joined the colonial service in Solomon Islands in 1904 and founded the government station of 'Aoke at Rarasu in west Kwara'ae in 1909, where he worked until he left the Solomons in 1915. Besides many prints from Beattie, Rose and other named photographers, his albums include photographs by himself and his wife Mary and some fine portraits from To'abaita.

In 1917 the traveller Martin Johnson, on a tour from 'Aoke with District Officer William Bell, took photographs in Langalanga and the Kwara'ae inland, some of which were published by his wife (Johnson 1944). The film-maker Edward Salisbury filmed and photographed west Kwara'ae dancers and Langalanga money-makers in 1921 (Salisbury 1922, 1928). In 1929 the anthropologist Eugen Paravicini took photographs, and collected some ornaments, from west Kwara'ae south as far as 'Are'are, and in the early 1930s the Anglican missionary David Lloyd Francis took some interesting photographs on an inland visit on the west Kwara'ae-Fataleka border. In the 1930s there were also well-documented photographs from Tae Lagoon by Toshio Asaeda and from To'abaita by the anthropologist Ian Hogbin (Hogbin 1939, 1945). In the 1940s, after the Second World War, the Melanesian Mission sponsored another photographic tour of the coasts of Malaita, producing a full (but undated) catalogue of images of Christians looking very different from Beattie's photographs two generations earlier, in clothes rather than ornaments. Then, from the 1960s, several more anthropologists began research among Malaita peoples, publishing photographs of local costume and ornaments from Baegu (H. Ross 1973, K. Ross 1981), Kwaio (Keesing 1983) and 'Are'are (de Coppet and Zemp 1978, Zemp 1995).

Between the 1910s and the 1960s, the best photographs of well-ornamented Malaitans were nearly all from the north, with none from Kwara'ae until the 1970s. When I first arrived in Malaita in 1979 only a few families in Kwara'ae still followed the dress code of the ancestral religion, mostly in the fiercely conservative community of 'Ere'ere. They and some Christians, mainly Anglicans, still put on shows of festival dancing, as shown by photographs of the great gathering of Kwara'ae chiefs at 'Aimela in 1976, taken by Levi Laka for UNESCO, but there was little sign of the full sets of ornaments which Kwara'ae elders described as worn by their parents' generation.

It was not only the Christians who were losing their ornaments in the course of the twentieth century. Zemp's photographs from 'Are'are (de Coppet and Zemp 1978) include particularly vivid illustrations of old-fashioned Malaitans of the 1960s and 70s, but even they lack most of the ornaments

described for south Malaita by Ivens, who had already noted a decline in ornaments in Sa'a in the 1920s (Ivens 1927:147). It seems that by the late twentieth century even those Malaitans who still wore local ornaments for important occasions had far fewer of them than did their ancestors a few generations before. But with the benefit of these collections, researches and photographs, we can begin to rediscover the rich diversity of body ornaments within the cultural traditions of Malaita and beyond.

Local styles of ornaments

Malaitans share a common identity which the Kwara'ae attribute to origin from their own founding shrine of Siale, although others have their own origin histories. All recognize the island as home to a number of related local traditions which are distinguished most of all by language.

The twelve or so languages and dialects of Malaita divide most clearly into north and south on the border between Kwara'ae and Kwaio, but people have always migrated and married between neighbouring language areas regardless of these distinctions. However, in the days before commercial shipping and roads, the difficulties of travel within the mountainous inland, inhabited by potentially hostile strangers, limited the cultural horizons of the inland people. By contrast, the sea people were long-distance travellers, taking fleets of canoes around the coasts of Malaita and to neighbouring islands to trade in goods which included things exchanged with their inland neighbours. Their trading relationships were secured by marriages to create long-distance kinship ties. The Langalanga in the west traded and intermarried with the Lau in the northeast, who are closely related to the sea people of Ata'a and Kwai further south, and to the Lau settlement at Walande in Sa'a. The Langalanga and Lau also travelled regularly to Gela, Guadalcanal and Gao on Isabel. In south Malaita, where there was less distinction between sea and inland peoples, the 'Are'are and Sa'a not only traded with Langalanga but also belonged to an inter-island network linking the 'Are'Are settlements at Marau at the east end of Guadalcanal, the Arosi area of west Makira and the small islands of Ulawa, Ugi and Orumarau (Naitoro 1993:26–8).

These sea contacts meant that valuable exchange objects such as ornaments and money were more widely shared around the coasts of Malaita than within the interior. The sea people had some ornaments in common all around the island, especially things made of sea materials such as brow-bindings (*fo'odara*) of money-beads and dolphin teeth, fish-teeth-cluster (*barulifaī'a*) straps and carapace (*bala*) fretwork ear-pendants of turtleshell, all of which the Kwara'ae more often bought from them than made themselves. Some ornaments were worn the length of Malaita, inland and coastal, like shell-disks (*sa'ela'o*) incised with frigate-bird designs, cowrie-row (*talabuli*) brow-bindings, patterned combs (*kafa gwaroa*), pattern-straps (*'abagwaro*) of money-beads for the arms, and pearlshell crescents (*dafe*). But the Kwara'ae have barely heard of the pearly stone (*fou'atoleeleo*) baton borne by warriors collecting rewards from Kwaio southwards, while the Kwaio do not wear the circle-fence (*barafā*) of *soela* beads of Kwara'ae

Plate 34 This inland man, photographed by an SSEM missionary in the mid-twentieth century, illustrates a north Malaita style of ornaments, with turtle-design and cowries on the head, fish-teeth-cluster at the neck, broad pattern-straps and conus rings on the arms, calico held by a leather strap and conus-rattles on the legs. (SSEM photo 108)

Plate 35 Filistas Kokosi of Ngongosila island, off the coast of east Kwara'ae, wearing her family's money-bead ornaments in 1983: a brow-binding, breast-fastening and cincture with an old-style skirt. (Burt photo)

Plate 36 A man from Roasi in Sa'a photographed by Beattie in 1906. He wears a south-Malaita-style comb, cowrie-row browband, nose-conus ring, glass-bead necklace, vine-strip bands and conus rings on the arms and a belt of glass beads with a Union Jack design. (Edge-Partington collection BM Oc,Ca41.82)

and the north, nor the *dala* head ornament, worn north and west as far as Papua New Guinea (source of its name *kapkap*). Then there are the northern and southern kinds of money, of which only the Kwara'ae used both (see pages 59–61).

Through the relationships between islands maintained by the sea peoples, Malaitans also shared in the wider regional culture of Solomon Islands. Not only were the prestigious shell and teeth ornaments traded between islands, but some less valuable ornaments of forest vine-strip, the speciality of inland people like the Kwara'ae, were also widely shared. The close links between south Malaita, west Makira and east Guadalcanal were reflected in shared styles of shell, money-bead and dolphin-teeth ornaments. The red and yellow patterning (*gwaroa*) used on ornaments such as combs, ear-reeds, armbands and girdles, described as characteristic of Malaita when such ornaments were still commonly worn, was also known throughout the southeast Solomons (Montgomery 1896:185, Ivens 1930:34, Fox 1924:298). Even as far abroad as New Georgia and Bougainville in the west, distinctive local styles of ornaments such as tridacna arm-rings, pearlshell pendants and patterned armbands had enough similarities with Malaita to identify them all as 'Solomon Islands'.

Makira provides the earliest account of Solomon Islands ornaments, by Leopold Verguet, a missionary to Arosi in the 1840s (Verguet 1885), as well as the most striking illustrations

Plate 37 A woman from Makira, photographed by Martin Johnson in 1917. She wears the combination of dog and dolphin teeth, strings of money-beads as bandoliers and belt and money-bead pattern-straps on the wrists, which distinguish the Makira style from Malaita, especially north of 'Are'are. (Johnson photo 250760)

in Hugo Bernatzik's photographs from Owarara (Santa Ana) in the east in the early 1930s (Bernatzik 1936, Conru 2002), and briefer accounts by Davenport (1968:19) and Mead (1973:35–8). These show that Makira shared with Malaita many shell ornaments such as white cowries for the head, conus rings for the neck, incised bird-design shell-disk pendants, crescent and disk pendants of goldlip pearlshell, several kinds of tridacna shell arm-rings, and multiple-string denominations of money-beads. These would have been among the valuables carried on trading voyages around and between islands, but the straps, belts and net-sashes of woven money-beads or dolphin teeth of Malaita seem to have been less favoured on Makira than multiple-string ornaments of money-beads and strings and tassels of teeth, from dogs as well as dolphins. Until the mid-twentieth century, young people of east Makira appeared on special occasions festooned in such things, in much greater quantity than inland Malaitans would have been able to afford. These were worn with various ornaments known in south Malaita but less so to the north, such as certain shell ornaments for the ears and nose, money-bead pattern-straps for the wrists and ankles rather than for the upper arms, and combs inlaid with pearlshell set in black putty (Ivens 1929:32–3). In Makira, as in Ulawa and Sa'a, valuable ornaments formed family heirloom sets, worn by boys at public initiation ceremonies, as well as by wealthy chiefs and their wives.(Ivens 1927:133–4, opp.148, Bernatzik 1935 and 1936: pls, Mead 1973:35–8).

To the west, although Gela traded shell goods from Malaita and supplied raw shell, including some of the

pearlshell for crescent pendants, it was culturally and politically closer to Isabel. While the people of Isabel also imported money-beads and dolphin teeth from Malaita and exported pearlshell for crescents, their ornaments seem to have been more like those of the western Solomons. These included belts of highly polished cone-shell beads, in strings rather than woven straps, ornamented with clusters of dolphin teeth, cuscus teeth and small shell rings, as well as dolphin-teeth straps worn at the neck and the waist. The Isabel people also used the tridacna shell rings made in New Georgia for exchange as money and as symbols of chiefly authority. Some of these were ornamented to wear as pendants (*bakiha rapoto*) and others (*bakolo*) were worn on the arms. Whereas Malaita men and women would usually wear one or maybe two such rings above each elbow, in Isabel and western Solomons they might wear ten or more, from elbow to armpit. Such ornaments distinguished chiefs and their families, who were more widely and formally recognized than on Malaita, but they were also worn by a couple at their wedding. They were regarded as new to Isabel, replacing local ornaments which were little more than a memory by the mid-twentieth century, probably as a result of Isabel being drawn into the trading and headhunting networks dominated by the western Solomons in the late nineteenth century (Bogesi 1948:228–91, 341, White 1991: 96, 186).

From Gela and Isabel to the western Solomons, people also wore neck-pendants of conus, tridacna or pearlshell, carved and pierced in various designs. Some from Gela from the 1860s resemble nose-pendants from Malaita and Makira

Plate 38 Inqava of Roviana, western Solomons, and his wife, photographed by the missionary George Brown in 1902. His ornaments are characteristic of New Georgia and Isabel chiefs, with many tridacna rings on the arms, shell-bead and dolphin-teeth belt and an ornamented tridacna ring pendant. (Edge-Partington collection, BM Oc,Ca42.52)

(see page 94), with angular or birds' head projections around a central hole (BM 6371 to 6375, Brenchley collection). Some pearlshell pendants are evidently related to older varieties of the Malaita crescent, but clam-shell pendants are quite different from Malaita shell-disks. In Gela, Isabel and western Solomons men also wore *dala* head ornaments similar to those of Malaita (and to the Papua New Guinea *kapkap*) and cowrie-row browbands, but not the other southeast Solomons head ornaments of shell-disks, money-beads and dolphin teeth.

Information for Guadalcanal is more limited, but shows ornaments similar to Malaita and Makira. Besides east Guadalcanal's involvement in the south Malaita and west Makira trading circuit, there was a regular trade in money-beads from Langalanga to Guadalanal, where they were strung into local denominations which could be worn as bandoliers. Other Guadalcanal ornaments included wigs of white fibre, browbands of beads and dolphin teeth or cowries, fish-teeth-cluster straps worn at the waist, dog teeth worn as a strap or necklace, earring-clusters with shell rings, tridacna nose-pins, pearlshell crescents, orchid-pattern and *sangisangi*-type armbands, enclosed-strap armbands of glass beads, conus arm-rings of tridacna and rattan girdles (Woodford 1890:30,

Brown 1910:104, Hogbin 1937:88, 1965:cover, 1, 48, BM Oc,7639, BM Oc,6311). When the Weather Coast spiritual leader Moro led a revival of traditional dress from the 1950s, his followers' ornaments also included woven money-bead straps and panels hanging from bandoliers on the chest and back, and Moro himself was covered in woven money-bead ornaments to symbolize the values of traditional wealth (Macintyre 1975).

The tradition of body ornaments in any local area of Malaita or Solomon Islands was a distinctive local combination of styles and conventions variously shared with neighbouring peoples and islands, often as a result of the trading relationships which have been remembered or documented over the last century and more. In describing a tradition such as Kwara'ae, so much of which has been lost, this allows us to draw upon and contribute to knowledge of a wider area of southeast Solomon Islands and beyond. Within Malaita it means that if something was once worn in both north Malaita and Kwaio or south Malaita, the Kwara'ae probably, but not certainly, wore it too, even if they have since forgotten. Whether even the ornaments remembered were characteristic of Kwara'ae rather than just known there is another matter, for some elders identify things generally worn in Kwara'ae as belonging to neighbouring peoples. These include not only the money-bead and dolphin-teeth ornaments bought from the Langalanga and Lau sea peoples, but also objects which other Kwara'ae recall making themselves, as when patterned-bamboo (*fa'i'augwaroa*) ear-sticks are said to be a Fataleka ornament.

Like other peoples of the world, the Malaitans often prefer to see their cultural traditions as unique, standardized and changeless, especially when comparing former times with the threatening changes brought about by colonization. The Whitemen who document and publish the cultures of such peoples have for their own reasons often represented them as the servants of rigid unchanging tradition. Those like the Kwaio, who are still making some ornaments exactly like those which have been in museums for a hundred years or more, do indeed feel strongly about conserving their cultural traditions, but this has not prevented them from developing their culture and enjoying exotic imports. Malaitans would always have acquired and imitated ornaments from near and far, leading to changes in local fashions which must have increased with the improved communications of the colonial period. Indeed, as for other Melanesians, there was prestige in 'pulling in' exotic valuables from abroad (Robbins and Akin 1999:19–20), demonstrated in the adoption of Whiteman ornaments and clothing.

Bearing this in mind, we should be wary of regarding anything as belonging since ancient times to one area or island, for ornaments travelled from one end of the Solomons archipelago to the other. There are photographs of a Bougainville man wearing a Malaita style shell-disk in the 1890s (Meyer and Parkinson 1900: pl. 45),[13] a Makira dancer wearing a shell-disk from Santa Cruz in the 1930s (Bernatzik in Conru 2002:239), and a Malaitan wearing a western Solomons shell-bead girdle in the 1940s (see above, page 27). A few Kwaio even keep as tabu relics *kafala* (implying 'foreign') ornaments modelled on neck pendants brought home from Samoa by migrant workers in the nineteenth century. Those most skilled in making the old styles of Malaitan ornaments would also have been best able to experiment with new ones, like Sulafanamae of Tofu in east Kwaio, whose work, both conventional and original, illustrates a number of types of ornament in this book. The makers of ornaments also had to respond to changes in demand, like the late twentieth-century fashion for money-bead and dolphin-teeth necklaces which led many young Kwaio to dismantle old fish-teeth-cluster straps (*barulifaī'a*) for the teeth, and the popularity of Langalanga money-bead net-design ornaments for displays of local culture in Malaita and Honiara. Although historical records do not allow us to trace such developments in much detail over the last century or so, we can glimpse them in the catalogue of ornaments which follows.

Plate 39 Malaitan body ornaments as worn for a dance at the 2008 Independence celebrations in Honiara. The man on the left wears a ten-string (*tafuli'ae*) money, and the man holding the wooden gong has a breast-fastening (*torisusu*), necklace (*'alu'alu*) and pattern-strap (*'abagwaro*, of the Kwara'ae 'arrows' design) of money-beads. Otherwise their ornaments include shell-disks (*sa'ela'o*) and crescents (*dafe*) of painted card, girdles (*fo'osae*) and bands (*obi*) for the arms of plastic strip, and new-style loincloths (*kabilato*) of bark-cloth. (Clive Moore photo)

Notes

1 This history was recorded in the 1950s in a government *Native Affairs Book, Langalanga*, now in the Solomon Islands National Archives (BSIP 27/1/4).

2 Information on the making and stringing of money-beads was supplied by men from or familiar with Langalanga in the 1980s and 1990s, supplemented by information from Woodford (1908a) and Bartle (1952).

3 The fact that the Kwaio call these beads *safi*, while in 'Are'are *safi* is a money denomination, illustrates the confusing variability of local terms for money.

4 See also Akin 1999 for a detailed analysis of the role of Malaitan local money during the twentieth century.

5 Although often described as 'porpoises', the various species caught are all of the Delphinidae family (Takekewa 1996).

6 Kwara'ae and other Malaitan terms for shell are not always easy to translate accurately, referring as they do to useful function as well as form. For example, in Sa'a *la'o* means conus shell, in Kwaio it means round or rounded (of shell and other objects), and in north Malaita it means conus and conus-disk, so the general Malaitan meaning may be shell(-disk). Likewise, in Sa'a *kokome* means conus arm-ring, while in Kwaio and north Malaita *kome* includes both conus and tridacna rings, so the general Malaitan meaning may be shell(-ring).

A generic term in one language may refer only to specific species or ornaments in another. For instance, the Kwaio *imai* or 'of the low-tide' denotes shells in general for the way they are collected, but in Kwara'ae is used specifically for trochus. The Kwara'ae *karango* (for which 'winkle' serves as a convenient but imprecise translation) describes univalve snail-like shells, including conus, trochus, cowries, and others, but in Kwaio it designates only cowries and in Lau it also referred to other creatures gathered at low tide. Since inland people know less about sea creatures, they are likely to borrow words from the languages of the sea peoples (Ivens 1929, Maranda).

7 *Bala*, which also means a pitched-roof shelter, refers to both the carapace and to turtleshell as a material.

8 In plain weave the strips cross one over one, while in twill they cross two over two (or more), each row overlapping the next one to give a stepped or herringbone effect.

9 In English 'weaving' implies a fixed set of threads or strips (the warps) with another set (the wefts) passing over and under it, so that both are at right angles to the edge of the material. 'Plaiting' implies that neither set is fixed and both are diagonal to the edge. 'Embroidery' means stitching the pattern onto a plaited or woven surface. These distinctions are not recognized in the Kwara'ae language, but all three techniques are used to produce similar patterns. For instance, patterns are woven in vine-strip on ear-sticks and in money-beads on pattern-straps, but armbands are plaited and the patterns added by embroidery.

10 That is, pairs of wefts are twisted around each other between the warps so that they hold them tight.

11 For the Lau, the hornbill is symbolic of the seclusion of women's reproductive power, from the way the female is walled into her nest hole while breeding (Maranda), but whether other Malaitans share this concern is unclear.

12 The history of the arts and crafts trade in Solomon Islands is documented in detail by Jari Kupiainen (2000), on whose work the following draws.

13 Although Parkinson says such shell-disks were made in Bougainville, the identical design is itself evidence of trade contact (Parkinson 1999:214).

Figure 7 Ornaments which might be worn by a Kwara'ae man in former times. They include a patterned comb (*kafa gwaroa*) with split-bright-strips (*'abafillutali*), cowries (*buli*), serrated-conus (*komegiria*), patterned-bamboos (*fa'i 'au gwaroa*) and earring-clusters (*barutege*) in the ears, a stud (*'otu*) and pin (*usuusu*) in the nose, a string of human teeth (*ūma ana lifa ngwae*) and a big shell-disk (*sa'ela'o doe*).

Figure 8 Ornaments which might be worn by a Kwara'ae woman in former times. They include a fish-teeth-cluster (*barulifa'i'a*), sawn-conus (*komefuria*), patterned-bamboos (*fa'i 'au gwaroa*) and bamboo-trees (*'ai 'au*) in the ears, a pin (*usuusu*) in the nose and a women's shell-disk-rattle (*ketesa'ela'o kini*) with a necklace (*'alu'alu*) of *safi* money-beads.

Chapter 4

A catalogue of Malaita ornaments

The objects with which the Kwara'ae ornamented themselves, crafted from the products of the inland and the sea, included money (more often exchanged than worn) and valuables (inherited rather than exchanged), symbols of men's power and of women's married status, intricately patterned artefacts and leaves plucked from home and forest. The values, histories and cultural associations of these things lent their diverse significances to the artistic effect of making people look attractive, impressive, intimidating, or just appropriate and respectable. But ultimately this effect depended on the objects themselves looking good on the body according to local standards of ornamental style.

Although this catalogue is focused on Kwara'ae ornaments, it also covers other parts of Malaita and makes comparisons with the traditions of other parts of Solomon Islands. The drawings come from photographs of particular ornaments, from Kwara'ae where possible, but also representing the styles of other areas. The ornaments are listed under their Kwara'ae names, or other language names when the Kwara'ae is unknown. Most names are descriptive and they often vary, as do the forms of the ornaments themselves. Styles of ornaments were not fixed and people often experimented and improvised or broke with convention, especially as fashions changed with growing experience of colonial culture. Nor were particular ornaments always worn in the same way, whether at the head or neck, in the ear or nose. The 240 or so ornaments featured in this catalogue can only illustrate the possibilities of this rich and varied tradition.

For an orderly presentation, we begin with the money system which was so deeply involved in personal ornamentation, before listing objects made specifically to wear, in order from the head downwards. We conclude with things worn as additions, bodily preparation and finally with some personal recollections on how people once ornamented themselves.

Money

Throughout Malaita strings of money-beads and dolphin teeth are exchanged for the necessities of life, goods, services and persons, mediating social and economic relationships, but they are also worn on public occasions to show the status of those who own and exchange them.

Money-beads are valued by length and made up into more or less standard denominations, while dolphin teeth are valued by counting individually. All can be valued in terms of each other and of cash (*selene* or 'shilling'), and they also provide a standard of value for artefacts such as body ornaments. Formerly this money formed a currency almost as flexible as cash. Small amounts could be used to pay for portions of food in the market, for minor services such as medicinal remedies, and in restitution for minor offences, although in most of Malaita such payments have now long been made in cash. Larger denominations are still important for major purchases such as gardens of food-crops and pigs for feasts, and they are essential for formal exchanges such as brideprice, restitution for serious offences and death-compensation payments. For this reason moneys are regarded as symbols of peace, and ten-strings (*tafuli'ae*) often bear tassels of red cloth at the ends representing the bloodshed they serve to prevent.

The money-beads used in north Malaita, including Kwara'ae, are mostly made in Langalanga on the west coast. For the Langalanga, formerly living on offshore islands with little garden land, producing money (*bata* in Langalanga) contributes to a livelihood based on fishing, trade and migrant labour. They travelled the length of Malaita and beyond, to Gela and Guadalcanal (Woodford 1908a:83), contributing to a trading network that extended throughout Solomon Islands, from Makira to Bougainville and beyond (see Connell 1977). The Langalanga produce various denominations to order. Formerly a Kwara'ae man and wife might commission a ten-string (*tafuli'ae*) by providing garden-food and betelnut to a Langalanga man and wife while they worked on it, presenting more food when it was complete. In recent times the money has been made to sell in markets or stores in 'Aoke or Honiara, or hawked around at public gatherings. Denominations of this northern money are all quite large and valuable, suitable for large-scale exchanges, and formerly dolphin teeth served as a more general-purpose money or small change, which was acceptable all around Malaita and beyond, as far as Makira and New Georgia (Ivens 1930:170).

But the Kwara'ae also use the money of the peoples to the south, in which Langalanga beads are reworked and combined with 'white money' *kofu* beads, mostly made by the inland people of Kwaio and strung in a quite different set of denominations. Unlike the northern money, short strings of white money are acceptable as small change for minor purchases and services (see Akin 1999 for details).

Maga mani or **money-beads** are valued by measuring strings against the arms and body. The measurements do not necessarily divide into one another and attempts to standardize denominations in terms of colonial measurements (feet and inches) have not met with general agreement. Perhaps because they have been using cash for so long, the Kwara'ae are often rather uncertain about the less common measurements, used especially for the southern money. Some terms such as *la'usu'u* are as much money denominations as measurements, and more measurements were probably used in the past, as they still are in Kwaio.

Although money-beads may be valued and exchanged as single strings, important exchanges require larger denominations, which are valued according to the kinds of beads and numbers of strings as well as the length. The ten-string (*tafuli'ae*) is the common high-value denomination of the northern type of money, also used by the Langalanga who make it (although the Lau say that formerly, in the early colonial period, the largest denomination was an eight-string *kwalu'ae;* Maranda). Its make-up and value varies, despite periodic attempts by colonial and then local authorities to standardize both length and cash equivalence during the twentieth century. From the standard navel-length (*kwa'ibuta*) or fathom (*tafana*), it can range from five to seven or eight feet, with cash value varying accordingly. The Langalanga value ten-strings in terms of a more standardized denomination of their own, the *fura*, which is four strings of unpolished white *galia* beads a full arm (*oirua*) long. The standard ten-string is worth two 'moneys' (*bata*) or 40 *fura*, but the value also varies with the type and quality of the beads. A more valuable ten-string has a mid-section of up to six inches of *fira'i* (instead of *safi*), strung in a 'net' (*furai*) design with *galia* and *fulu* at the intersections. The Langalanga value this at five moneys or 100 *fura*. An old ten-string which has been re-ground to make the beads smaller and smoother might be valued at 50 *fura* instead of 40.

A common smaller denomination in Kwara'ae is *la'usu'u*, a length of red *safi* money-beads from the thumb to the place where a band would be worn on the upper arm, which is also the basic measurement for the southern kind of money in Kwaio. The southern white money (*mani kwao*) has a much larger range of denominations, providing the flexibility for exchange which dolphin teeth give to the northern money. Many Kwara'ae are unsure what these denominations are, but use the low denomination *māmalakwai* and the high denominiation *bani'au* (notionally equivalent to a ten-string), as general terms for the southern money. However, Kwara'ae experts explain a system which is similar to Kwaio, with most denominations named for the number of strings and the length measured in *la'usu'u* (for instance, a seven *bani'au* (*bani'au fiu*) is six strings, seven *la'usu'u* long).[1] Further south, the 'Are'are use other denominations again, with the southern white money for small purchases, red money in higher value units of up to ten strings, plus a rare twenty-string (Naitoro 1993:42–3).

Measurements for money used in Kwara'ae

a'e'u'u / ma'e'u'u or **thumb-base**; from the tip to the base of the thumb

malafunu or **span**; end of thumb to end of middle finger

ma'e obi or **band**; end of thumb to place of (wrist)-band (*obi*) (equivalent to a span)

alasikaba or **shaver**; end of thumb to mid-forearm, where the end of an arrow-shaft is held while shaving it (*alasia*)

la'umilima or **elbow**; end of thumb to inner bend (*la'u*) of hand / arm (*lima*)

fafo'ikome or **above-the-conus**; end of thumb to top of the conus (*fa'ikome*) ring worn above the elbow

la'usu'u (untranslatable); end of thumb to place of a band worn on upper arm

gwau'aba or **shoulder**; end of thumb to top of shoulder

gwa'i'aba'aba or **great-arm**; end of thumb to breastbone

suli kaula 'iburi or **behind-the-collar-bone**; end of thumb to the opposite collarbone

tafanga or **fathom**; straight distance between outstretched arms

kwa'ibuta or **navel**; between outstretched arms, hanging to level with the navel (reckoned as 6 feet)

gugurū'ingwae or **man's-knee**; between outstretched arms, hanging to the knee (reckoned as 8 feet)

siga'u'una or **toenail**; between outstretched arms, hanging to the toe (reckoned as 9 feet)

Money denominations used in Kwara'ae

mani or **(shell)-money**

tafuli'ae or **ten-string** (lit. ten-legs) is typically made up, from middle to end, of:

- *safi* or *fira'i* midsection
- spacer of wood or turtleshell
- *galia-kurila-galia-kurila*, from about three to about ten of each
- *galia* alone for about 3 spans
- *safi-galia-fulu-safi-galia-fulu* for 1-to-1½ spans
- spacer of wood or turtleshell
- *galia-fulu-galia-fulu* to complete the full length
- rattle (*kete*) or tight-lip (*mumu*) seeds with red cloth tassels to decorate the end, sometimes with conus rings

la'usu'u	one string of *safi*, from end of thumb to place of band worn on upper arm
gwau'aba or **shoulder**	one string of white money from the end of thumb to top of shoulder
māmalakwai	one string of white money 3 *la'usu'u* long
'au	one string of white money 5 *la'usu'u* long
gairabi	two strings of white money 5 *la'usu'u* long with *safi* at one end, named and valued according to the number of (wrist)bands (*ma'e obi*) of *safi*
gani'ulu	three strings of white money
fa'afa'a	four strings of white money
lima'ae	five strings of white money
bani'au	five strings of white money, sometimes with 1 *la'usu'u* of *safi* at one end
tofu'afu	ten strings of white money
lifa kirio or **dolphin teeth**	
robo	the largest and most valuable dolphin teeth
unubulu	medium dolphin teeth
taka'idiri	normal-size dolphin teeth
nengenenge	smaller than *taka'idiri* (Kwaio)
rī or *i'asina*	the smallest dolphin teeth (Kwaio)

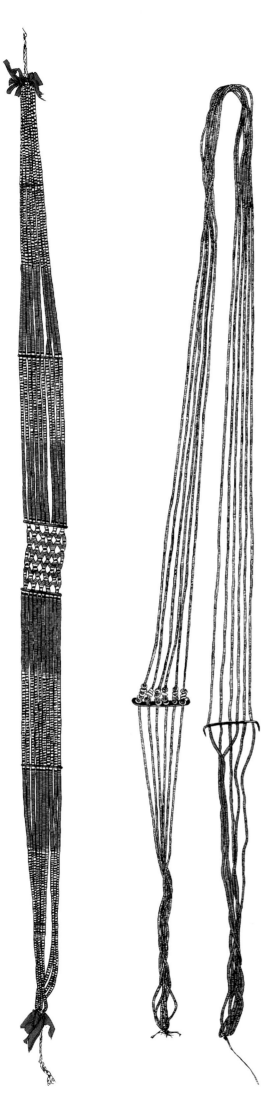

Lifa kirio or **dolphin teeth** are of several kinds of different values. Those who catch the dolphins distinguish six types of teeth, of which three or four are used as money around Malaita (Ivens 1930:169, Takekewa 1996), including inland areas such as Kwaio, but some Kwara'ae distinguish only two. In Lau the value of dolphin teeth in terms of other money remained stable for most of the twentieth century, at 50 large *robo* or 200 medium-sized *unubulu* dolphin teeth for one ten-string (*tafuli'ae*) money (Ivens 1930:278, Maranda). In Kwara'ae a ten-string was said to have been exchanged for 1,000 teeth in former times, but only 100 in the late twentieth century. The complexity of dolphin teeth values is illustrated by the treatment of *robo* teeth in southern Kwaio and 'Are'are, where perfect examples are made up into high-value denominations of 30 teeth or less, kept wrapped in local cloth and formally displayed during certain ceremonial exchanges.

Money can be worn to ornament the body, particularly when it is to be exchanged, but also as a demonstration of power and prestige on public occasions. Some ways of wearing it are shown in the photograph of the Kwara'ae chiefs at the 1976 meeting at 'Aimela (page 16), wrapped around the neck and shoulders or across the chest with the central net of a ten-string in the middle, rather like the breast-fastening (*torisusu*) of money-beads specially made as ornaments. Dolphin teeth, when threaded on a single string for exchange purposes, can also be worn draped around the head or as a simple necklace. When made into fish-teeth-cluster (*barulifaī'a*) straps they retained their use as money and were still valued by the number of teeth.

Other islands had their own local money denominations of money-beads, dolphin teeth and other valuables, whether locally produced or traded from Malaita or elsewhere, and they too used these as ornaments. In Arosi, west Makira, denominations of four or more strings of money-beads were distinguished by the addition of teeth of dophin, dog or bat, and shorter ones were commonly worn as a pair of single bandoliers (Scott, Bernatzik 1936: pls). Guadalcanal people also wore their money-bead denominations as bandoliers and dolphin and dog teeth as straps around the neck (Hogbin 1937:88, 1965:48).

Figure 9 A fathom-long ten-string money (*tafuli'ae*) from the 1990s. (Burt)

Figure 10 A six-string *bani'au* from the 1990s. (Burt)

Head ornaments

Rū fuana laungilana gwauna ngwae or **things
to ornament the head** included combs with various
attachments, shell-disks, browbands and brow-bindings, some
of which could also be worn at the neck.

Kafa kī or **combs** were used not only to comb the hair but
also as an ornament by men, stuck in the hair, and the finest
combs were made only to wear.

It is said that the way men wore their combs showed
their status; an important man would wear it with the neck
pointing upward at the top of the head, a single man on the
right side of the head and a married man on the left. There
is a saying that a comb pointing downwards from the side of
the head shows a man who doesn't want to share his food,
shielding his eyes from the disapproving gaze of others.

Combs were used to hold certain other ornaments,
particularly feathers (*eloelo*) and split-bright-strips
(*'abafilutali*) of red-stained palm-leaf.

Gau'adi'o or **bound-comb** (lit. Vitaceae-bound) is a comb
of sticks, usually of *maoa* (*Melastomataceae*) wood bound
(*gau*) together with Vitaceae (*'adi'o*) or other vine-strips,
used for combing the hair but sometimes also worn in the hair
as an ornament. Some combs are ornamented by including
stripes of dark *Gleichenia* (*luluka*) vine-strip or simple patterns
of yellow orchid (*'adi*), red coconut cuticle (*taketake niu*)
and bare sticks. Such combs can also be bound with coloured
nylon-strip (*'abanaelon*).

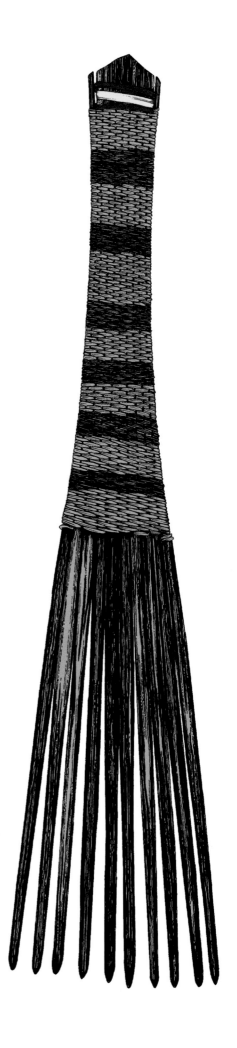

Figure 11 A bound-comb (*gau'adi'o*) of the simplest
kind from east Kwaio (known there as *ga'u'adiko*),
made by 'Ru'uboo▲ of Gaunaakafu in 1981. This is the
simplest kind, with bands of light Vitaceae (*'adi'o*)
and dark *Gleichenia* (*luluka*) with a few strips of
yellow orchid (*'adi*) and red coconut cuticle (*taketake
niu*) at the top. (Akin)
100%

Figure 12 A bound-comb (*gau'adi'o*) made by Gāgafe▲ of Tofu, southeast Kwaio, in 1981, ornamented with yellow orchid (*'adi*). (Akin)
100%

Figure 13 A bound-comb (*gau'adi'o*) bound with nylon-strip (*'abanaelon*), made by Arumae▲ of 'Ere'ere, east Kwara'ae, in the early 1980s. (Burt)
100%

Kafa gwaroa or **patterned comb** is worn in the hair by men. It resembles bound-combs (*gau'adi'o*) in being made of separate sticks, but the main bindings of coconut thread (*fisifisi niu*) holding the sticks at the crossbar would not withstand regular use for combing. The neck or base (*luana, 'a'erū*) at the top of the comb is of orchid (*'adi*) interwoven with the black sticks, and on the body or belly (*nonina, ogana*), orchid is woven on red-stained coconut cuticle (*taketake niu*) which winds around the sticks. The pattern is on both sides, although on the neck one side is the reverse of the other.

There are many variations on the basic patterned comb. In Kwaio in the early twenty first century, imaginative makers continue to experiment with new designs with their own descriptive names, as well as repeating basic designs which date back at least to the mid-nineteenth century.

This ornament is characteristic of Malaita, although it was probably also traded to other islands. It was made by inland people in most of the island, and was still made in north Malaita, Kwaio and perhaps 'Are'are in the late twentieth century.

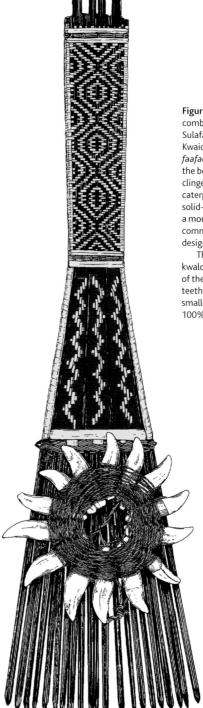

Figure 15 A basic patterned comb (*kafa gwaroa*) made by Sulafanamae▲ of Tofu, southeast Kwaio, in 1981 (known there as *faafao*). The common pattern on the belly is called woven-tree-clinger (*susudau'ai*) after an edible caterpillar and that on the neck is solid-solid-seed (*lodo'efuufuu*), a more complex version of the common solid-seed (*lodo'efuu*) design on the north Malaita comb.
The 'string-of-fish' (Kwaio *kwaloi'a*) attached to the bottom of the comb is of large lobo dolphin teeth instead of the more usual smaller kind. (Akin)
100%

Figure 14 A basic patterned comb (*kafa gwaroa*) made in Baegu or Baelelea, probably in the 1960s (known there as *kafa nira*). (Maranda)
100%

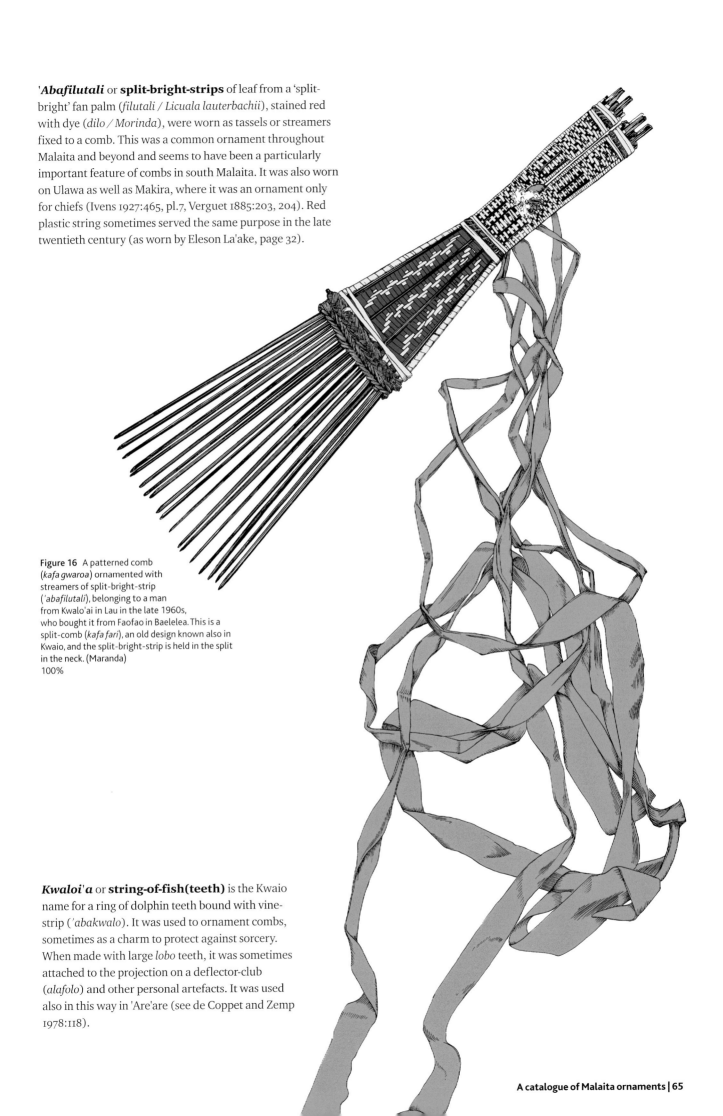

'*Abafilutali* or **split-bright-strips** of leaf from a 'split-bright' fan palm (*filutali / Licuala lauterbachii*), stained red with dye (*dilo / Morinda*), were worn as tassels or streamers fixed to a comb. This was a common ornament throughout Malaita and beyond and seems to have been a particularly important feature of combs in south Malaita. It was also worn on Ulawa as well as Makira, where it was an ornament only for chiefs (Ivens 1927:465, pl.7, Verguet 1885:203, 204). Red plastic string sometimes served the same purpose in the late twentieth century (as worn by Eleson La'ake, page 32).

Figure 16 A patterned comb (*kafa gwaroa*) ornamented with streamers of split-bright-strip ('*abafilutali*), belonging to a man from Kwalo'ai in Lau in the late 1960s, who bought it from Faofao in Baelelea. This is a split-comb (*kafa fari*), an old design known also in Kwaio, and the split-bright-strip is held in the split in the neck. (Maranda)
100%

Kwaloi'a or **string-of-fish(teeth)** is the Kwaio name for a ring of dolphin teeth bound with vine-strip ('*abakwalo*). It was used to ornament combs, sometimes as a charm to protect against sorcery. When made with large *lobo* teeth, it was sometimes attached to the projection on a deflector-club (*alafolo*) and other personal artefacts. It was used also in this way in 'Are'are (see de Coppet and Zemp 1978:118).

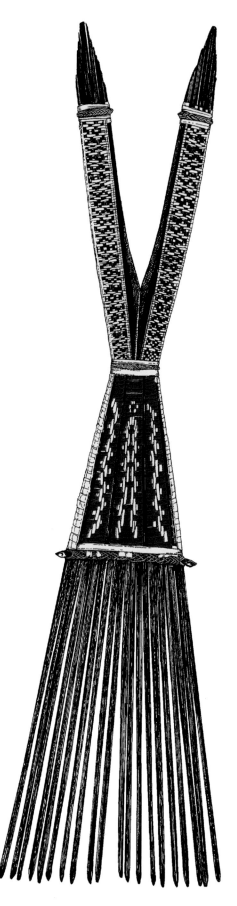

Figure 17 A 'wagtail-comb' (*Kwaio fāla'e*) design of patterned comb (*kafa gwaroa*). It was made in 1982 by Sulafanamae▲ of Tofu, southeast Kwaio, who took the general design from an old comb in the Solomon Islands National Museum. The pattern on the neck is called *susufolo* (plait-across) (Akin)
100%

Figure 18 A patterned comb (*kafa gwaroa*) of novel design made by Arimae▲ of Furii'au, east Kwaio, in 1987. The sticks are of *maoa* wood, like a bound-comb (*gau'adi'o*), instead of the usual tree-fern. (Akin)
100%

Kafa gwaroa doe or **big patterned comb** is a larger version of the basic patterned comb, but curved to fit the shape of the head. These were once made in Kwara'ae but were no longer to be seen there in the late twentieth century, although they were still being made in north Malaita in the 1960s or later. Big patterned combs were probably a central and north Malaita ornament, generally not made in Kwaio and the south. This was also a man's ornament, although in Lau and perhaps elsewhere a maiden would wear it as part of her wedding ornaments (Ivens 1930:96).

Figure 19 A big patterned comb (*kafa gwaroa doe*) made by Oimae▲ of Agia in Baegu, north Malaita, probably in the 1960s. Although the design is similar to many other combs, this one is unusual in having the same pattern repeated on the back. (Maranda) 100%

Figure 20 A big patterned comb (*kafa gwaroa doe*) from Malaita, which until 1869 belonged to the Revd R.H. Codrington of the Melanesian Mission. (BM Oc,1944,02.1688)
100%

Figure 21 A big patterned comb (*kafa gwaroa doe*)
which came to the British Museum in 1894.
(BM Oc,1894.420)
100%

Fā'au or **protruding-comb** is the Kwaio name for a patterned comb (*kafa gwaroa*) with an extra body protruding from the front, its sticks lodged between the teeth and the join bound and consolidated with putty as on a big patterned comb (*kafa gwaroa doe*). Kwaio elders of the late twentieth century recalled seeing examples long ago but no longer knew how it was made. It was probably known elsewhere in Malaita too, at least in the south, and perhaps also in Ulawa.[2]

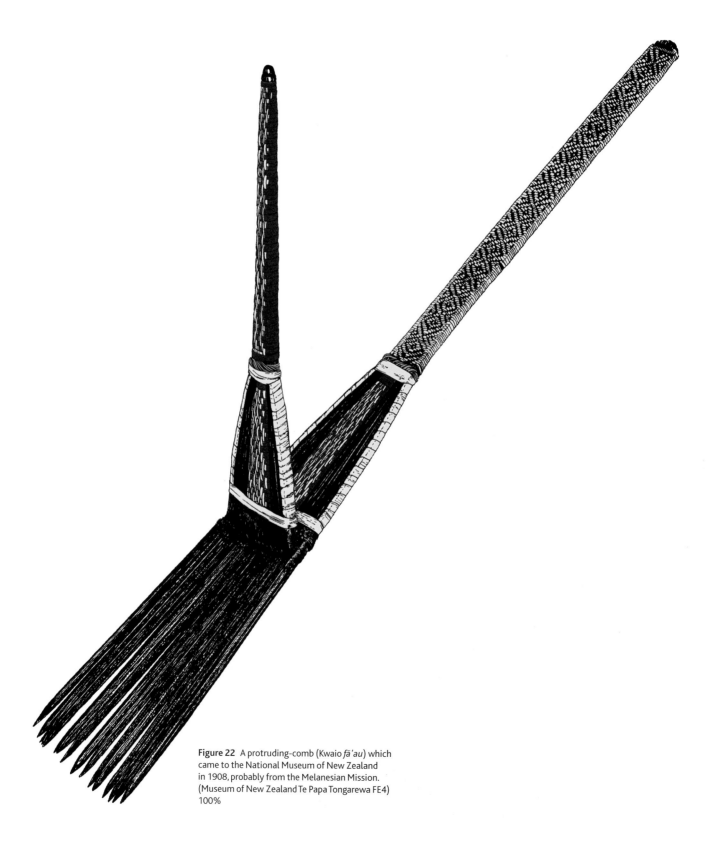

Figure 22 A protruding-comb (Kwaio *fā'au*) which came to the National Museum of New Zealand in 1908, probably from the Melanesian Mission. (Museum of New Zealand Te Papa Tongarewa FE4) 100%

Arapa reoreo or **pearly comb** is the Sa'a name for a comb with the body ornamented with pieces of pearly nautilus shell (Sa'a, *reoreo*) set in black putty (*saia*) (Ivens 1929:32–3). This is an ornamented version of a plain comb of tapering sticks which is bound at the bottom of the body with a crossbar, and at the top, and consolidated with putty. Usually a stick, sometimes two or three, protrude as spikes from the top, but there are many variations in design, such as a neck with yellow orchid patterning (BM Oc,6361, BM Oc,6363).

This type of comb, pearly or plain, was more characteristic of Makira and made especially on Ulawa (Ivens 1927:47), but it was worn in south Malaita and occasionally in Kwaio as an alternative to the Malaitan patterned comb (*kafa gwaroa*).

Figure 23 A pearly comb (Sa'a *arapa reoreo*) from the British collection of the Melanesian Mission. The crossbar is carved with birds' heads at the ends and a loop of twine is attached to hold ornaments such as split-bright-strips of leaf ('*abafilutali*). (Burt) 100%

Kafa kala or **carved comb**, made from a single piece of wood is said to have been introduced to Malaita from the western Solomons in colonial times. The Kwara'ae make them from hardwood trees such as *Planchonella* (*riru*) and solid *Neonauclea* (*malanunu fau*). Incised designs are blackened with putty (*saia*), and sometimes imitate the shell inlay used on other objects in parts of Solomon Islands. The wood is shaped with an axe and rasp, smoothed with a flake of flint or glass and polished with an abrasive (*samota, Ficus* sp.) leaf. Although made to comb the hair, these combs are also worn as ornaments in Kwara'ae and elsewhere in Malaita (see e.g. Keesing 1983:33, de Coppet and Zemp 1978:62).

Figure 25 A carved comb (*kafa kala*) made in 1979 by Robert Sulufia of Lama, east Kwara'ae. (Burt) 100%

Figure 24 A carved comb (*kafa kala*) made by Jimmy Damiakalo of Lama, east Kwara'ae, in the 1970s. (Burt) 100%

Eloelo or **feathers** were worn by men in the hair or in a comb, singly or bound together as a plume attached to a comb. The feathers used included pigeon (*bola*, *kurukuru*), cockatoo, cockerel and probably many others (as Rannie's account implies, page 9). In Kwaio, and no doubt elsewhere, cockatoo-plumes (*susukui'ege*) were worn by festival dancers. Hornbill feathers, worn by a man who had killed, were associated with warriors. They might be fitted into a bamboo socket attached to a comb to spin or to tremble in the wind. Photographs of Malaitans in Fiji also show plumes of cockerel feathers worn in pattern-straps (*'abagwaro*) on the arms; no doubt a fashion from home, although only leaves were worn in this way in recent times.

Figure 26 A cockatoo-plume (Kwaio *susukui'ege*) for the hair made by Sulafanamae▲ of Tofu, east Kwaio, in the early 1980s. The split feathers include some coloured parrot feathers. (Akin 45)
100%

Figure 27 A hornbill feather from Lau from the 1960s, ornamented with glass beads and twists of woollen yarn, made to fit in a socket in a comb. (Maranda)
100%

Funifunu or **turtle-design** (known to Whitemen as *kapkap* and as *dala* elsewhere in Solomon Islands) is a turtleshell disk cut into openwork designs and secured to a tridacna disk by a hole in the centre.[3] The Kwara'ae do not always agree on its correct name; some call it *bero*-disk (*sa'ebero*), others 'flat-disk' (*sa'ebebe*), or simply 'big shell-disk' (*sa'ela'o doe*) or 'incised shell-disk' (*sa'ela'o rokoa*), but these names are also used of other shell-disk ornaments with which the turtle-design seems to be identified or confused. Turtle-designs were worn at the head, formerly on a band plaited of red-stained vine-strip or braid, to judge from museum examples from Malaita.

Kwara'ae describe the turtle-design as something to be worn on public occasions only by a very important tabu-speaker caring for a large congregation. There are only two examples of this ornament definitely identified as Kwara'ae: one is in the Solomon Islands National Museum and the other belonged to Timi Ko'oliu, last senior tabu-speaker of 'Ere'ere in east Kwara'ae. According to a tradition from 'Ere'ere, a turtle-design would be made by a woman while in the birth seclusion house (*bisi kale*). Then when someone was killed they would consecrate it by 'pursuing a ghost with it' (*lali akalo 'ania*) at the ceremony to collect the reward for the killing. This implies that the extreme defilement surrounding its making was inverted by the killing into the extreme tabu

appropriate for something worn on the head of the most senior tabu-speaker and mediator with the ghosts. When the tabu-speaker died it had to be deposited with his body, and his son could only wear it if it emerged from the ground as a sign that he could take it.

Turtle-designs were also worn in north Malaita (where they are known as *dala*, also a general name for big shell-disks) but seldom in Kwaio or south Malaita or Makira.[4] Of the few clearly attributed to Malaita, most have a central star or flower (*fa'i bulubulu, takarū*) surrounded by circles of snake-shape (*ma'e tafo*) wriggly lines, with triangular hills or arrows (*ma'e ua, ma'e sima*) at the outer edge. This basic design is shared by many turtle-designs from elsewhere in Solomon Islands, which also have other motifs found in only a few Malaita examples. These include a square central motif, the circles interrupted by human figures, and a squared branching motif which seems related to the figures. Since variations of the basic design are so common and widespread, it is interesting to find that the two Kwara'ae examples are quite different, quartered with frigate-bird (*gaula*) zigzags very similar to certain *kapkaps* from Papua New Guinea (e.g. BM Oc,1919.453) and with a general effect like the so called eye-narrowing (*sisimā*) dazzle of patterned walling (see Kwa'ioloa and Burt 2001:71–3).

Figure 28 This turtle-design (*funifunu*) belonged to Timi Ko'oliu, last senior priest of Kwara'ae, who described how had been made by a woman while in childbirth seclusion. The only feature its design shares with other Solomon Islands turtle-designs is the border of triangles.

Ko'oliu, born about 1900, was the sixth generation to wear this ornament, so it may have been made in the late eighteenth century. It was buried with him when he died in 1984, and since his son then joined the church there was no-one to inherit it.

By Ko'oliu's time the centre of the turtleshell was broken and had been repaired with twine. This drawing reconstructs its probable original appearance. (Burt)
100%

Figure 29 A turtle-design (*funifunu*) from Baelelea, north Malaita (where it is called *dala*); an heirloom said to be twelve generations old in 1987. Its style is similar to others from Malaita but also resembles those from the western Solomons in having the snake-shapes (*ma'e tafo*) radiating from centre to edge. (Fulbright photo)
100%

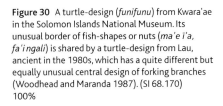

Figure 30 A turtle-design (*funifunu*) from Kwara'ae in the Solomon Islands National Museum. Its unusual border of fish-shapes or nuts (*ma'e i'a, fa'ingali*) is shared by a turtle-design from Lau, ancient in the 1980s, which has a quite different but equally unusual central design of forking branches (Woodhead and Maranda 1987). (SI 68.170)
100%

Turtle-design ornaments were probably always particularly valuable and scarce, for the fine carving of the turtleshell on the best examples would have required remarkable skill and patience. A recruiter who bought one in north Malaita in 1913 for fifty sticks of tobacco noted that 'The natives usually place a high value on these' (Herr 1978:171). They appear to have been traded between Malaita and the islands to the west, including Gela and Savo, Guadalcanal, Isabel and the western Solomons, where they were the principal head ornaments for senior men or chiefs. (A brief comment from the 1930s implies that those made in Isabel were traded to Guadalcanal by people from Gela; Hogbin 1964:50).

Figure 31 A particularly fine old turtle-design (*funifunu*) of the most usual Malaita design, labelled 'from Malanta. Solomon Isl.'. It is one of several given to the British Museum by the Revd R.H. Codrington of the Melanesian Mission in 1874. (BM Oc,RHC32)
100%

Because no two turtle-designs are quite alike in the way these various forms are rendered or combined, and so few of them have histories, all we can say about local styles is that they were not very local. Those from the western Solomons have more and finer concentric circles with kinked radial lines and more of the human figure and branching motifs, but these were also known and maybe made on Malaita. Examples like the fine turtle-design of western-Solomons style worn by Irobaoa of Suaba in the 1900s or 1910s might well have inspired Malaitan craftworkers (see page 28). As rare valuables, these ornaments must have been both traded and imitated from one island to another (as reflected perhaps in the name for them, *dala*, used in both north Malaita and western Solomons). A revival in the making of turtle-designs in the 1980s continued this diffusion of styles, as Malaitan makers using mechanical tools took designs from museum collections. The resulting ornaments are as finely made as most old examples and have been sold to foreign collectors for high prices in Honiara shops, sometimes attached to red money-bead necklaces.

Figure 32 Another of the turtle-designs (*funifunu*) 'from Malanta. Solomon Isl.' given to the British Museum by the Revd R.H. Codrington, with particularly fine and fragile turtleshell, broken long ago. The headband is plaited from braided pandanus vine-strip in a manner more characteristic of the western Solomons. (BM Oc,RHC33)
100%

Buli or **cowrie** is a white cowrie shell worn as a head ornament. Men might wear one or two cowries on one or both sides of the forehead, tied to the hair by a hole at one end. Cowries were said to have been valuable and may have been scarce, for the inland people of north Malaita made imitations of tridacna (Maranda).

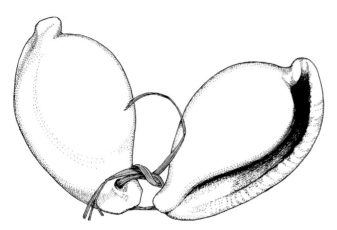

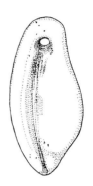

Figure 33 Two cowries (*buli*) for wearing in the hair, tied together for safekeeping. They were kept as relics by Gwa'alebe of the Atōbi clan of Latea, east Kwara'ae, in 1979, with the pattern-straps (*'abagwaro*) on page 133. (Burt)
100%

Figure 34 A cowrie (*buli*) from north Malaita, probably Baelelea, made of tridacna shell, with the underside carefully carved even though it would be hidden when worn in the hair. (Akin)
100%

Suuriri is a Kwaio name for a small shell-disk incised with a frigate-bird design, like those worn as neck pendants (see pages 94–103), but worn tied in the hair. Men wore these in the same manner as cowries (*buli*), on the side of the head, in Kwara'ae as in Kwaio. This was also a style of south Malaita (Ivens 1929:160), while in north Malaita a small shell-disk with a central hole was worn in the same way.

Figure 35 A *suuriri* shell-disk (*sa'ela'o*) from Nānakinimae in east Kwaio, made in 1981. (Akin)
100%

Talabuli or **cowrie-row**, also called 'twine-cowries' (*bulidadalo*), is a set of cowries, from five or six to fifteen or more, strung on two lengths of twine by holes in the sides and tied as a 'brow-binding' (*fo'odara*) around the forehead.

Some say that the cowrie-row was not a Kwara'ae fashion but was copied from Fataleka, but cowries were worn throughout Malaita, more often as single large shells in north Malaita and in rows especially in the southern half of Malaita, to judge from old photos (Beattie photos 500, 502, Edge-Partington photos, Hogbin 1945, de Coppet and Zemp 1978:100, 101, 109).

The cowrie-row was also characteristic of Makira, sometimes with money-beads and dolphin teeth added (Verguet 1885:200, 201, 203, Rannie 1912:301, Beattie photo 480; Bernatzik 1935:frontispiece, pls 1, 12), and was also worn in north Guadalcanal, but cowries do not seem to have been common head ornaments elsewhere in Solomon Islands.

Figure 36 A cowrie-row (*talabuli*) assembled by Laeniamae▲ of Kwailala'e, east Kwaio, in the 1980s, (usually known there as *tale'ekalango*) (Akin 99) 100%

Obidala or **brow-band** is a Kwaio name for a strap of plaited dark vine-strip, patterned with red and yellow embroidery, made like orchid-pattern (*gwaro'adi'adi*) armbands and with similar designs. There are circular bands in museum collections which seem to have been made for the head (besides those used to hold the turtle-design, *funifunu*, ornament). Another type is a narrow strap with ties at the ends, originally devised in east Kwaio in 1980 for the anthropologist David Akin to keep his hair in place. Circular headbands were also made in Guadalcanal (e.g. Queensland Museum E.7000).

Fo'odara or **brow-binding** usually describes a strap of money-beads, usually white *galia*, red *safi* and black *fulu*, with the lower part strung as a net and fringed with dolphin teeth. Less valuable versions are also made using glass beads and tight-lip (*mumu*) seeds. Brow-bindings are made by the sea people, but are sometimes purchased from them by the Kwara'ae, to be worn by men for dancing and by maidens particularly as part of their marriage ornaments.

Formerly this ornament was probably worn only by the sea people of central and north Malaita, but by the late twentieth century it had become characteristic of the whole island, except in inland Kwaio. It was also taken up on Makira, where strings of money-beads and dolphin teeth had sometimes been worn as brow-bindings (Bernatzik 1936:pls 10, 143) and has come to feature as Solomon Islands national costume for publicity and tourist purposes.

Figure 37 A brow-band (*obidala*) from the British Melanesian Mission collection, with a design familiar in west Kwara'ae. (BM Oc1991,08.29)
50%

Figure 38 A brow-band (*obidala*) strap from east Kwaio made by Lagabata● of Fouafo'afo'a in 1981. (Akin)
50%

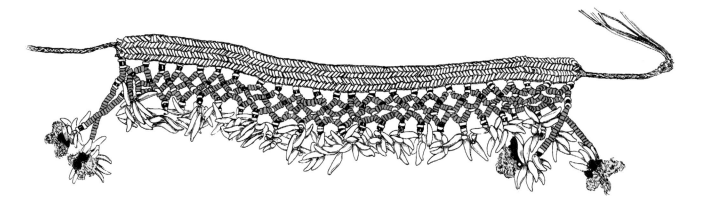

Figure 39 A brow-binding (*fo'odara*) with dolphin teeth, with a complex history among the sea peoples of northern Malaita. It was worn as a set with cross-design carapace (*bala*) ear pendants (page 90), a breast-fastening (*torisusu*) of safi and a necklace (*'alu'alu*) of *safi* and dolphin teeth, all made by Maefiti, a man from Lau living in Langalanga. In 1991 they were kept by his sister Ethel Tangoia, who lived with her husband's family on Ngongosila island off the east coast of Kwara'ae. (Burt)
50%

Figure 40 A brow-binding (*fo'odara*) of glass beads and dolphin teeth belonging to Lovea, tabu-speaker of Uru island off the northeast coast of Kwaio, in 1984 (known there as *e'edala*). The pattern at the centre of the strap is in red, white and blue, with other colours substituted at the ends and red and yellow beads on the net. It was worn with carapace (*bala*) ear pendants (page 90). (Burt)
50%

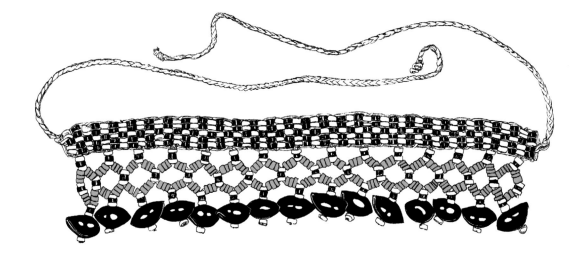

Figure 41 A brow-binding (*fo'odara*) of money-beads with tight-lip (*mumu*) seeds instead of dolphin teeth. This is a less valuable ornament from Langalanga, popular for traditional costume in the late twentieth century. The strap of white and black money-beads is woven by the technique used for glass beads, with the beads square to the edge, and the twine is of nylon-strip (*'abanaelon*). (Jane Huxley-Khng)
50%

Barulifaī'a or **fish-teeth-cluster** is a set of several hundred dolphin teeth, of the medium-sized *unubulu*, woven into a strap. Some call it simply 'fish teeth' (*lifa ī 'a*), others 'necklace' (*'alu'alu*, a general name), or by the common Malaitan name 'fence' (*biru*, implying bristling and enclosing). It was worn around the brow or the neck by both men and women.

This ornament was worn throughout Malaita. The Kwara'ae usually bought them from the sea people who caught the dolphins, particularly from Lau, but inland people made them too. Until the 1940s there was a fashion in east Fataleka for senior men to wear fish-teeth-clusters around German mariners' hats obtained from the northern Solomons while they were under German control until the First World War (see Plate 21, page 27, Russell). As a strap, the fish teeth could still be presented in exchanges and even treated as a money denomination, valued by the number of teeth.

Fish-teeth-clusters were also worn on Guadalcanal and Makira, and dog teeth were also woven into straps in both Guadalcanal and Arosi, west Makira (Plate 37, page 54; BM Oc,7639: Hogbin 1964:48, Macintyre 1975, Verguet 1885:203), although on Makira, where great quantities of dolphin teeth were worn, they were more usually made into strung ornaments (Bernatzik 1936:pls). A rather different type of fish-teeth-cluster, with separate broad panels worn as a loose necklace or a belt, was worn on Gela, Savo and Isabel (Paravicini 1931:pl 5, Melanesian Mission photo 31, Tetehu 2006).

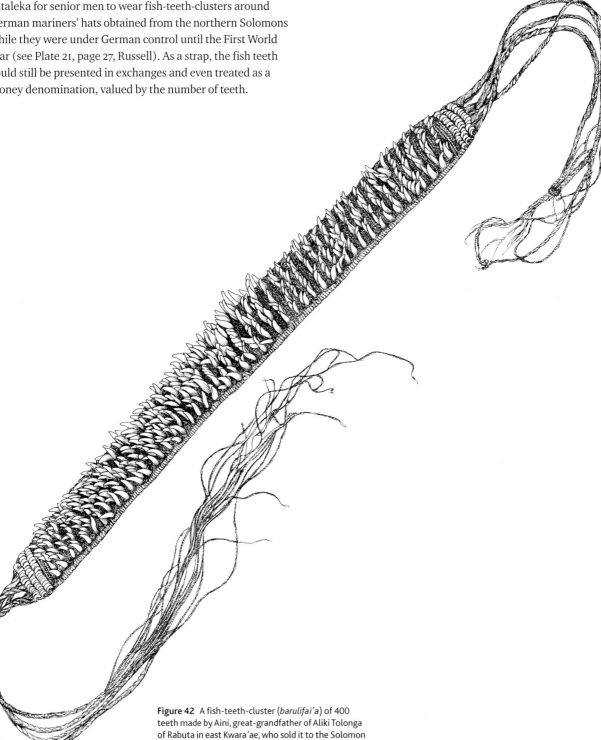

Figure 42 A fish-teeth-cluster (*barulifaī'a*) of 400 teeth made by Aini, great-grandfather of Aliki Tolonga of Rabuta in east Kwara'ae, who sold it to the Solomon Islands National Museum in 1978. (SI 78-276) 50%

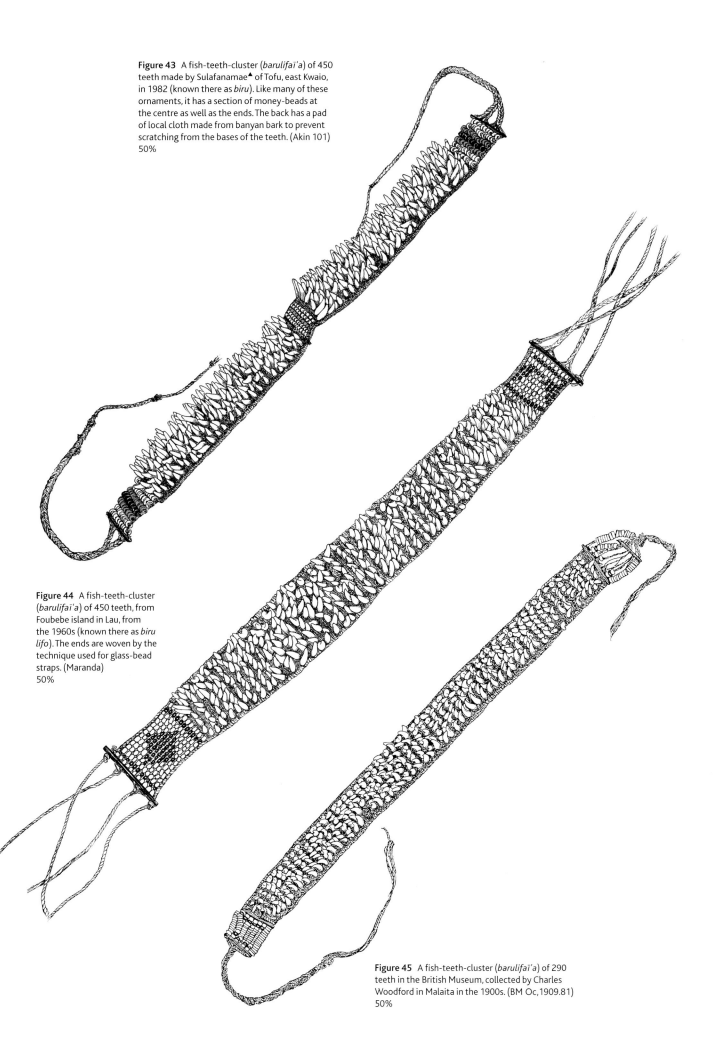

Figure 43 A fish-teeth-cluster (*barulifaī'a*) of 450 teeth made by Sulafanamae▲ of Tofu, east Kwaio, in 1982 (known there as *biru*). Like many of these ornaments, it has a section of money-beads at the centre as well as the ends. The back has a pad of local cloth made from banyan bark to prevent scratching from the bases of the teeth. (Akin 101) 50%

Figure 44 A fish-teeth-cluster (*barulifaī'a*) of 450 teeth, from Foubebe island in Lau, from the 1960s (known there as *biru lifo*). The ends are woven by the technique used for glass-bead straps. (Maranda) 50%

Figure 45 A fish-teeth-cluster (*barulifaī'a*) of 290 teeth in the British Museum, collected by Charles Woodford in Malaita in the 1900s. (BM Oc, 1909.81) 50%

Ear ornaments

Rū fuana sa'ilaungi ana alingana ngwae or **ornaments to insert in the ear** were many and varied, including obscure and unusual ornaments which are now barely remembered. Formerly men and women might have holes at the bottom, middle and top of each ear, plugged with rolls of cordyline (*sango*) leaf if they had no other ornaments. Throughout Malaita, men and women sometimes pierced holes all around the edges of the ears to hold small pegs as well as more elaborate ornaments (Paravicini 1931:157, Cromar 1935:247, Vandercook 1937:332, Zemp 1995:pl. 12).

Komefuria or **sawn-conus** is a conus ring with a gap 'sawn' through it by grinding on stone, so that it can be inserted through a hole in the top of the ear, or pinched onto the top edge of the ear without a hole. Although no longer seen in Kwara'ae, many old photographs show simple rings of conus (*kome*) shell worn in this way, especially by women. Some men seem to be wearing only part of a conus ring, perhaps indicating the fragility of these ornaments, which may also account for their absence from most museum collections.

Old photographs show this to be among the ear ornaments most commonly worn by men and women throughout Malaita, although not elsewhere.

Figure 46 A reconstruction of a sawn-conus (*komefuria*).
100%

Komegiria or **serrated-conus** is like a sawn-conus (*komefuria*), but made from a flat piece of shell with the outer edges cut into pointed serrations and a gap for it to be clipped to the top of the ear, or maybe inserted through a hole. From old photographs it seems to have been less common than the simple sawn-conus, but more have survived, although not in Kwara'ae and most without provenance. There are several forms, some of which may have had their own names. Hence *fafangalalo* (a name also given to a type of nose-stud, see page 95) is said to be a ring of tridacna (*'ima*) worn by men at the top of the ear when collecting rewards for killing. Some are so similar to certain nose ornaments that they may have been worn in nose or ear.

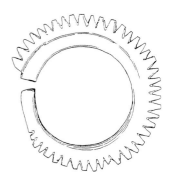

Figure 47 A serrated-conus (*komefuria*) from the Solomon Islands National Museum, of the kind shown in the photograph from north Malaita, Plate 4, page 10. (Carlier 2002:no. 12)
100%

Figure 48 An old serrated-conus (*komefuria*) from Lau, probably made inland in Baegu or Baelelea, with one end missing. (Maranda)
100%

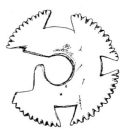

Figure 49 A serrated-conus (*komefuria*) ornament of unknown origin. As one of a pair, it would certainly have been worn in the ear. (Attenborough)
100%

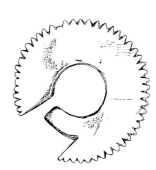

Figure 50 A serrated-conus (*komefuria*) of unknown origin, but very similar to a broken one from north Malaita (Maranda). The narrow projection would have allowed it to be worn in either ear or nose. (Attenborough)
100%

Figure 51 A serrated-conus (*komefuria*) from the Solomon Islands National Museum (70.524). (Carlier 2002: no. 14)
100%

Figure 52 A reconstruction of a simple earring (*tege*) cut from turtleshell and theaded with *soela* rings.
100%

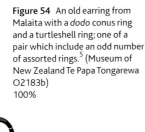

Figure 53 An old earring (*tege*) with *dodo* conus rings, from the British Melanesian Mission collection. (SI Museum)
100%

Figure 54 An old earring from Malaita with a *dodo* conus ring and a turtleshell ring; one of a pair which include an odd number of assorted rings.[5] (Museum of New Zealand Te Papa Tongarewa O2183b)
100%

Figure 55 Earrings (*tege*) from 'North Mala', collected by Revd H. Nind of the Melanesian Mission before 1912 and now in the British Museum. They include four turtleshell earrings, seven *dodo* conus rings and a large trochus ring (*fa'isiare*). The two *dodo* at the bottom must have been threaded by springing the trochus ring apart where it is broken. (BM 1944 Oc,2.1339)
100%

Tege or **earring** is the simplest of ear ornaments, a narrow ring of turtleshell with a break allowing it to be inserted in a hole in the bottom part of the ear. Small ones were cut as a circle from the turtleshell and larger ones were made from a strip bent into a circle.

This was a basic ornament for men and women throughout Malaita and beyond, worn singly or in clusters, often with other rings threaded on them, such as white *galu* money-beads, *soela* beads or *dodo* conus rings. Men also seem to have used additional earrings to link together shell and turtleshell rings, some almost as large as arm-rings, but there were also some more standard ornaments based on earrings.

Soela is an earring (*tege*) with a number of white *soela* beads threaded on it, perhaps up to ten.

Barutege or **earring-cluster** is a group of six or more earrings, each threaded with one or more white *soela* beads, *galu* money-beads or small conus (*kome*) rings, worn in the same hole in the ear. One kind has each shell ring threaded on two adjacent earrings, so linking them all together and making the shell rings form an overlapping row (e.g. Rose 12, 287, Beattie 514).

Old photographs show this to have been a common ornament for men and women throughout Malaita and beyond, including Guadalcanal (e.g. Hogbin 1964 cover).

Baru'isoela or **soela-cluster** describes a kind of earring-cluster (*barutege*) in which about six earrings with ten or more *soela* rings threaded on each are bound together, with short strings of beads hanging down and ending in dolphin teeth or tufts of wool. This was an ornament of north Malaita which was known in Kwara'ae and traded south at least as far as Kwaio.

Figure 56 A reconstruction of a large earring-cluster (*barutege*), as shown in old photographs. Each *dodo* conus ring is threaded through two earrings to keep the whole cluster together.
100%

Figure 57 A *soela*-cluster (*baru'isoela*) from Baelelea from the 1960s (known there as *alinga barafa*). (Maranda)
100%

Fa'i'augwaroa or **patterned-bamboo**, also called *fa'irade* or reed, was a common ear ornament for men and women. It is made from a length of thin *Schizostachyum* (*keketo*) bamboo shoot growing from a fallen pole, patterned with red-stained coconut cuticle (*taketake niu*) shreds and sometimes black *Gleichenia* (*luluka*), wound around it and interwoven with yellow orchid stem (*'adi*) running lengthwise. The name 'reed' suggests that it might also be made from reed (*rade / Miscanthus / Phragmites*). Some have a tuft at the end, formerly of feathers, more recently of woollen yarn.

Patterned-bamboos were usually worn through a hole at the bottom of the ear, mostly to the front and pointing downwards, well beyond the mouth if they were long. Sometimes, perhaps when a hole had been stretched by larger ornaments, the earlobe might be twisted so that the front end of the bamboo pointed backwards, held in place by pressing against the side of the neck. Very long ones might even be tied together behind the head to keep them in place. But patterned-bamboos were also sometimes worn at the top of the ear (see Paravicini photo 3959) or even through the nose instead of a nose-pin (*usuusu*).

Some Kwara'ae say patterned-bamboos were usually made by the Fataleka, from whom they bought them, but they remember making them too. Throughout the Malaita inland patterned-bamboos were made in many shapes, sizes and patterns which seem to have been shared from one area to another. Most are between 6 and 12 inches long (see Asaeda photo 3807-72), and from the thickness of a pencil to half that, but there were also special types with their own names. The woven patterns also vary a great deal.

There are similar patterned-bamboos from west Makira, and very short thick ones from Savo, Guadalcanal and New Georgia,[6] but these ornaments were particularly characteristic of Malaita.

Figure 58 A patterned-bamboo (*fa'i'augwaroa*), one of a pair made in Baegu in the mid-twentieth century (known there as *rade*). (Maranda)
100%

Figure 59 A patterned-bamboo (*fa'i'augwaroa*) from Baelelea from the 1980s or 1990s. Since the Kwaio also made this design it is likely that the Kwara'ae did too. (Burt)
100%

Figure 60 A fine patterned-bamboo (*fa'i'augwaroa*) made by Nene'au So'ogeni[▲] of Kwaina'afi'a, east Kwaio, in the late 1980s (known there as *'ausakwalo* and *'aukwa'ikwa'i*). (Akin 308)
100%

Figure 61 A patterned-bamboo (*fa'i'augwaroa*) from the 1910s, from Mary Edge-Partington's collection, one of a pair labelled 'made by bushmen of Mala'. (BM Oc,1921,1102.31)
100%

Figure 62 A small patterned-bamboo (*fa'i'augwaroa*) from Malaita, one of a pair from Mary Edge-Partington's collection. (BM Oc,1921,1102.32)
100%

'Ausakwalofari or **forked-sakwalo-bamboo** is the Kwaio name for a patterned-bamboo (*fa'i'augwaroa*) which has the end worn to the front split into two or three parts, often splayed out by stuffing a wad of fibre into the base of the fork. The Kwaio, who make these, also recall buying a kind from Kwara'ae which had three groups of three *ī'asina* dolphin teeth at intervals along the single stem.

'Aususu or **pin-bamboo**[7] is a Kwaio and south Malaita name for a short bamboo peg, patterned like a patterned-bamboo (*fa'i'augwaroa*) or simply wrapped with red coconut cuticle (*taketakeniu*) and with a pearlshell stopper in the front end. These were worn by men and women, usually several in holes around the edge of the ear as a 'pin-bamboo-row' (Kwaio *talee'aususu*), so that the pearlshell ends would glitter (Ivens 1928:39, Paravicini 1931:157 and photo 3734, Cromar 1935:247, Zemp 1995 pl.12a). Short patterned-bamboos (*fa'i'augwaroa dokodoko*) are also remembered in Kwara'ae, but without the pearlshell stoppers.

Figure 63 A forked-patterned-bamboo (*'ausakwalofari*), one of a pair made by Moruka● of Ga'enaafou,[8] east Kwaio, in 1979. (Akin 304) 100%

Figure 64 A simple double-bamboo-shoot (*ruafiifito*) bound with coloured shreds instead of woven, one of a pair made by Rifuala▲ of Naa'umi, southeast Kwaio in 1982. (Akin) 100%

Figure 65 A forked-double-bamboo-shoot (*ruafiifitofari*), one of a pair made by Sulafanamae▲ of Tofu, southeast Kwaio, in 1983. (Akin 320) 100%

Ruafiifito or **double-bamboo-shoot** is the Kwaio name for a kind of patterned-bamboo which, instead of being inserted through the ear, has one end hooked and twisted into the hair by an arrow-barb so that it rests above the ear.

Figure 66 A pin-bamboo (*'aususu*) in the British Museum labelled 'SOUTH MALA', one of a pair collected by Revd Hubert Nind of the Melanesian Mission some time before 1913. (BM Oc,1944,2.1329) 100%

'Ai'au or **bamboo-tree** is an ear ornament made of a flower or rosette of dolphin teeth or bat teeth around a circle of glass beads, or formerly of *'afi'afi* money-beads, which is mounted on the end of short patterned-bamboo (*fa'i'augwaroa dokodoko*). It usually has strings of glass beads hanging down, sometimes forming a loop to fasten around the bamboo and secure it behind the ear. Both men and women wore them in a hole in the earlobe, often with a patterned-bamboo (*fa'i'augwaroa*) in a hole immediately above it.

This is an ornament of Malaita only, also known in the north and in Kwaio (where it is associated with sea people).

Oranaī'a or **fish-(teeth)-tassel** (or *ora'i ī'a*) describes a short patterned-bamboo (*fa'i'augwaroa*) with four or six strings of small *'afi'afi* beads or glass beads, with dolphin teeth inserted into one end to hang down from the front of the ear as a tassel. Some use the name for the bamboo-tree (*'ai'au*).

Figure 71 A reconstruction of one kind of fish-tassel (*ora'i ī'a*), based on a short patterned-bamboo (*fa'i'augwaroa dokodoko*) with pearlshell ends, from the British Melanesian Mission collection. (SI Museum)
100%

I'alolo'ia or **bowed-fish(teeth)** is a Kwaio name for an ear ornament with dolphin teeth and fine *'afi'afi* beads strung on a bamboo stick as if on a bow-string. A peg holding the string into one end of the bamboo can be removed to insert the bamboo through a hole in the bottom of the ear.

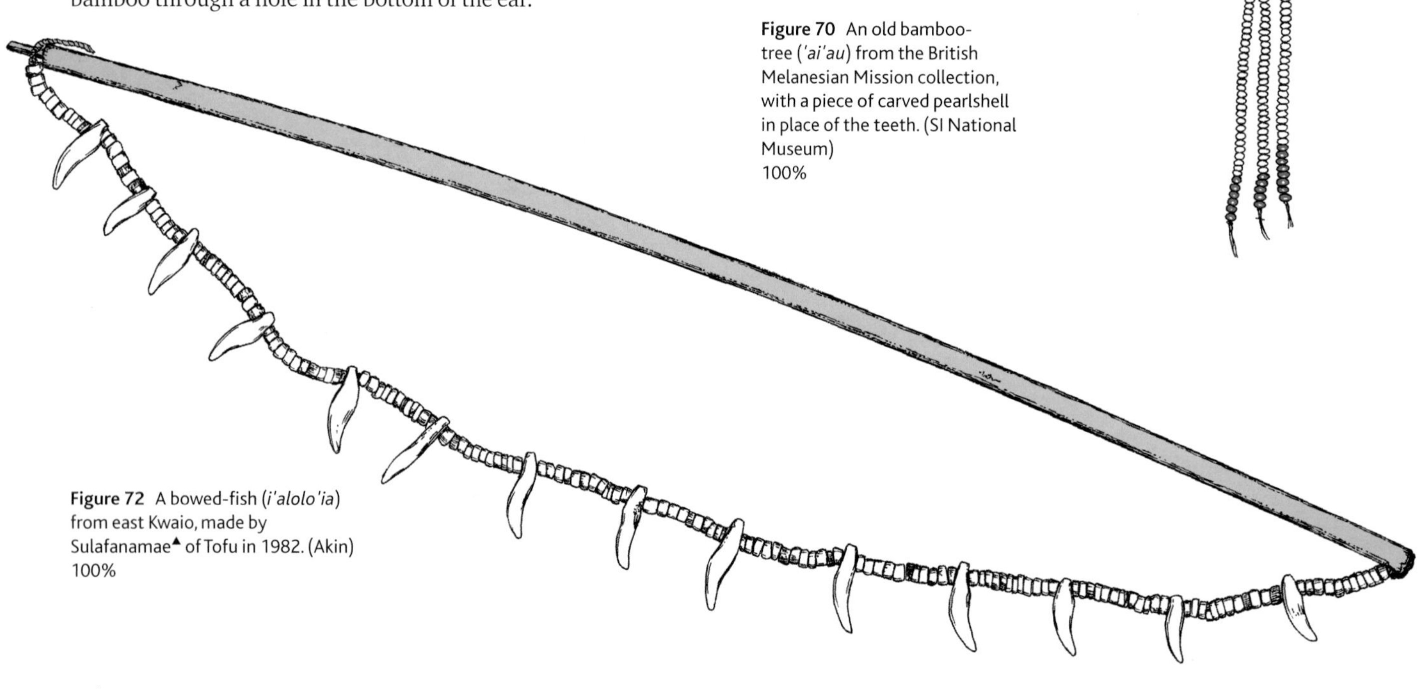

Figure 67 A bamboo-tree (*'ai'au*) with bat teeth, made in Fataleka and belonging to a family at Tabāngwao in east Kwara'ae in 1984. (Burt)
100%

Figure 68 A bamboo-tree (*'ai'au*) with bat teeth, one of a pair from north Malaita from the 1960s (also known as *'ai'au* there and in Kwaio). (Maranda)
100%

Figure 69 An old bamboo-tree (*'ai'au*) with dolphin teeth from the British Melanesian Mission collection. (SI Museum)
100%

Figure 70 An old bamboo-tree (*'ai'au*) from the British Melanesian Mission collection, with a piece of carved pearlshell in place of the teeth. (SI National Museum)
100%

Figure 72 A bowed-fish (*i'alolo'ia*) from east Kwaio, made by Sulafanamae▲ of Tofu in 1982. (Akin)
100%

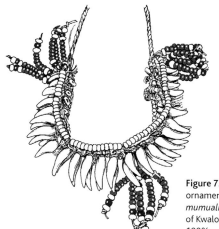

Figure 73 An ear-fringe ornament from Lau (also called *mumualinga*), made by Malefo▲ of Kwalo'ai. (Maranda) 100%

Figure 74 A tridacna (*ima*) ornament in the British Museum, of unknown origin. It is very similar to the stopper (*'afudu'udu'u*) nose-stud, page 95, but has a larger peg with a bamboo sheath which would allow it to be worn in a hole in the ear, if not on an earring. (BM Oc,1947,1.6) 100%

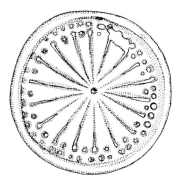

Figure 75 An *eho* ornament from Makira, given to the British Museum by Revd Richard Comins of the Melanesian Mission in 1891. (BM Oc,+4908) 100%

Mumualinga or **ear-fringe** describes certain dolphin-teeth ear ornaments of Kwara'ae and north Malaita. A Fataleka description is of a long patterned-bamboo (*fa'i'augwaroa*) decorated with beads to the front of the ear and a row of dolphin teeth behind, quite different from the Lau example shown here.

'Ima or **tridacna** is described in Kwara'ae as a small disk of tridacna incised with patterns like a shell-disk (*sa'ela'o*) with a stem at the back like a stud for the nose (*otu*). This was inserted into a piece of bamboo which was inserted through the earring-cluster (*barutege*).

Eho is the Sa'a name for a shell-disk ear ornament made and worn in south Malaita. The tridacna (*'ima*) is ground thin to leave a raised outer edge and pierced with radiating cuts and holes. It was worn by men and women, hanging from the ear by a string through the central hole, and could be ornamented with a set of short money-bead strings with bat teeth, the pair linked by a string of money-beads under the chin (Ivens 1918:19, 1927:89).

This ornament was worn in Sa'a and possibly 'Are'are but not elsewhere on Malaita, and it was more common on Makira (Bernatzik 1936:pls 55 and 56, Mead 1973:35).

Ta'ota'ofunu or **turtleshell** (sometimes pronounced *ta'uta'u*), also called *ulifunu doe* or big turtle-skin, is a large cylinder of turtleshell with pointed ends to clip through the hole at the bottom of the ear. It is said that only tabu-speakers and important men would wear them, although they can be seen quite commonly in old photographs (as in a Beattie 540, in which they are worn by four out of a group of nine men at Fote in west Kwara'ae)

This ornament was worn from Kwaio to north Malaita, but not elsewhere. The Kwaio say it should properly be worn alone, with no other ear ornaments, as some (but not all) old photographs confirm.

Figure 76 A single turtleshell (*ta'ota'ofunu*), an heirloom worn by Timi Ko'oliu, last senior tabu-speaker of 'Ere'ere, east Kwara'ae. (Burt) 100%

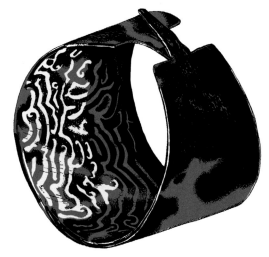

Figure 77 A turtleshell (*ta'ota'ofunu*) from east Kwaio (known there as *'ule'efonu* and *'uri'ifonu*) made by Sulafanamae▲ of Tofu in 1980. Unlike older examples, the ends of the coil are cut down to fit through the ear, and the natural pattern of the turtleshell still shows. (Akin 105) 100%

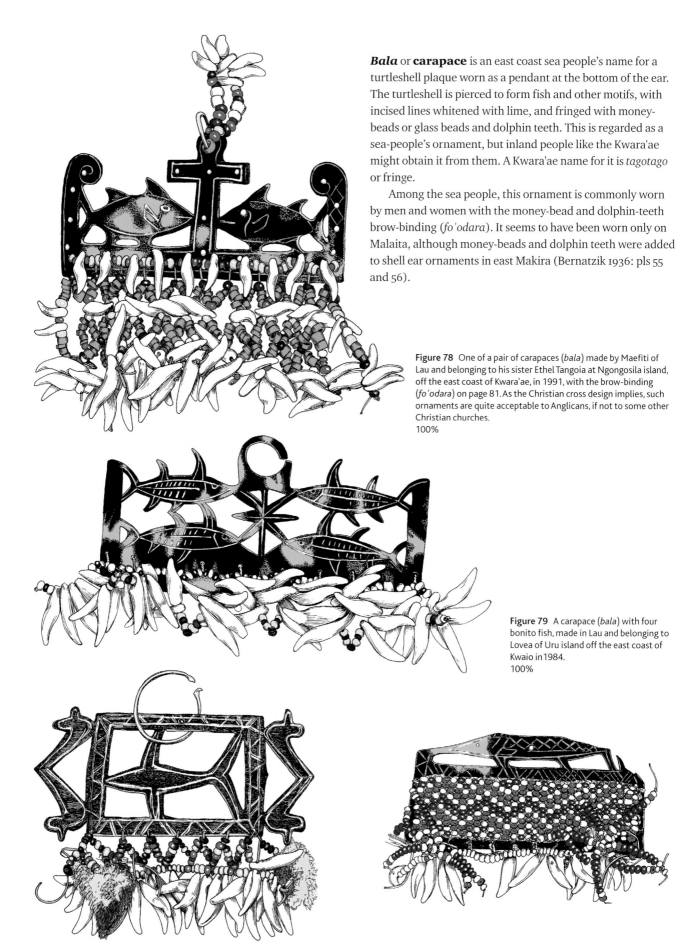

Bala or **carapace** is an east coast sea people's name for a turtleshell plaque worn as a pendant at the bottom of the ear. The turtleshell is pierced to form fish and other motifs, with incised lines whitened with lime, and fringed with money-beads or glass beads and dolphin teeth. This is regarded as a sea-people's ornament, but inland people like the Kwara'ae might obtain it from them. A Kwara'ae name for it is *tagotago* or fringe.

Among the sea people, this ornament is commonly worn by men and women with the money-bead and dolphin-teeth brow-binding (*fo'odara*). It seems to have been worn only on Malaita, although money-beads and dolphin teeth were added to shell ear ornaments in east Makira (Bernatzik 1936: pls 55 and 56).

Figure 78 One of a pair of carapaces (*bala*) made by Maefiti of Lau and belonging to his sister Ethel Tangoia at Ngongosila island, off the east coast of Kwara'ae, in 1991, with the brow-binding (*fo'odara*) on page 81. As the Christian cross design implies, such ornaments are quite acceptable to Anglicans, if not to some other Christian churches.
100%

Figure 79 A carapace (*bala*) with four bonito fish, made in Lau and belonging to Lovea of Uru island off the east coast of Kwaio in 1984.
100%

Figure 80 One of a pair of carapaces (*bala*) from Ngongosila in 1984, with a shark and pairs of sea birds They belonged with a brow-binding (*fo'odara*).
100%

Figure 81 One of a pair of carapaces (*bala*) belonging to Lovea of Uru Island in 1984, made by his father and worn with the glass-bead brow-binding (*fo'odara*) on page 81. The woven glass beads of red, white and blue cover the original fish design.
100%

Ba'o is a Kwaio name for an ear ornament of turtleshell fringed with bat teeth, like a simpler inland kind of carapace (*bala*) ornament.

Figure 82 A *ba'o* made by Rifuala▲ of Naa'umi, southeast Kwaio, in 1982. (Akin 280)
100%

Figure 83 A *ba'o* made to his own original design by Sulafanamae▲ of Tofu, southeast Kwaio, in 1982. (Akin)
100%

Giringali alinga or **ear-cut-nut** is a woman's ear ornament made from a nut (*Canarium*) with one side cut into a peg for the ear, the other ornamented with pearly nautilus shell stuck with black putty (*saia*), and a cluster of bat teeth hanging from strings of fine *'afi'afi* beads or glass beads at the bottom.

In Kwaio cut-nuts are made as a pair of nuts bound together, with clusters of 200 to 250 bats' teeth which often hide the beads. These are worn front and back on a stick which passes through the bottom of the ear. In south Malaita a single nut was sometimes hung with human teeth instead of bat teeth, a style shared with Makira (Akin).

Figure 84 A double cut-nut (*giringali*) made by Nene'au So'ogeni▲ of Kwaina'afi'a, east Kwaio, in 1983 (known there as *kwari'ingari*). The pearlshell is inlaid in grooves carved into the nut. (Akin 112)
100%

Figure 85 A cut-nut (*giringali*) of the south-Malaita type. As part of Charles Woodford's collection, it dates from before 1914. The bats' teeth hang from strings of greyish glass beads, chosen perhaps for their resemblance to *'afi'afi* beads. The pearlshell is stuck rather crudely to the surface of the nut. (BM Oc,1929,0713.47)
100%

Nose ornaments

Rū fuana sa'ilaungi ana rakana ngwae or **ornaments to insert in the nose** were of many kinds, some common, others probably local fashions unfamiliar in other districts. Bishop Montgomery described their effect in the 1890s. Besides the nose-pin (*usuusu*),

> … some of them will pierce as many as eighteen holes in a circle round the nostrils, and plug them all neatly with pieces of mother-of-pearl, giving the appearance of a ring set with stones. If in addition to this they insert in a hole in the very tip of the nose a shell ornament ending in the head of a tropic bird, and projecting straight out from the face, you have some idea of the elegant appearance of a Maleita beau … (Montgomery 1896:185)

(Similar accounts from the 1890s to the 1920s include de Tolna 1903:307, Mytinger 1943:34–6, London 1971:264).

Usuusu or **(nose-)pin** was much the most common nose ornament, a pin of tridacna (*'ima*) worn through a hole in the septum of the nose. In Kwara'ae it is said that men wore long ones and women short ones, but old photographs from various parts of Malaita also show men with short nose-pins and women with long ones (Beattie photo 238x, Paravicini 1931:pl.61 and photo 3956, Maranda). In Kwaio the longest are called 'turn-the-boys-aside' (*dudu'alakwa*) as if when worn by a maiden the points would clear a space in an admiring crowd. The Kwaio also recall nose-pins sometimes being worn in the ear.

Nose-pins were similar throughout Malaita. They usually have one or several narrow bands of fine black twine around each end, of fibres such as *bunabuna* or *'abe*, or sometimes blue thread. In Kwara'ae some had four fibre 'whiskers' (*nonganonga*) on each band with two or three *safi* money-beads or glass beads strung on them. Among other variations, women in 'Are'are wore a curved pin of pearlshell (Geerts 1970:34), and in Langalanga they wore a nose-pin, apparently of reed, with the small nose-conus (*kome rakana*) (Rose photos 12272, 12287).

Pins of tridacna were also worn in Guadalcanal and Isabel (Bogesi 1948:228), as well as in various islands eastwards as far as mainland New Guinea. Very short ones were among a wide variety of nose ornaments worn in Makira (Bernatzik 1936:pls 49–60).

Komerakana or **nose-conus** is a sawn-conus (*komefuria*) ring worn through the septum of the nose. Men sometimes wore one large enough to hang down over the mouth and this is documented for various places around Malaita, so it was no doubt sometimes worn in Kwara'ae, although now forgotten (see Plates 5, 17 and 36, pages 12, 22 and 53, Beattie photos 43, 501, 528, 539, Melvin 1977:50). Early photographs also show women as well as men wearing a smaller conus ring, just covering the upper lip. This seems to have been particularly popular in Langalanga in the 1900s, worn with a nose-pin (*usuusu*) of reed (Rose photos 12272, 12287).

A sawn-conus was also worn in the nose in Arosi, west Makira (BM photo Oc,B34.10), and a turtleshell ring in Ulawa (Beattie photo 575, Ivens 1927:19).

Figure 86 A short nose-pin (*usuusu*) that belonged to a woman of 'Ere'ere, east Kwara'ae, and was kept by her grandson Michael Bare in the 1980s. (Burt) 100%

Figure 87 A short nose-pin (*usuusu*) from Malaita given to the British Museum in 1891 by Revd Richard Comins of the Melanesian Mission. (BM Oc,+4904) 100%

Figure 88 A particularly fine long nose-pin (*usuusu*) belonging to Ramo'itolo, last tabu-speaker of Latea in east Kwara'ae, who died in 1969. The bands at the ends are of blue woollen thread. (Burt) 100%

Figure 89 A very fine long man's nose-pin from Lau (also known there as *usuusu*). (Maranda) 100%

Figure 90 A reconstruction of a nose-pin (*usuusu*) with whiskers (*nonganonga*) (as described by Frank Ete Tu'aisalo). 100%

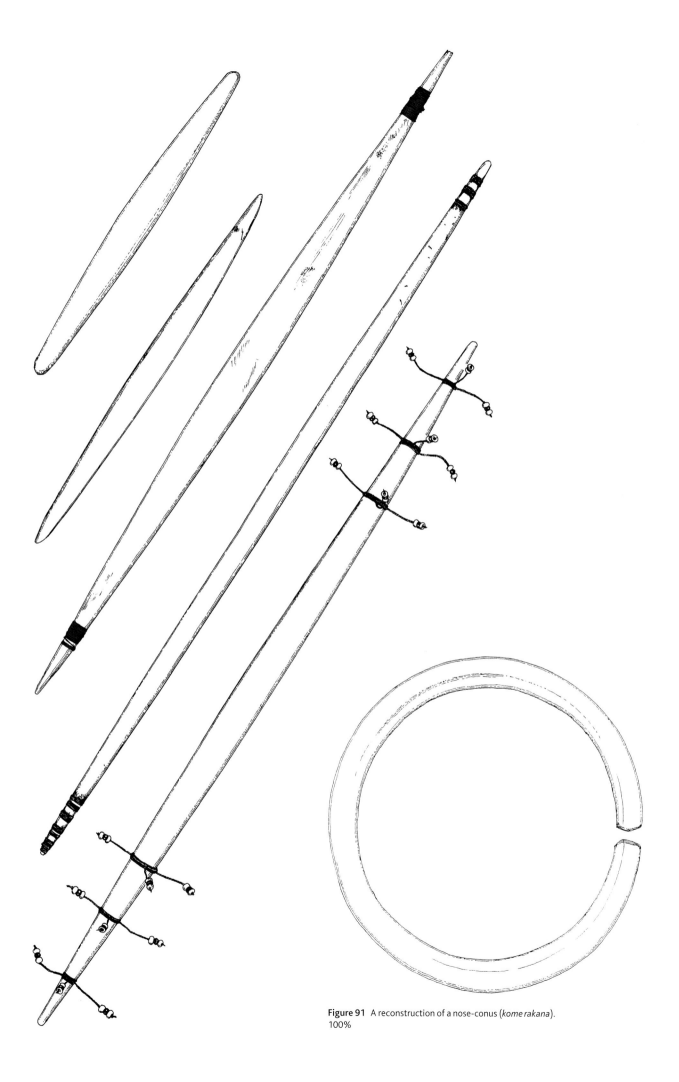

Figure 91 A reconstruction of a nose-conus (*kome rakana*).
100%

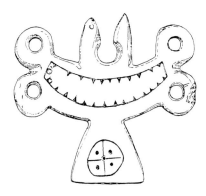

Figure 92 A scorpion (*farifari*) nose-pendant from Lau (where it is known as *fafari* or *komefari*). This was an heirloom seven generations old in the late 1960s, when it belonged to Malefo, a man of the Rere clan of Funafou island. The two pairs of rings were said to be the scorpion's legs, and the incised crescent, a canoe. (Maranda)
100%

Farifari or **scorpion** is a pendant of tridacna (*'ima*) named for the pair of 'claws' by which it was clipped to the septum of the nose. The various forms, with rings, bird-heads and a central flange, probably had their own names.

Scorpion nose ornaments were also worn, by men and sometimes by women, in north Malaita, in Langalanga (see Plates 21, 22 and 23, pages 27, 28 and 31; Ross 1973:21) and in Kwaio, as a less common alternative to the nose-pin (*usuusu*).

Ornaments like the scorpion were worn also in Ulawa, west and east Makira (Brenchley 1873:254, Wilson painting 1854, Bernatzik 1936: pls 13, 49–52, Davenport 1968:409), and some resemble pendants worn at the neck in Isabel (BM photo Oc,B90.12) and western Solomons.

Figure 93 A scorpion (*farifari*) nose-pendant from Lau. (Maranda)
100%

Figure 94 A scorpion (*farifari*) nose-pendant from Malaita, resembling that worn by Irobaoa of Suaba, north Malaita, in Plate 22, page 28.[9] (Edmundson and Boylan 1999: pl. 64)
100%

Figure 95 A scorpion (*farifari*) nose-pendant which came to the Solomon Islands Museum in 1974. (SI Museum 74.85)
100%

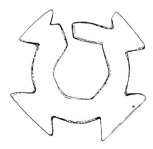

Figure 96 A *uikome* nose-pendant from Baelelea, north Malaita. (Maranda)
100%

Uikome (possibly meaning clam-conus) is a north Malaita name for a tridacna (*'ima*) nose-pendant clipped to, or inserted through the hole in, the septum of nose (Maranda). It resembles some of the serrated-conus (*komegiria*) rings worn at the top of the ear, which could have been interchangeable with it.

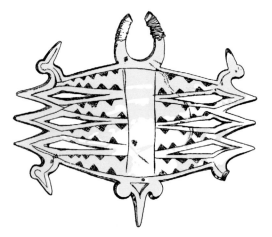

Parapara ni i'e or **shoal-of-fish** is the Sa'a name for a nose-pendant of pearlshell (*'umari*) or turtleshell (*ulifunu*) with a design of mackerel tails, worn in south Malaita (Ivens 1927:143, 1929) and in Makira (Bernatzik 1936:pls 62, 64, 65).

Figure 97 A shoal-of-fish (*parapara ni i'e*) nose-pendant of dark pearlshell from Sa'a or Ulawa, collected by Revd Walter Ivens in the late nineteenth or early twentieth century. (BM Oc,1940,3.9)
100%

'Otu or **(nose-)stud** is a general name for an ornament worn in a hole in the tip of the nose. Although usually associated with men, some women in Lau also had holes for such ornaments.

'Afudu'udu'u or **stopper** is a nose-stud (*'otu*) in the form of a disk of tridacna (*'ima*) incised with a black flower (*takarū*) pattern, with a spike at the back for inserting into the tip of the nose. This is what people usually describe when they recall the nose-stud, but *'afudu'udu'u* is more specific, named for the stopper of a bamboo flask or a hole. It is said that this ornament was worn only by a man to show that he had killed, the hole being bored after the deed. Some say that it was the only stud worn in Kwara'ae, as distinct from districts such as Lau, but others contradict this. It is shown in a number of old photographs of Malaitan men (including Beattie 540, 546, 239X, at Fote and Fiu in west Kwara'ae), although in Kwara'ae it seems to have gone out of fashion with the last generation to carry out publicly approved killings, fathers of the late twentieth-century elders.

Fafangalalo or **man-eater** is described as a long curved nose-stud (*'otu*) of tridacna (*'ima*) worn pointing upwards from the tip of the nose. As the name implies, it is said to have been worn by a man who had killed and eaten someone. Studs of this kind are also shown in old photographs, and they sometimes appear to be made from fragments of conus (*kome*) rings (e.g. Beattie photo 513 from Uru, east Kwaio).

Itoli is the Sa'a name for a nose-stud (*'otu*) of dark pearlshell (*'umari bulu*) in the form of a bird's head (Ivens 1927:82). This ornament is remembered in Kwaio and was also worn in Ulawa. Similar studs, but of turtleshell and more elaborately carved, were worn in east Makira (Bernatzik 1936:pls 53, 54, Mead 1973:36).

'Otousilea or **decorated (nose)-stud** is a Kwaio general name for various forms of nose ornament now no longer to be seen. Some glimpsed in old photographs seem to be ornamented with dolphin teeth (e.g. SSEM photo 112).

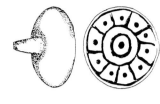

Figure 98 This ornament in the British Museum is evidently a 'stopper' (*'afudu'udu'u*) nose-stud, as described in Kwara'ae and shown in old photographs. As part of Charles Woodford's collection, it dates from before 1914. (BM Oc,1929,0713.61) 100%

Figure 99 A reconstruction of a man-eater (*fafangalalo*) stud. (from Beattie photo 513) 100%

Figure 100 An *itoli* nose-stud of dark pearlshell from Ulawa, given to the British Museum in 1891 by Revd Richard Comins of the Melanesian Mission. (BM Oc,+4906) 100%

Figure 101 An *itoli* nose-stud of tridacna from Ulawa, given to the British Museum in 1891 by Revd Richard Comins. (BM Oc,+4905) 100%

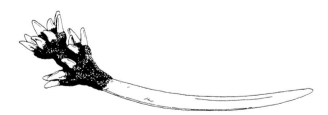

Figure 102 A decorated-stud (*'otousilea*) from east Kwaio made by Nene'au So'ogeni▲ of Kwaina'afi'a in 1982, from recollections of an old ornament long since lost. It is of tridacna with *i'asina* dolphin teeth attached with putty (*saia / Panari*). (Something similar is shown in Beattie photo 513 from Uru, east Kwaio). (Akin) 100%

Binui'asina is a Kwaio name for an ornament of small dolphin teeth (*i'asina*) bound with coconut thread (*fisifisinaniu*), worn around the nose and held by passing the two ends of fibre through a hole in each side of the nose and down the nostrils. It is made rather like the string-of-fish (Kwaio, *kwaloi'a*) ornament (page 64), which it resembles when worn. A similar ornament with bat teeth was also worn in Dorio (Paravicini 1931:170).

Ma'esufusufu is a Kwaio name for three small *'afi'afi* beads worn in holes in the tip and sides of the nose by women.

Ma'efurumou is a Kwaio name for three dolphin teeth worn in holes in the tip and sides of the nose by men.

Tamutamula or **tufty** is the Kwaio name for a short tuft of coconut-threads (*fisifisinaniu*) which was worn by young men through the nose in place of the nose-pin (*usuusu*), with a stud (*'otu*) in the tip of the nose.

Ruame'etofi is the Kwaio name for a man's nose ornament of pearly nautilus shell covering the nose. Two pieces of nautilus, glued with tree resin onto a strip of bark, have three small sticks mounted in the natural holes in the shell and in the join between them, which are inserted into holes in the nose to keep the ornament in place. Sometimes three plates were used (known as a pearly-row, *tale'eleeleo*). It was worn by men only in Kwaio and inland 'Are'are, where it was apparently quite popular; in one photograph from 1910 (Burnett 1911:100) four men out of ten wear them (Ivens 1927:82–3, 1929:143; photos in Young 1925:38, 70, Edge-Partington Oc,Ca44.266 and 267).

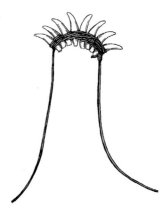

Figure 103 A *binui'asina* made by Sulafanamae▲ of Tofu, southeast Kwaio, in 1982. (Akin 295) 100%

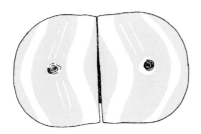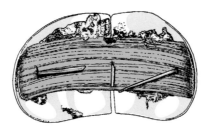

Figure 104 Front and back of a *ruame'etofi* made in 1981 by Basiberi▲ of Gwāgwari, southeast Kwaio. (Akin 170) 100%

Tala'reoreo or **pearly-row** could also describe a row of seven small squares of pearly nautilus shell, as formerly worn around the nose in Sa'a. Several men wearing this ornament were photographed aboard HMS *Royalist* at Port Adam in the early 1890s (including the young man in Plate 33, page 51). The British Museum once had an example obtained by the *Royalist*'s captain, Edward Davis, described as 'small square pieces of pearl shell fastened to a curved strip of wood' (BM Oc,1904,0621.16).

Neck pendant ornaments

Laungi fuana fa'alana ana luana ngwae or ***ornaments to hang from the neck*** included several kinds of pendant, mostly of shell, and a variety of strung ornaments of money-beads and teeth which can be described in general terms as necklaces (*'alu'alu*). Some of these ornaments such as shell-disks (*sa'ela'o*) could also be worn on the head, just as the fish-teeth-cluster (*barulifaī'a*) could also be worn at the neck.

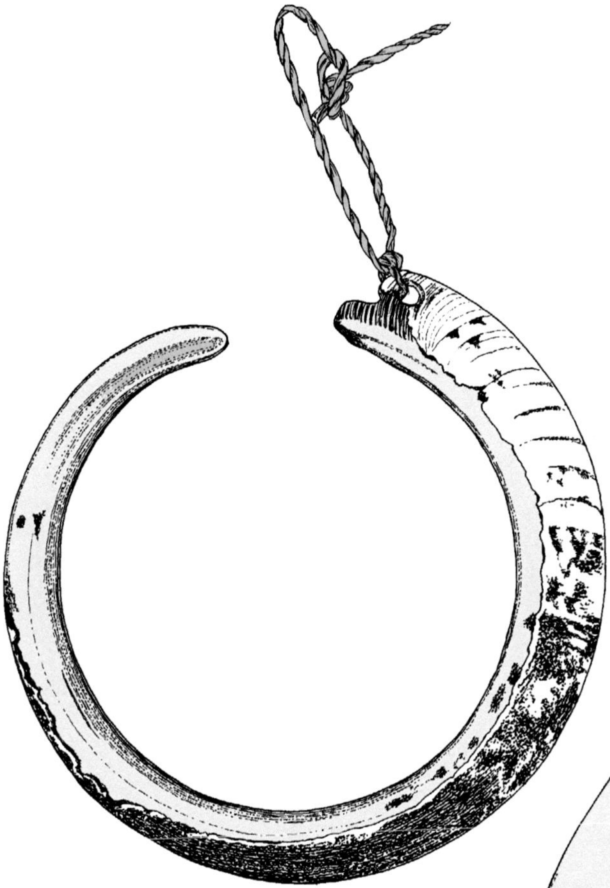

Lifagwata or **pig-tooth** could be worn by men as a neck pendant. Pigs were a sign of wealth and prestige for the inland people of Malaita, who raised them particularly as sacrificial meals for their ancestral ghosts and to feed relatives and neighbours at festivals and marriage feasts. Some pigs had their top canine teeth knocked out so that the lower canines, without anything to wear them down, would continue to grow and sometimes form a complete circle, adding to the value of the pig. Pigs were also an important part of the reward (*fo'oa*) offered for killing an enemy and in the old histories 'the pig tusks had curved round' is a way of saying how long a reward had stood waiting to be claimed.

Some men wore the teeth as trophies of pigs they had stolen to eat, a popular sport for young men which they would proclaim in public, without identifying the particular theft. Such teeth might be treated as tabu because of the magic of the ghosts which had enabled them to steal. Others were mementos of pigs received as presentations and rewards, particularly the curved teeth, which were often worn at the back of the neck on the string of an ornament such as a crescent (*dafe*) or big shell-disk (*sa'ela'o doe*).

Although this ornament was well known in Kwaio, it seems to have been less common in north Malaita (Maranda).

Figure 105 A pig-tooth (*lifagwata*) pendant belonging to Timi Ko'oliu, last tabu-speaker of 'Ere'ere. This was an heirloom from a pig given to his grandfather in reward for a killing, perhaps around 1870, which he presented to Ben Burt in 1979. (Burt)
100%

Figure 106 A pig-tooth (*lifagwata*) pendant from Malaita from before 1932, now in the British Museum. Its surface has been smoothed and polished. (BM Oc,1944,02.1340)
100%

Sa'ela'o or **shell-disk** (sometimes simply 'shell', *la'o*)
is a general term for a disk of tridacna (*'ima*) with incised
and blackened designs, which was worn as a neck or head
pendant. There were two basic types of design throughout
Malaita. The one to which the name shell-disk usually refers
hangs from a hole at the top edge and has a frigate-bird (*gaula*)
design. The other, usually described in Kwara'ae as a woman's
shell-disk (*sa'ela'o kini*), has the hole in the centre and a
simpler star design (see below). Some shell-disks have designs
on both sides, either because the original had begun to wear
and fade or because someone wanted to create his own design
without going through the long labour of grinding a new shell-
disk. The making of shell-disks had almost died out by the late
1970s, but in 1980 people began to make them again at the
Kwaio Cultural Centre, particularly for the export market, and
soon other Malaitans also began making them again.

The frigate-bird shell-disks were usually worn at the neck
by men in Kwara'ae, but women sometimes wore the smaller
ones. In Kwaio they are worn more by married women, often
in pairs, and in Kwaio and 'Are'are men also wore very small
ones tied to the hair (see page 78). One Kwara'ae elder also
recalled a *bero*-disk (*sa'ebero*), a frigate-bird shell-disk with
a hole at each side so that it could be worn on the wrist like a
watch.

The frigate-bird design has many variations. Most shell-
disks have a pair of birds flying to left and right, usually with
a third diving bird below, often reduced to a pair of wings
without a head. The tails of the pair of birds usually end in
shapes derived from fish tails rather than forked frigate-bird
tails, recalling their association with bonito, so important in
the economy and ceremonial life of the sea peoples of south
Malaita and Makira. This could also account for the occasional
inclusion of canoes, sometimes with human figures. Whether
other Malaitans identify these designs with bonito fishing is
another matter, and bird tails can also become fern-scrolls or
moth antennae. Almost all shell-disks have borders based on
rows of frigate-birds (*tala 'i gaula*) as paired hill-shapes (*ma'e
ua*), either alternating to form a row of frigate-birds between or
opposing to form cowrie- or fish-shapes (*ma'e buli, ma'e ī 'a*).

Some designs can be identified with certain parts of
Malaita and as more or less ancient but, since shell-disks were
exchanged far and wide, it is often impossible to be certain
where even those which have kept their histories were actually
made. This is shown by shell-disk-rattles (*ketesa'ela'o*) in
which no two are alike. Designs from one area may well have
been imitated in another and it is even possible that those who
made shell-disks in quantity chose designs preferred by those
to whom they wished to sell them, much as the Langalanga
varied their production of money-beads. The most common
styles of recent generations may not all be very ancient, for
the older sides of some double-sided shell-disks often have
designs which seem to have otherwise disappeared. Three
old Kwara'ae heirlooms, from Siale, Manadari and Kwalufafo,
although very different, seem to show older styles in which
the pair of birds are separate and have curved tapering wings.

The Kwara'ae shell-disks illustrated here give a fair
impression of the range of frigate-bird designs used

throughout most of Malaita, apart from the north. They were
not necessarily made in Kwara'ae, and some certainly were
not. If there was a distinctive Kwara'ae or mid-Malaita style,
it could be the three separate and rather linear birds on the
shell-disk from Latea (opposite) and on the newer sides of the
Manadari and Kwalufafo shell-disks (page 100), also seen on
some Langalanga examples.

Like the newer Kwara'ae designs, shell-disks from Kwaio
and south Malaita usually have the birds joined in a single
motif. Most have straight wings with a projection to indicate
the elbow and, in south Malaita, usually three crescent shapes
at the end of the fish tails. A style distinctive of east Kwaio
has a strongly curved outline around a continuous motif.
From north Malaita there are several shell-disk designs with
the birds so stylized as to be hardly recognizable, resembling
each other only when they are all compared with frigate-bird
designs from further south. These also share features with
other north Malaitan designs which seem to bear no relation
to the frigate-bird at all.

Within these more or less local styles there is still much
variation. Some of this could be due to casual workmanship
by individuals making their own ornaments. The more
standardized designs could be the products of a few gifted
craftsmen who were able to sell large numbers to others,
locally and abroad. In general it seems that the makers of
shell-disks felt free to reinterpret the basic motifs without
paying much attention to what they represented, sometimes
changing them almost beyond recognition.

The only other island where incised shell-disks were
commonly worn was Makira. Some of these had the three-
frigate-bird design, indistinguishable from those of Malaita
and perhaps traded from there (Bernatzik 1936:pls 69,
70), but others had a distinctive Makira design. Instead of
the pair of frigate-birds there is a pair of fish with human
bodies or legs, sometimes reduced to abstract curves, with
a diving frigate-bird below. This design, documented for
Arosi as early as the 1850s as well as for east Makira (Webster
drawings, Bernatzik 1936:pl. 168), also travelled and
sometimes appears on the older sides of shell-disks with a
Malaitan design on the other (one such disk was kept in east
Kwaio in the late twentieth century). Incised shell-disks were
also made on Bougainville and Buka in the late nineteenth
century, by 'only a few artists', but their Malaita-style frigate-
bird design suggests a close trade connection between the
islands (Parkinson 1999:214, Meyer and Parkinson 1894:
pl. 45).

Sa'ela'o doe or **big shell-disk**, also called *raga*, was worn
singly, either as a neck pendant or at the side of the head.
Most are incised with the frigate-bird design with the hole
at the top, but some have the star design and central hole
like the woman's shell-disks (see below). Big shell-disks
were important and valuable heirlooms, associated with
tabu-speakers (some identify or confuse them with the rare
and important turtle-design, *funifunu*, also said to be a tabu-
speaker's ornament). Like the smaller shell-disks, the big ones
were worn throughout Malaita.

Figure 107 An old heirloom shell-disk (*sa'ela'o*) with two *'aimamu* conus rings, worn with the nose-pin (Figure 88, page 93) by Ramo'itolo, last tabu-speaker of Latea in east Kwara'ae, who died in 1969. This example demonstrates that the more important old objects are not always the best made. The rudimentary third frigate-bird has a sun (*sina*) between its wings. (Burt) 100%

Figure 108 A big shell-disk (*sa'ela'o doe*) which belonged to the tabu-speakers of 'Aimomoko in central Kwara'ae. The frigate-birds, in an old style, have their tails adapted to form coiled *Dennstaedtia*-fern crowns (*gwa'i unuunu*), said to look like eyes.

It is said that twelve generations ago (to the 1990s) the 'Aimomoko people fled to Kwaio to escape a feud, bought some land at Rara'ifata, and the senior man for that land gave this shell-disk to their tabu-speaker in memory of the land transfer. It was passed down the generations to Filo'isi of 'Aimomoko, the last tabu-speaker to practise the ancestral religion at Siale, which most Kwara'ae regard as their most ancient shrine. The shell-disk became a tabu ancestral relic and was not worn, except perhaps for sacrificial festivals.

Filo'isi joined the church in 1943 and after his death in about 1954 the 'Aimomoko people gave the shell-disk to their son-in-law Adriel Rofate'e Toemanu of Gwauna'ongi. Rofate'e later wore it on important occasions as a Paramount Chief in the Kwara'ae tradition movement. (Burt) 100%

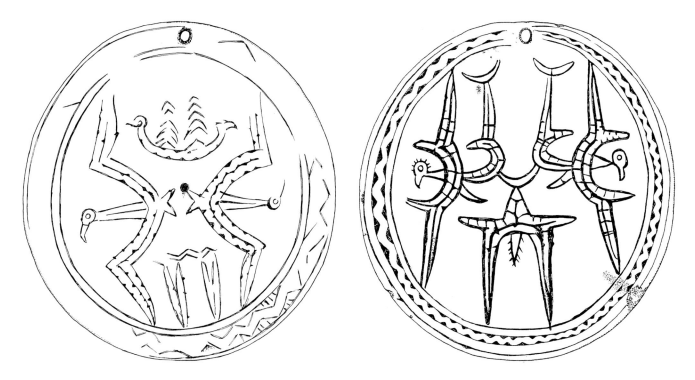

Figure 109 Two sides of an ancient big shell-disk (sa'ela'o doe) which belonged to the tabu-speakers of Daroa in central Kwara'ae. It was kept in their tabu-sanctum, since abandoned, until salvaged in about 1990 by James Abera'u of Ualakwai. It is said to have been made 15 generations before by Idumae, tabu-speaker of Mānadari, the ancient tabu-sanctum from which Daroa-Ualakwai clan derives, founded soon after Siale. The original design, now worn and faint, includes what could be a canoe with birds' heads, while the newer side is is in a more recent style. (Burt)
100%

Figure 110 Two sides of a big shell-disk (sa'ela'o doe) formerly belonging to Lui of Kwalufafo in east Kwara'ae, who died about 1959. It was then inherited by Patterson Suidufu. The older side has a man in a canoe between the birds. (Burt)
100%

Figure 111 An old shell-disk (*sa'ela'o*) bought by an east Kwara'ae man on a visit to Kwaio 1984 (where they are known as *la'oniasi* or shell-of-the-sea). (Burt)
100%

Figure 112 A shell-disk (*sa'ela'o*) made in east Kwaio in the 1990s to sell in Honiara. The distinctive design was developed by Mede▲ of Naanakinimae in the 1980s. (Burt)
100%

Figure 113 A big shell-disk (*sa'ela'o doe*), belonging to Lovea▲ of Uru island in 1984, but made in east Kwaio, possibly by Lausimae.▲ The continuous motif, outlined with strong curves with circular heads and eyes, is the distinctive style of east Kwaio, and is used on most of the shell-disks still made there. (Burt)
100%

Figure 114 A shell-disk (*sa'ela'o*) of a style associated with south Malaita (Sa'a *ulute*, see Ivens 1918:pl. 8, 1927: pl. 15),[10] which came to the British Museum in 1921. Its other, older, side has a simple mid-Malaita design. (BM Oc,1921,1014.59)
100%

Ketesa'ela'o or **shell-disk-rattle**, also called 'shell-disk-string' (_usisa'ela'o_), is a group of about six small frigate-bird shell-disks strung together, usually on a string of white _galu_ money-beads laid edge to edge. The name refers to the way they rattle against one another when moved.

This was a man's ornament, particularly associated with warriors. It was a way of wearing shell-disks throughout Malaita, and a mixture of disks from various sources, as in the Kwara'ae examples shown here, was probably common (one with eight disks collected by Paravicini in 1929 somewhere between west Kwara'ae and 'Are'are has an equally wide range of designs; 1940:153). However, in north Malaita the disks were commonly made as a matching set of about ten.

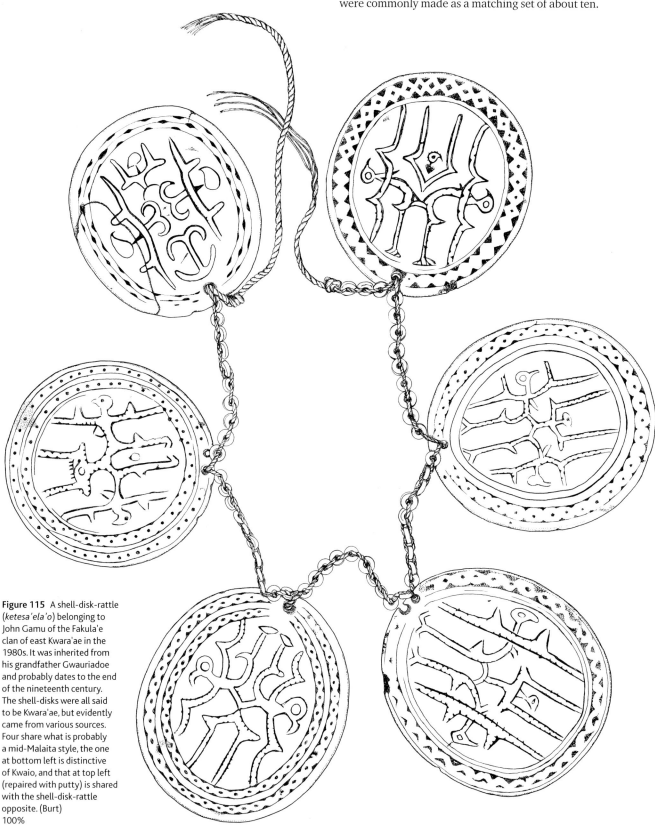

Figure 115 A shell-disk-rattle (_ketesa'ela'o_) belonging to John Gamu of the Fakula'e clan of east Kwara'ae in the 1980s. It was inherited from his grandfather Gwauriadoe and probably dates to the end of the nineteenth century. The shell-disks were all said to be Kwara'ae, but evidently came from various sources. Four share what is probably a mid-Malaita style, the one at bottom left is distinctive of Kwaio, and that at top left (repaired with putty) is shared with the shell-disk-rattle opposite. (Burt) 100%

Figure 116 A shell-disk-rattle (*ketesa'ela'o*) from Fiu in west Kwara'ae, assembled from shell-disks of different styles and states of wear. It came to the Auckland Museum in 1932. While most of these resemble other mid-Malaita shell-disks, the abstract one at top right is more typical of north Malaita. (Auckland Museum 18386) 100%

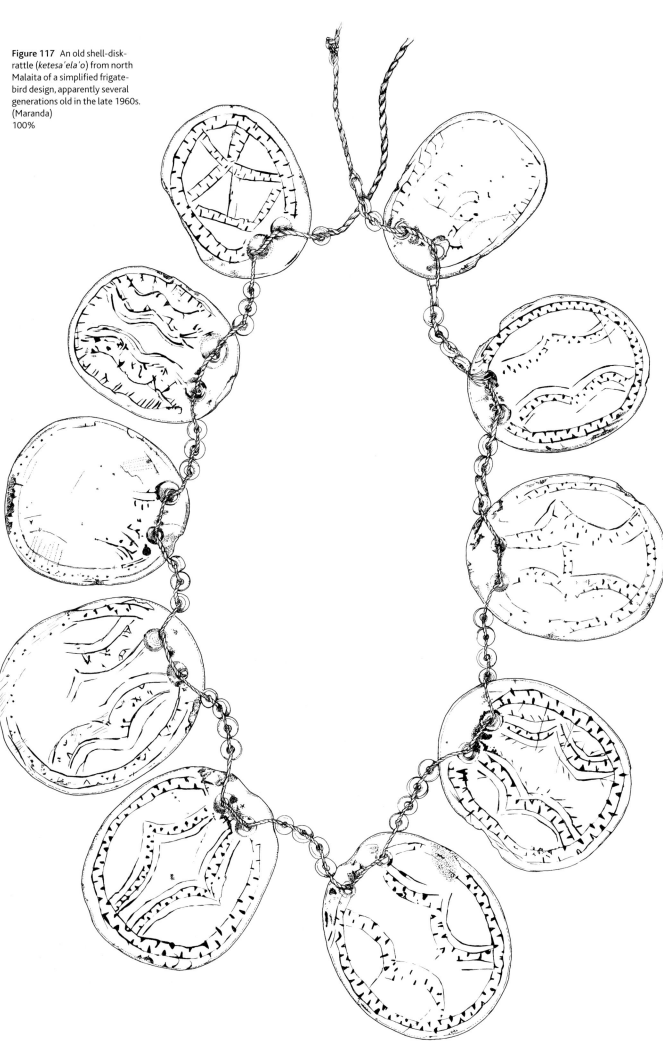

Figure 117 An old shell-disk-rattle (*ketesaʼelaʼo*) from north Malaita of a simplified frigate-bird design, apparently several generations old in the late 1960s. (Maranda)
100%

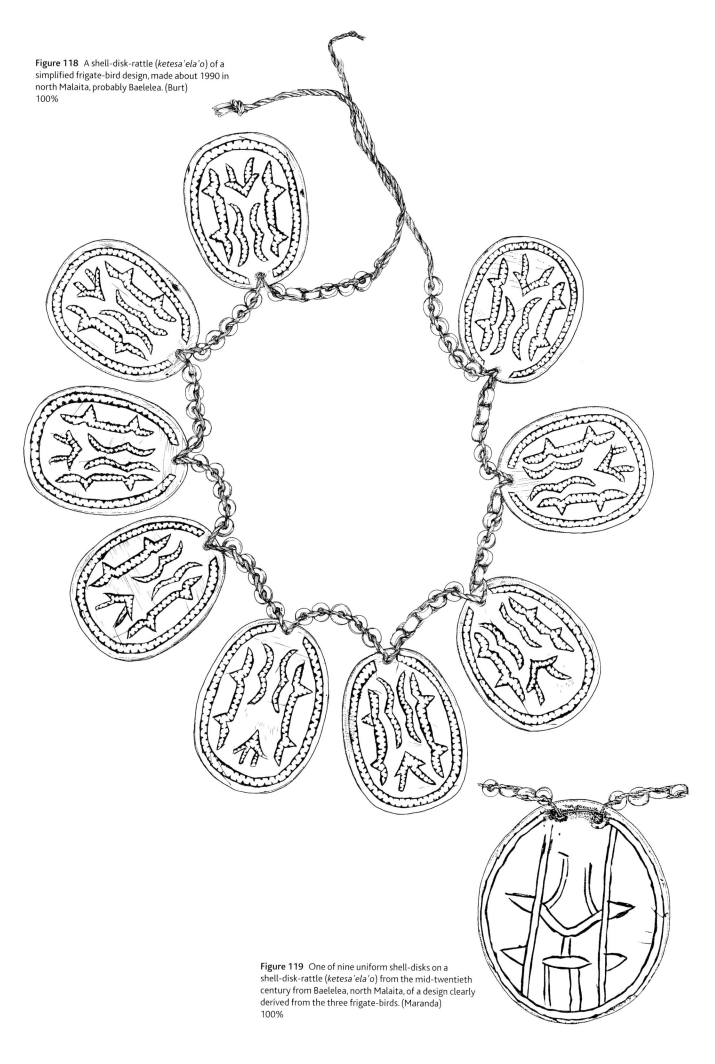

Figure 118 A shell-disk-rattle (*ketesa'ela'o*) of a simplified frigate-bird design, made about 1990 in north Malaita, probably Baelelea. (Burt) 100%

Figure 119 One of nine uniform shell-disks on a shell-disk-rattle (*ketesa'ela'o*) from the mid-twentieth century from Baelelea, north Malaita, of a design clearly derived from the three frigate-birds. (Maranda) 100%

Sa'ela'o kini or **woman's shell-disk** is a small shell-disk with an incised star (*fa'i bulubulu*) design and the hole in the centre. It was worn by women at the neck, although some say only by maidens, several shell-disks being threaded on a string which was poked through the hole from behind and secured by a knot or a money-bead at the front. Some examples have the frigate-bird design on one side, the other evidently reworked with the central hole and cross because the original hole at the edge had worn through. Men only wore the star on a big shell-disk for a head ornament.

The small cross shell-disks were also worn by women in north Malaita, Kwaio and south Malaita (Ivens 1927:392). The Kwaio distinguish two designs: 'incised-fish-shoal' (*girigwei'a*), with pairs of fish at the ends of the star is said to have originated with the sea people to the north, and is supposed to be worn in pairs by marriageable maidens; 'incised-mountain-ridge' (*girimalaile*) has triangular 'mountains' along the star, and should be strung in a row of up to ten as 'threaded woman's shell-disks' (*usi sa'ela'o kini*).

Figure 120 A woman's shell-disk (*sa'ela'o kini*) of the incised-fish-shoal (*girigwei'a*) design, made by Winiamae▲ of Nānakinimae, east Kwaio, in 1983. (Akin 55)
100%

Figure 121 A big shell-disk (*sa'ela'o doe*) for the head, of the incised-fish-shoal (*girigwei'a*) design. It was made in Kwaio (where these large disks are called *'eteomea*), and kept as an heirloom by Lovea, tabu-speaker of Uru island in 1984. (Burt)
100%

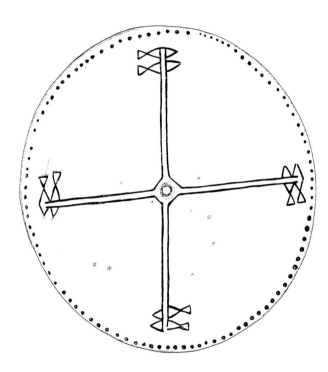

Dala is a name for a big shell-disk with a star-design distinctive of north Malaita. Unlike the woman's shell-disk (*sa'ela'o kini*), the hole is at the edge and the arms of the cross usually end in crescents within the border of the disk. *Dala* were worn by men at the neck or head (like the *funifunu* or turtle-design head ornament, also called *dala* in north Malaita), sometimes one on each side of the head. In Lau they were said to be worn particularly by priests, and the star-design is said to represent the identity of people with their patron sea-spirits (Maranda).

A Kwara'ae elder could have been describing a variation of this northern style when he recalled seeing long ago a row of star-design shell-disks strung edge-to-edge by holes at each side, worn around the waist by an old man.

Figure 122 A *dala* shell-disk from inland north Malaita, with the local version of the star design, from the mid-twentieth century. This one is unusual in having a hole at each side. (Maranda)
100%

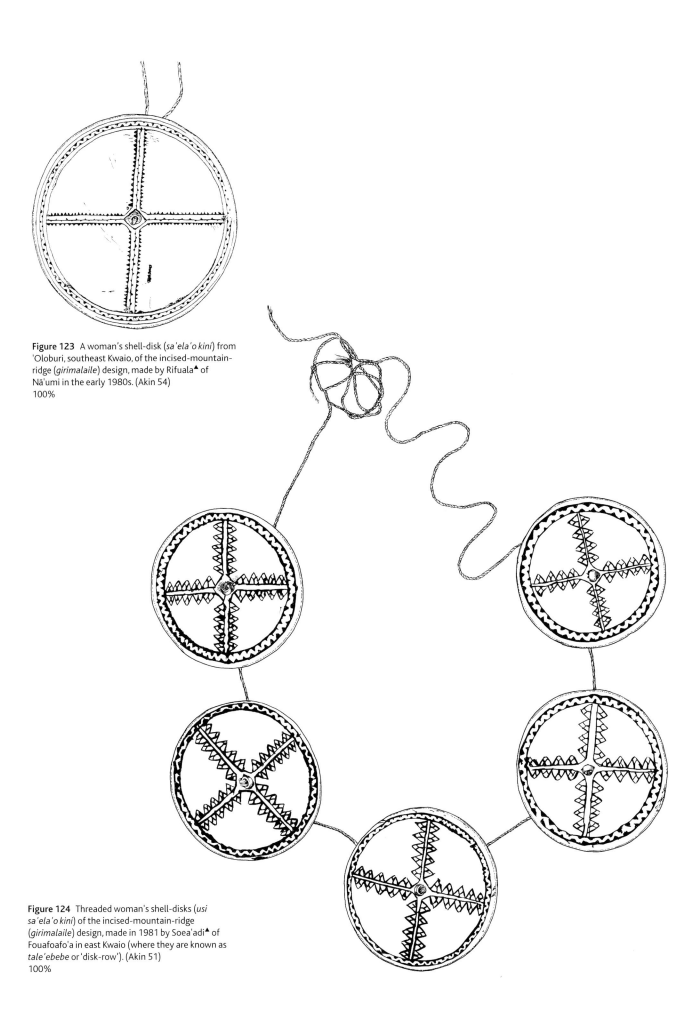

Figure 123 A woman's shell-disk (*sa'ela'o kini*) from 'Oloburi, southeast Kwaio, of the incised-mountain-ridge (*girimalaile*) design, made by Rifuala▲ of Nä'umi in the early 1980s. (Akin 54)
100%

Figure 124 Threaded woman's shell-disks (*usi sa'ela'o kini*) of the incised-mountain-ridge (*girimalaile*) design, made in 1981 by Soea'adi▲ of Fouafoafo'a in east Kwaio (where they are known as *tale'ebebe* or 'disk-row'). (Akin 51)
100%

La'otari or **cut-shell** is a Kwaio name for a pendant ground from a broken shell-disk (Kwaio, *la'oniasi*), commonly worn in Kwaio by maidens and infants. It was probably known in Kwara'ae and other parts of Malaita too.

Figure 126 A cut-shell (*la'otari*) from Kwaio. (Akin)
100%

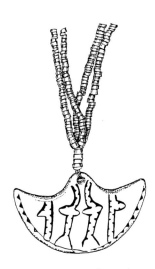

Figure 127 A cut-shell (*la'otari*) from Kwaio, made from a frigate-bird shell-disk (Kwaio *la'oniasi*) strung on a necklace of *'afi'afi* beads. (Akin 57)
100%

Figure 125 An old big shell-disk (*sa'ela'o doe*), given to the British Museum in 1880. On the back of the Malaita design is an older, more worn design including a pair of fish, characteristic of Makira. The blacking, mostly lost, has been restored in the drawing, and the old collection label containing all that is known of the shell-disk's history, is glued to the surface. (BM Oc,+1160)
100%

Foufoulā or **orator-pendant** is the Kwaio name for a locally made disk of chalky white stone, with an incised frigate-bird design and two hornbill heads projecting from the top. It was made by the people of Gounaakafu in east Kwaio in former times and was said to have been worn only by a powerful feast-giver and orator on big public occasions. They regard it as the model for the tridacna shell-disks (Kwaio *la'oniasi*) made by the sea people.

Figure 128 A *foufoulā* made by 'Otomae of Gounaakafu, east Kwaio, in 1982. With no surviving example to copy, he made it from a historical description. (Akin)
100%

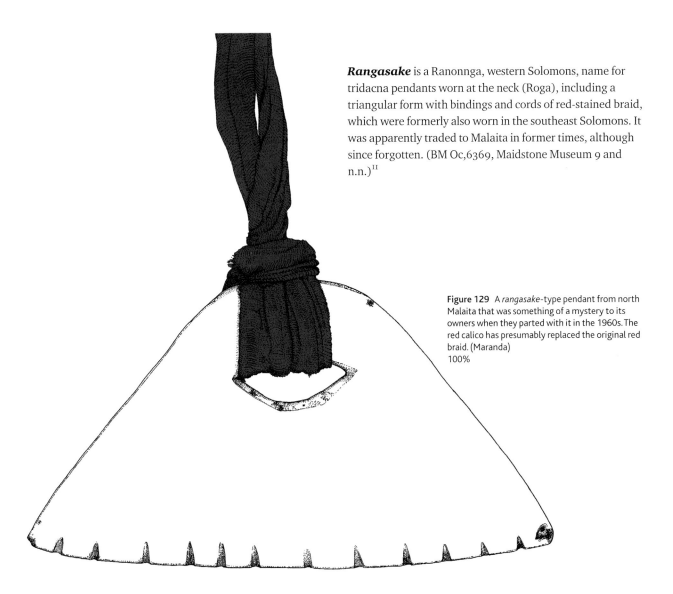

Rangasake is a Ranonnga, western Solomons, name for tridacna pendants worn at the neck (Roga), including a triangular form with bindings and cords of red-stained braid, which were formerly also worn in the southeast Solomons. It was apparently traded to Malaita in former times, although since forgotten. (BM Oc,6369, Maidstone Museum 9 and n.n.)[11]

Figure 129 A *rangasake*-type pendant from north Malaita that was something of a mystery to its owners when they parted with it in the 1960s. The red calico has presumably replaced the original red braid. (Maranda)
100%

Dafe or **crescent** is a pendant of pearlshell (*'umari*) shaped like a crescent moon with the shiny iridescent inner side of the shell facing outwards and the back ground smooth. Many crescents have a frigate-bird of turtleshell mounted in the centre secured by the two suspension cords, and a few have the tips of the crescent carved as bird heads. The crescent is generally a man's ornament, said by some to be worn by tabu-speakers, but more probably worn by any man, as others say. Small ones were also worn by women in Kwara'ae and elsewhere (as in Plate 7, page 14, and Paravicini photo 4021 from Buma, Langalanga). Formerly, as early twentieth-century photos show, crescents were often worn on a single string of large *buruburu* glass beads, more recently on one or several strings of money-beads, often fastened with a button and loop. The older style, still followed in Kwaio, was to wear the crescent close to the throat, but in Kwara'ae in the late twentieth century it was hung lower on the chest. As a common Malaita ornament, crescents have also been imitated in wood, plywood and board as a dance ornament, especially in the late twentieth century.

The Kwara'ae examples shown here illustrate the large and simple forms of crescent, usually of important pearlshell (*'umari 'inoto'a* / goldlip) common throughout Malaita, but there were some local variations in style. The Kwaio prefer slightly smaller crescents and sometimes grind down larger ones traded from elsewhere. In north Malaita some crescents were further ornamented with incised fish and rows of circles (made with a wire compass; Akin 1988). A fringe of money-beads strung in a net design was added occasionally in the past, and more commonly in the later twentieth century, especially in Langalanga.[12] A very few crescents have a carved projection from the bottom (see Rose photo 12,254 from Dala,

west Kwara'ae). Although the turtleshell attachment is usually a frigate-bird, flying or occasionally diving, other motifs were also used in various parts of Malaita.

While the large crescent of important pearlshell was a characteristic Malaita ornament during the twentieth century, it is not a very ancient tradition there. The Kwaio and Sa'a trace its origin to Gela and Isabel islands (Ivens 1927:393–5), and the similarity of its names around Malaita and neighbouring islands supports the probability that it only became common on Malaita with an increased supply of this shell in the late nineteenth century (see page 41).[13] However, large pearlshell crescents were common on Makira from at least the 1840s (Verguet 1885:201, 203) and many other Solomon Islands pearlshell pendants were of similar shape, that is, with the lip of the shell forming a curved lower edge. Some of those in museum collections, smaller and of dark pearlshell (*'umari bulu* / blacklip), might be from Malaita, but old photographs also show such ornaments to have been worn from Makira to the western Solomons. Many have a central projection at the top for hanging, some with another at the bottom, in a few cases making the pendant resemble a bird with spread wings. Others, with a flat top edge, bottom projection and birds' heads at each end, look like the profile of a feast bowl (as noted for one western Solomons-style crescent when given to the British Museum in the 1880s; BM Oc,+1159). Further variations include ends rounded into fern-like coils and smaller or larger projections from the lower edge. Pearlshell crescents were among the pendants characteristic of New Georgia, western Solomons, in the colonial period, and examples from there range from simple straight-topped crescents to complex frigate-bird and scroll designs (Williamson 1914:23, Woodford photo BM Oc,B34.14, Somerville photo BM Oc,B36.3).

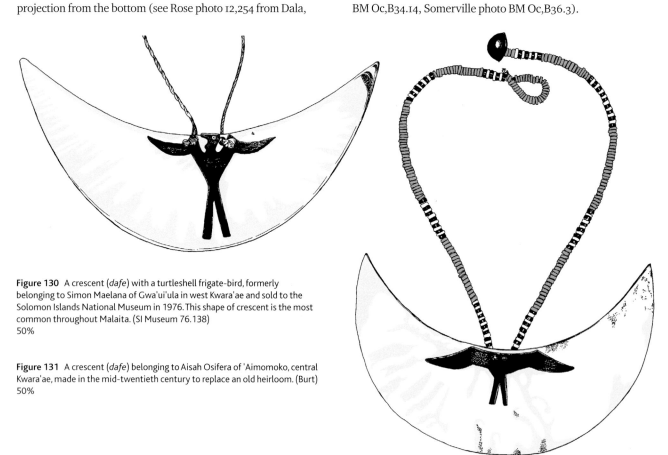

Figure 130 A crescent (*dafe*) with a turtleshell frigate-bird, formerly belonging to Simon Maelana of Gwa'ui'ula in west Kwara'ae and sold to the Solomon Islands National Museum in 1976. This shape of crescent is the most common throughout Malaita. (SI Museum 76.138)
50%

Figure 131 A crescent (*dafe*) belonging to Aisah Osifera of 'Aimomoko, central Kwara'ae, made in the mid-twentieth century to replace an old heirloom. (Burt)
50%

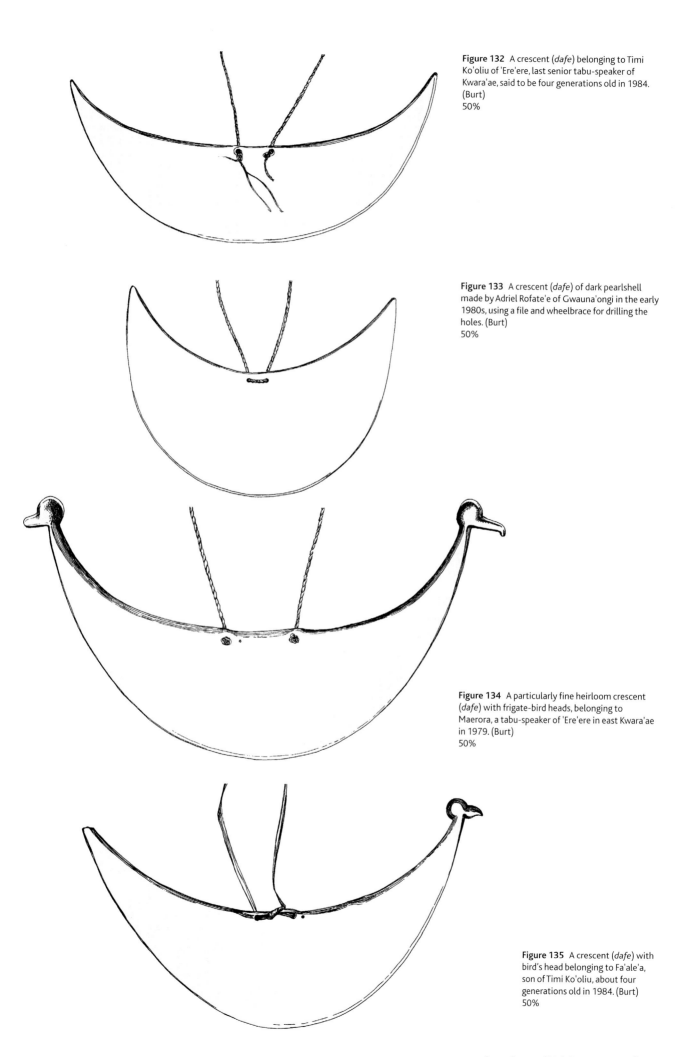

Figure 132 A crescent (*dafe*) belonging to Timi Ko'oliu of 'Ere'ere, last senior tabu-speaker of Kwara'ae, said to be four generations old in 1984. (Burt)
50%

Figure 133 A crescent (*dafe*) of dark pearlshell made by Adriel Rofate'e of Gwauna'ongi in the early 1980s, using a file and wheelbrace for drilling the holes. (Burt)
50%

Figure 134 A particularly fine heirloom crescent (*dafe*) with frigate-bird heads, belonging to Maerora, a tabu-speaker of 'Ere'ere in east Kwara'ae in 1979. (Burt)
50%

Figure 135 A crescent (*dafe*) with bird's head belonging to Fa'ale'a, son of Timi Ko'oliu, about four generations old in 1984. (Burt)
50%

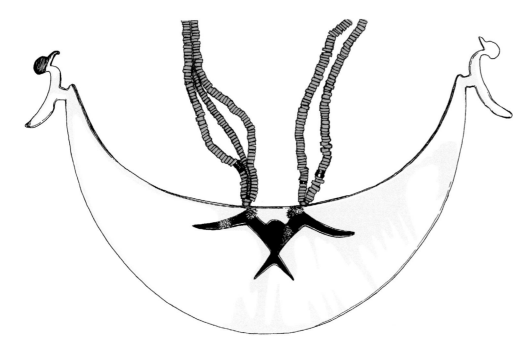

Figure 136 An unusual and especially fine crescent, an heirloom belonging to Ma'aanamae of 'Ai'eda in east Kwaio (known there as *dafi* and *dami*). It was already at least two generations old when he was born at the beginning of the twentieth century, and must have been treated with great care to avoid breaking the fragile frigate-bird tips. (Akin)
50%

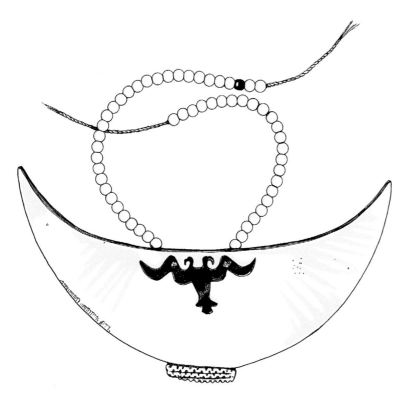

Figure 137 A crescent from Baelelea (known there as *dafi*) which is unusual in having the flat projection at the bottom, apparently related to the 'feastbowl' design. The double-headed bird is also unusual, but the large glass beads (*buruburu*) are typical crescent-beads (*kekefe dafe*), as shown in early-twentieth-century photographs. (Maranda)
50%

Figure 138 Some turtleshell motifs from otherwise simple crescents (left to right, top then bottom):

A pair of frigate-birds from Baegu, north Malaita. (Maranda)
50%

A pair of *Dennstaedtia*-fern crowns (*gwa'i 'unu'unu*) from north Malaita. (BM Oc,1944,02.1336)
50%

A design from north Malaita. (BM Oc,1944.02.1337)
50%

A frigate-bird made by Sulafanamae▲ of Tofu, southeast Kwaio. (Akin 66)
50%

A bird from southeast Kwaio, in a style from 'Are'are to the south. (Akin 67)
50%

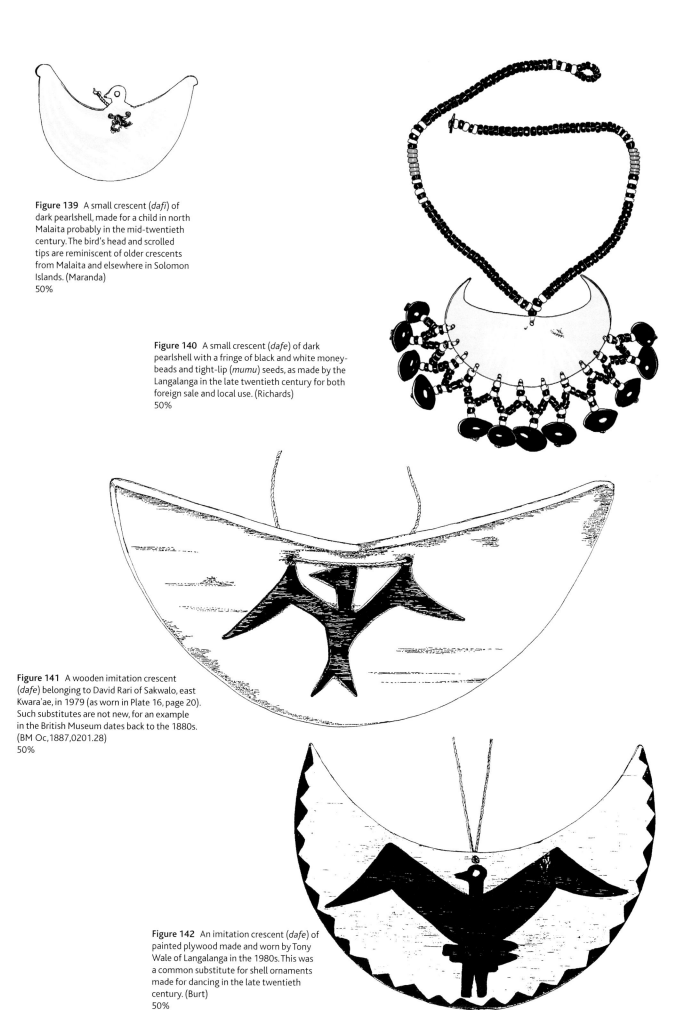

Figure 139 A small crescent (*dafi*) of dark pearlshell, made for a child in north Malaita probably in the mid-twentieth century. The bird's head and scrolled tips are reminiscent of older crescents from Malaita and elsewhere in Solomon Islands. (Maranda)
50%

Figure 140 A small crescent (*dafe*) of dark pearlshell with a fringe of black and white money-beads and tight-lip (*mumu*) seeds, as made by the Langalanga in the late twentieth century for both foreign sale and local use. (Richards)
50%

Figure 141 A wooden imitation crescent (*dafe*) belonging to David Rari of Sakwalo, east Kwara'ae, in 1979 (as worn in Plate 16, page 20). Such substitutes are not new, for an example in the British Museum dates back to the 1880s. (BM Oc,1887,0201.28)
50%

Figure 142 An imitation crescent (*dafe*) of painted plywood made and worn by Tony Wale of Langalanga in the 1980s. This was a common substitute for shell ornaments made for dancing in the late twentieth century. (Burt)
50%

Gwa'ila'o or **great-shell**, also called **kwaro** (meaning a ground pearlshell, as used for a vegetable knife), is a whole important pearlshell (*'umari 'inoto'a* / goldlip) with a black border of putty (*saia* / *Parinari*), worn as a neck pendant or sometimes at the side of the head, like a big shell-disk. The exterior of the shell faces outwards, requiring a fine shell, free of worm-holes, which had to be laboriously ground and polished to reveal the pearl, and this probably made it particularly valuable.

The great-shell was known throughout Malaita and generally regarded as belonging to the most senior leaders. Some Kwara'ae say it was worn only by a tabu-speaker or a lord (*aofia*), a legendary powerful leader with authority beyond his own clan, although others regard it as not particularly special. In Lau it was an ornament for aristocrats, but for inland peoples like the Kwara'ae, where lords were more an ideal than a political reality, it would have been no more than a claim to be an important man (*ngwae 'inoto'a*) (In Plate 21, page 27, four out of six chiefs from one local community are wearing them.) A Kwaio name for the ornament, *dafialafa*, has the related meanings of 'chief's-*dafi*' and 'wide-*dafi*', chiefs (*alafa*) being those of 'wide' authority and *dafi* implying 'pearlshell' as well as 'crescent'. In Sa'a and Lau it was said to represent the full moon, while in Sa'a and Kwaio it was said to be the way important pearlshells were first worn, when they were still scarce and particularly valuable (Ivens 1927:395, Maranda). It was also worn on Makira (Bernatzik 1936:pls 8, 67, 82, 131, Mead 1973:36).[14]

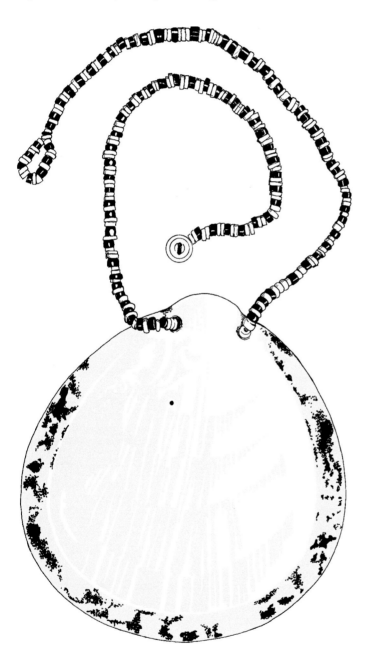

Figure 143 A great-shell (*gwa'ila'o*) belonging to Lovea, tabu-speaker of Uru island, east Kwaio, in 1984, which he called his 'lord's crescent' (*dafi alova*). The putty border, always fragile, had mostly cracked and fallen away. (Burt) 66%

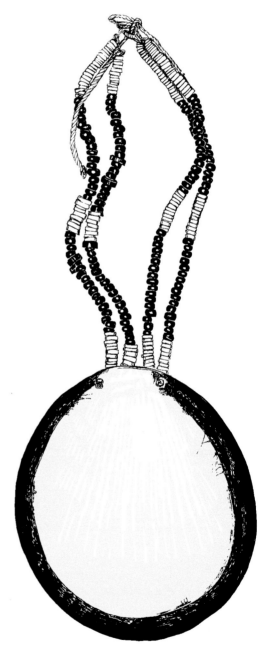

Figure 144 A great-shell (*gwa'ila'o*) made by Ru'uboo▲ of Ga'enāfou, east Kwaio, in 1983 (known there as *dafiburua, dafilalao, dafilalalo* and *dafialfa*) which shows how the ornament should look when the putty is intact. (Akin 269) 66%

Figure 145 A great-shell (*gwa'ila'o*) made by Jack Ramosaea from Fataleka, living in Honiara, which he wore as his 'lord's crescent' (*dafe aofia*) in 1984. The net of money-beads with tight-lip (*mumu*) seeds and tufts of plastic string is a recent innovation, following the net sometimes added to crescents (*dafe*). (Burt)
66%

Talakome or **conus-row**, also called *baru'ikome* or conus-
cluster, is a set of conus-rings worn at the neck on a string of
money-beads, often bound tight to stand out from the throat.
The rings might be graduated in size from smaller at the ends
to larger in the middle and were sometimes bound together
to keep them in order. This ornament was worn by children as
well as by men and women, with rows from about six to more
than twenty rings. Conus rings were also worn loosely on a
necklace (*'alu'alu*) a few at a time (as in Figure 107, page 99).

Conus-rows and other arrangements of conus rings were
also worn in Kwaio and Langalanga, and in south Malaita
where they were sometimes worn hanging lower on the
chest (Raucaz 1928:225, Paravicini 1931:157 and photos 3757,
3775, 3781, 3794, de Coppet and Zemp 1978:100, 101, 109,
Holdsworth 1977: photo), as well as in Makira (Denham photo,
Bernatzik 1936:pl. 57), but perhaps not in north Malaita.

Lalemanu or **make-a-bird** is a Kwaio name for a conus ring
with a projection carved in the form of a bird's head, which
was sometimes worn as the middle ring on a conus-row. This
ornament was also known throughout southeast Solomon
Islands, with the head more or less realistically carved.

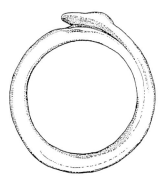

Figure 146 A make-a-bird conus
ring (Kwaio, *lalemanu*) from
the British Melanesian Mission
collection. The bird's head is
formed from the projecting
end of the cone-shell spiral.
(BM Oc,1991,08.48)
100%

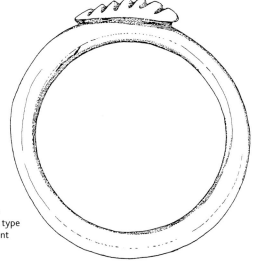

Figure 147 A make-a-bird (Kwaio, *lalemanu*) from
Guadalcanal from the early twentieth century, of a type
common on Malaita with the bird's head reminiscent
of a hornbill beak (though not identified as such).
(BM Oc,1920,0322.46)
100%

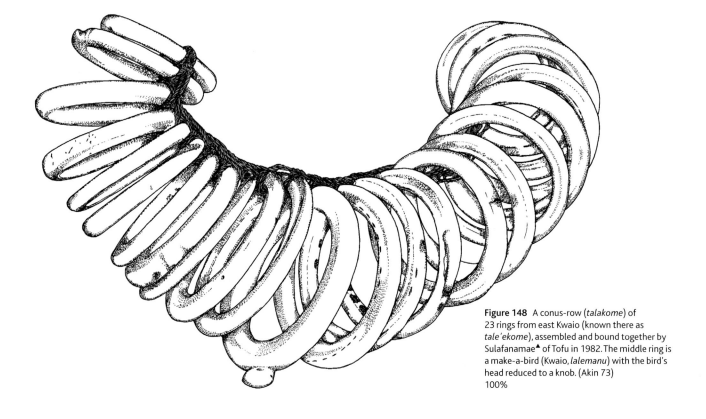

Figure 148 A conus-row (*talakome*) of
23 rings from east Kwaio (known there as
tale'ekome), assembled and bound together by
Sulafanamae▲ of Tofu in 1982. The middle ring is
a make-a-bird (Kwaio, *lalemanu*) with the bird's
head reduced to a knob. (Akin 73)
100%

Tala 'i dodo or **dodo-row** is a necklace of small *dodo* conus rings bound together in a row, like a kind of circle-fence (*barafā*), as some might identify it. In Kwara'ae this is remembered as an ornament for maidens, but in north Malaita and perhaps elsewhere it was also worn by youths (Asaeda photo 3807:62 shows a youth wearing one with a circle-fence).

Similar ornaments of small shell rings mounted in rows on flat braids of red-stained vine-strip were worn in Isabel and western Solomons (Woodford 1890:152, Tetehu 2006, BM Oc,1915.58).

Figure 149 A *dodo* necklace from Lau (where it is known as *'usikome* or threaded-conus). The *dodo* rings are held between a strip of red calico (*kaliko*) and a length of coarse twine (*dadalo*), which are bound together with vine-strip (*'abakwalo*). (Maranda) 100%

Usikarango or **threaded-winkles** is a row of small annulus-cowrie (*golo*) shells worn close around the neck by men and women. The shells are laid edge to edge, with the slit undersides of the shells outwards and the upper sides ground away, allowing them to be tied together through the slits. Such simple ornaments, of little value, were probably common throughout Malaita and beyond in former times.

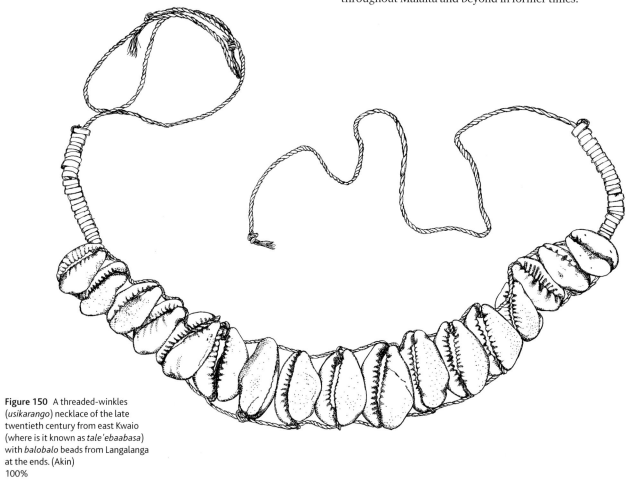

Figure 150 A threaded-winkles (*usikarango*) necklace of the late twentieth century from east Kwaio (where is it known as *tale'ebaabasa*) with *balobalo* beads from Langalanga at the ends. (Akin)
100%

Barafā or **circle-fence** is a length of rattan vine-strip with a row of white *soela* rings bound along it, worn as a coil which can pass over the head to hang around the neck.[15] The *soela* are threaded on a length of twine which is bound to the rattan with vine-strip winding between each bead. Some say it was only worn by men, others that it was worn by girls, particularly for marriage.

This is an ornament of north Malaita, where it was used as a money denomination and worn by men and women, and perhaps also of Langalanga (Ross 1973:268,280, Paravicini photo 3956), but it was not worn in Kwaio and the south.

Figure 151 A circle-fence (*barafā*) of eight coils, originating from Ironunu in Fataleka in 1974. (BM Oc,1976,11.270) 100%

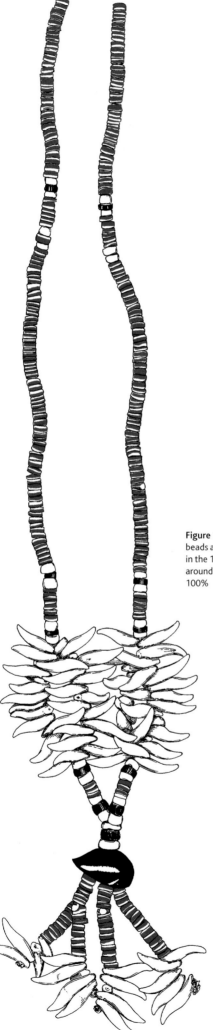

'Alu'alu or **necklace** is a general term for strings of money-beads with dolphin teeth or *dodo* conus rings threaded on them to wear around the neck, and it covers many kinds of ornaments. Men and women may wear simple strings of money-beads or glass beads, dolphin teeth or foreign materials such as chain, but there were some more or less standard forms, depending on the fashions of the time.

A simple kind of necklace remembered from the past and common throughout Malaita was one or more strings of red *safi* money-beads hanging to the breast, with clusters of dolphin teeth at intervals along it (see Hogbin 1939:88 for To'abaita and Ross 1973:272 for Baegu). These became fashionable in the mid-twentieth century, leading some young people in Kwaio to dismantle fish-teeth-cluster (*barulifaī'a*) straps for the teeth. Men of possessions in north Malaita sometimes wore necklaces of hundreds of the large *robo* dolphin teeth (as in the photo of Irobaoa, Plate 22, page 28). In the early twentieth century there was a fashion for tight necklaces of large glass beads (as in Plates 1, 2 and 4, pages viii, 6 and 10), and in the 1920s for short necklaces with a few long strings of beads hanging from the front down the chest (Paravicini photo 3956).

Many of these necklaces would have had their own particular names, in Kwara'ae and elsewhere. (While *'alu'alu* refers to decorative beads of white shell in Kwara'ae, the equivalent *'aru'aru* in Kwaio and south specifies red money-beads.)

Figure 152 A necklace (*'alu'alu*) of red shell beads and dolphin teeth, of a kind popular in the 1990s, made in south Malaita for sale around Malaita and in Honiara. (Burt) 100%

Figure 153 A necklace (*'alu'alu*) from Lau, mostly of red *safi* money-beads with a shell-disk of conus (*kome*), of a style popular in Solomon Islands in the 1980s. (Maranda) 100%

Figure 154 A necklace (*'alu'alu*) of fine *'afi'afi* money-beads with dolphin teeth, made in 1996 by Ita Foolamo of Gwagwa'efunu, east Kwaio (known there as *bokoi'a*, clumped-fish [teeth]). It has four sections of red and blue plastic beads, made from electrical wire insulation. (Akin) 100%

Figure 155 A string of *'afi'afi* beads with black winkle-shells, from east Kwaio from the late twentieth century. (Akin) 100%

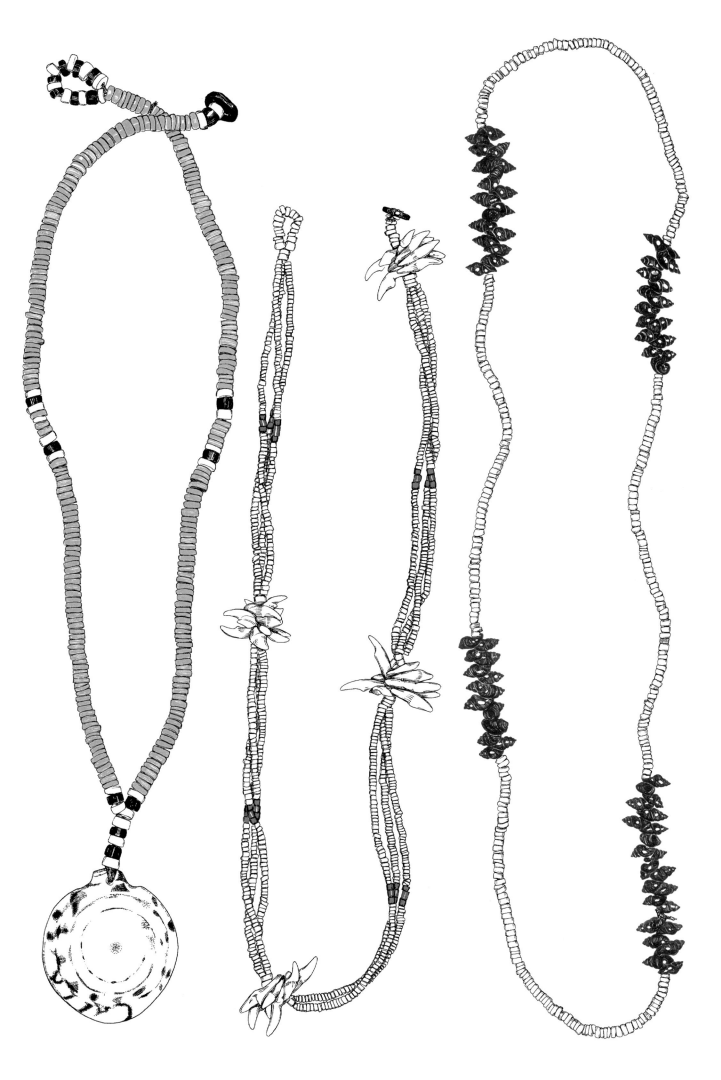

Figure 156 A necklace (*'alu'alu*) of red *safi*, white *galia* and black *kurila*
money-beads, with the net design and tight-lip (*mumu*) seed fringe typical of
Langalanga ornaments of the late twentieth century. (Richards)
50%

Fulu is a Baegu, north Malaita, name for a necklace of ten strings of beads with eight large valuable *robo* dolphin teeth at the middle of each string. The ornament is named for the predominance of black *fulu* seed beads, which have *dodo* conus rings threaded on them. It is said to have been worn by unmarried youths and maidens (Ross 1981:23; as shown in Plate 1, page viii).

Afi'afi'oia or **broken-'afi'afi** is a Kwaio name for a necklace of several strings of *'afi'afi* (*'afe'afe*) beads, 'broken' into sections by small *i'asina* dolphin teeth and turtleshell spacers. It is worn tight around the neck in southeast Kwaio.

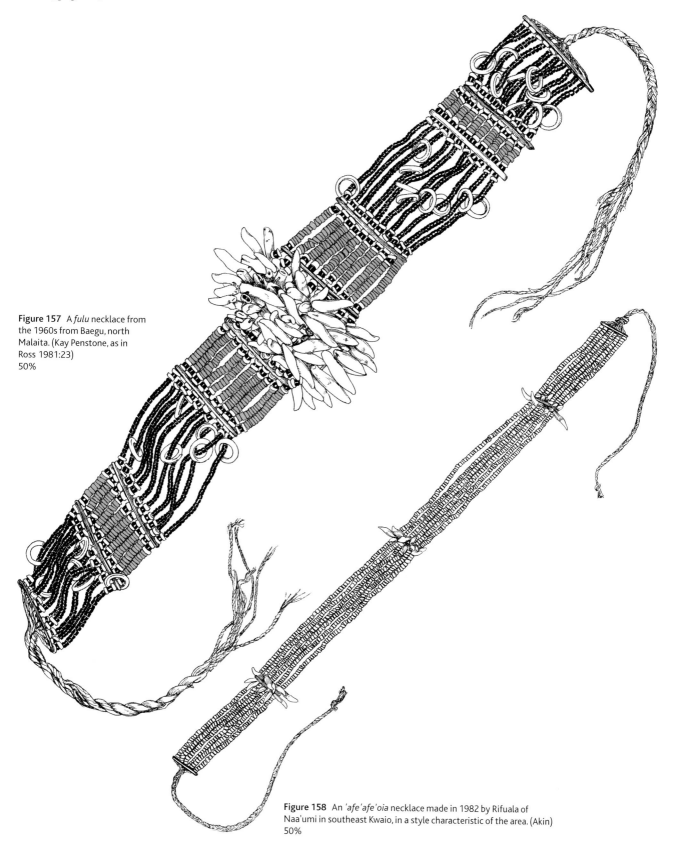

Figure 157 A *fulu* necklace from the 1960s from Baegu, north Malaita. (Kay Penstone, as in Ross 1981:23)
50%

Figure 158 An *'afe'afe'oia* necklace made in 1982 by Rifuala of Naa'umi in southeast Kwaio, in a style characteristic of the area. (Akin)
50%

Ūma ana lifa ngwae or **string of human teeth** was sometimes worn around the neck (as in Plate 20, page 26). As recalled today and confirmed by Whiteman visitors in the 1930s, when these ornaments were still often worn, the teeth came from people who had been eaten (Francis photo 129, *SCL*, June 1936:92). Local history recounts how a man in east Kwara'ae was discovered to have eaten his brother-in-law when seen drilling the man's teeth for such an ornament.

Strings of human teeth were probably worn around the neck throughout Malaita, and included the teeth of ancestors as well as enemies (*SCL* 1902:80, Paravicini 1931:172, Maranda).

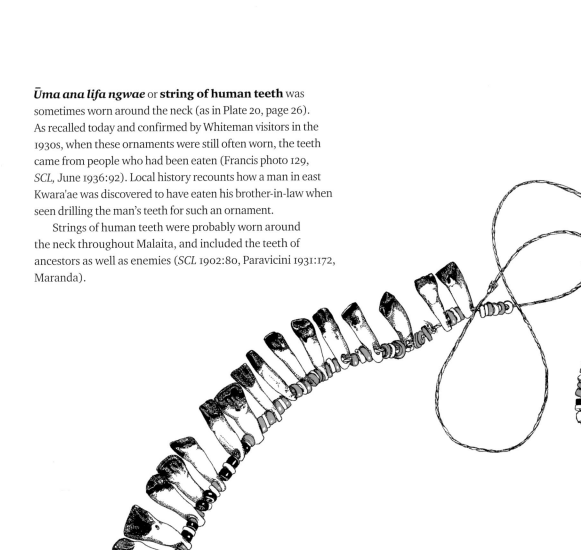

Figure 159 A string of human teeth (*ūma ana lifa ngwae*) spaced with money-beads, from Lau in the nineteenth century. It was given to John Renton, a Scottish castaway who lived there from 1868 to 1875, by Kabou of Sulufou island, apparently as a sign of protection. Renton brought it home and it is now in the National Museums of Scotland. (A.1893.296)
100%

'*Umāru* or **teeth-and-red-money** is a Kwaio and 'Are'are name for a sash, made of red *safi* money-beads strung in a net and fringed on one side with human incisor teeth, that was worn by men around the neck or as a bandolier. Ivens, who was familiar with the whole of Malaita, described this as 'A characteristic Mala ornament', which was worn over the left shoulder and under the right arm as a festival ornament in Sa'a (1897, 1927:213, 391). Another way of wearing it is across the back, the ends coming up under the arms to cross below the throat and fasten at the back of the neck (see photo in Bennett 1987:329).

Teeth-and-red-money is most commonly worn by chiefs in south Malaita and in southern Kwaio (de Coppet and Zemp 1978:109, de Coppet 1995:239), but it was also known, if less common, in north Malaita (see Plate 21, page 27; Russell 2003:66, Woodhead and Maranda 1987). Although Kwara'ae elders do not recall this ornament, some of their ancestors probably wore it too.

There were subtle differences in the teeth-and-beads ornaments in different areas. In Sa'a the teeth were from ancestors, while in 'Are'are and Kwaio they also came from slain enemies, and in Kwaio a type made only with canine teeth was distinguished as a *safi*-(bead)-and-canine (*kwa'usafi*). A similar ornament, but with dogs' teeth, was worn in north Guadalcanal.

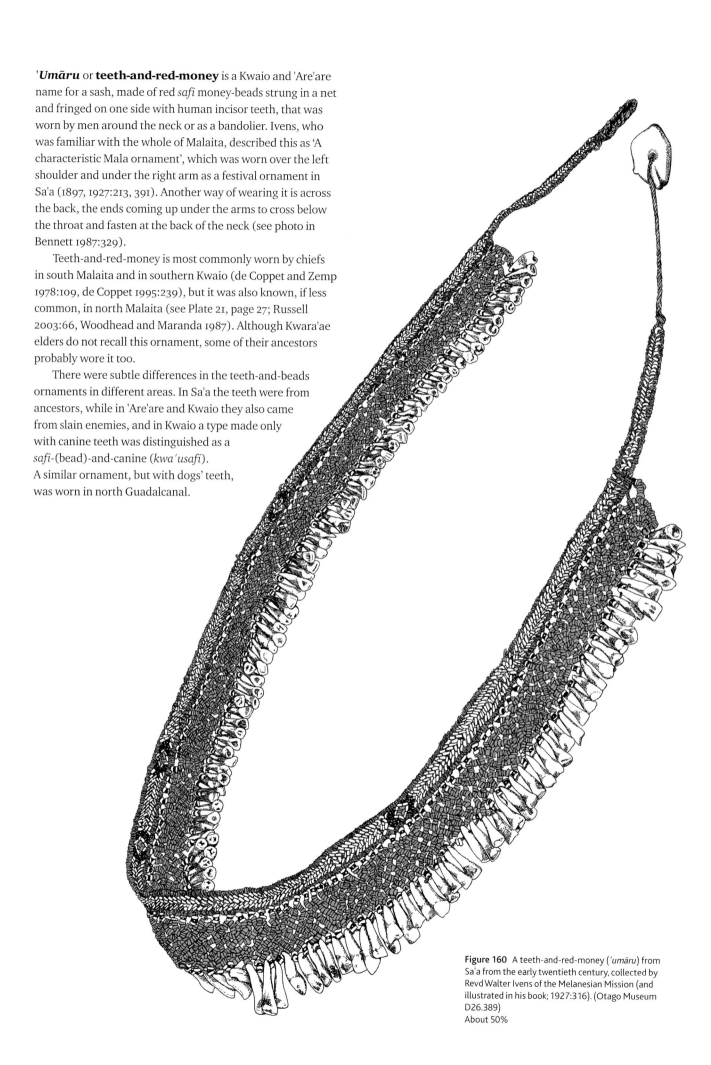

Figure 160 A teeth-and-red-money (*'umāru*) from Sa'a from the early twentieth century, collected by Revd Walter Ivens of the Melanesian Mission (and illustrated in his book; 1927:316). (Otago Museum D26.389)
About 50%

Torisusu or **breast-fastening**, also called *galisusu* or
'around-the-breasts', is a set of money-bead strings made
to wear on the upper body, which appear to tie a woman's
breasts, although they are also worn by men. Other names are
'abarara'o or bandoliers (after the string-figure 'cat's cradle'
game, *rara'o*), *tagotago* or fringe, from the row of tight-lip
(*mumu*) seeds fringing the ends, or simply the names of the
money-beads; white *galu*, red *safi* or white-money *a'afi*.

Some breast-fastenings are no more than two separate
sets of money-beads, like small money-bead denominations
with turtleshell spacers, tied into circles to be worn over one
shoulder and under the opposite arm. The more elaborate
ones are of four, six or more strings of money-beads, divided
into two sets which are interwoven in a net design where
they cross front and back and where they hang down to each
side. These are made by the Langalanga and bought by inland
people like the Kwara'ae as ornaments for dancers and for
women at marriage.

Breast-fastenings were worn around north and south
Malaita, although not in the Kwaio inland, mainly as a sea
people's ornament. As a simple way of wearing money-beads,
similar ornaments were worn in other islands, but usually as
single bandoliers, as in Makira and Guadalcanal (Bernatzik
1936:pls, Hogbin 1937:pl. 1A, Macintyre 1975, Scott). Double
breast-fastenings of glass beads also feature in the nineteenth-
century photographs of Malaitans in Fiji (see Plate 3, page 8).

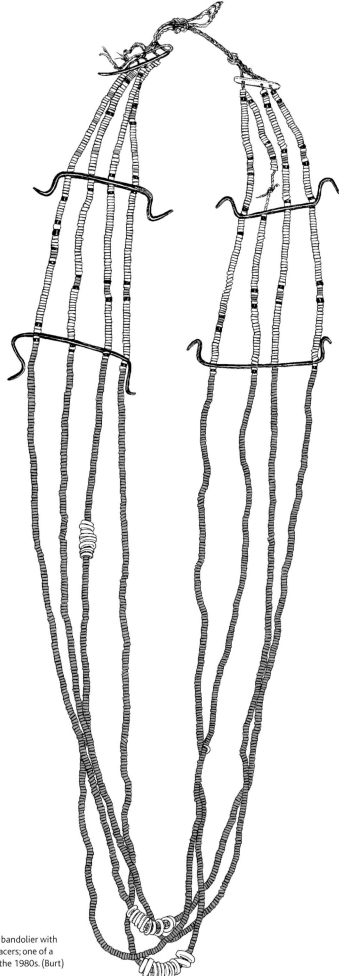

Figure 161 A *safi* red money-bead bandolier with
dodo conus rings and turtleshell spacers; one of a
pair worn by Lovea of Uru Island in the 1980s. (Burt)
33%

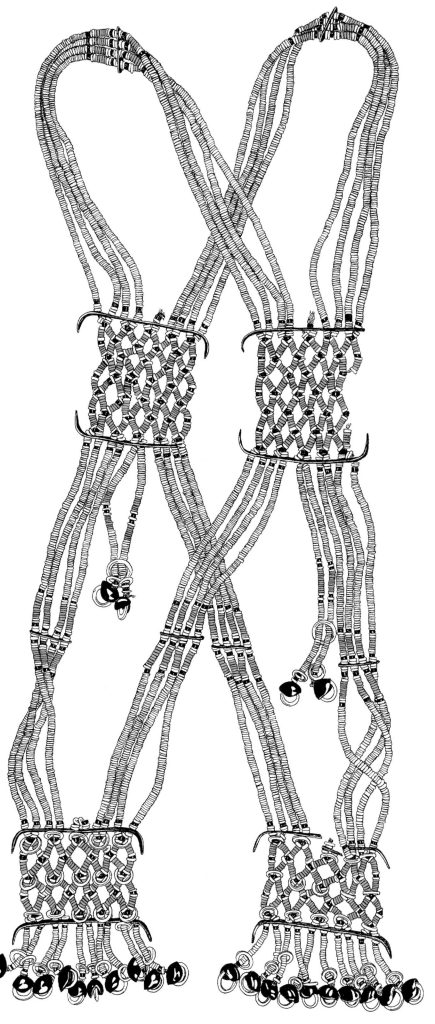

Figure 162 A breast-fastening (*torisusu*) from Langalanga (known there as *sausako*) from the late twentieth century. The eight strings of white *galu* beads are separated with turtleshell spacers and ornamented with red *romu* and black *gorila* beads, *dodo* conus rings and tight-lip (*mumu*) seeds. (Maranda)
33%

Arm ornaments

Rū fuana laungilana limana ngwae or **ornaments for the arms** included plaited bands, straps and bands of money-beads and glass beads for the upper arm or wrist, and rings of shell worn above the elbow.

Obi or **band** is a general name for plaited bands worn on the arms and legs, as well as for circular decorative lashings in general, as used to secure the beams of a house. As an ornament, 'band' can describe any kind of vine-strip circlet, but it refers particularly to the simplest bands made of rattan-strip (*'abakalita'u*). These include the large band-rattan (*obi*) named for this use, often stained with red 'dye' (*dilo*). Both men and women had their wrists and ankles 'banded' (*obia*) by plaiting one or several of these ornaments around them for festivals and other special events. Larger 'great-bands' (*gwa'iobi*) were worn on the upper arm mainly by men, some say only married men. This simple and basic ornament was worn around Malaita and beyond.

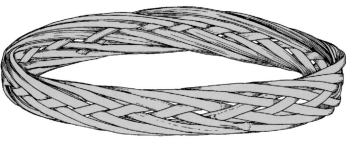

Figure 163 A band (*obi*) of rattan strip for the upper arm, made in east Kwara'ae in the 1980s. (Burt)
100%

Figure 164 A band (*obi*) of rattan strip for the upper arm, made in east Kwara'ae in the 1980s. (Burt)
100%

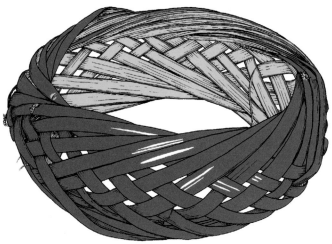

Figure 165 A band (*obi*) of rattan strip for the wrist, stained red with dye (*dilo*), from east Kwaio in the 1980s. (Akin 147)
100%

Figure 166 An fine band of red rattan and white *kwasakwasa* or *kwalekwale* (*Flagellaria*) vine-strip (green when new), made by Sulafanamae▲ of Tofu. The design is patented by the Kafu clan of east Kwaio for their own use. (Akin 156)
100%

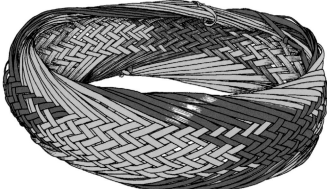

Gwaroa'adi'adi or **orchid-pattern** is one name for a kind of patterned band (*obi gwaroa*) worn on the upper arm, which is plaited from shreds of vine-strip and then patterned by embroidering with shreds of yellow orchid (*'adi*) and often also of red coconut cuticle (*taketake niu*). Other names are *gwarotaketake* or (coconut) cuticle-pattern, or simply orchid (*'adi*). (Some call it *sangisangi* or *gwarosangisangi* instead, but others describe this as a different kind of band; see below). Orchid-pattern bands are finer and more flexible than the rattan bands (*obi*), ranging in width from about ten to thirty or more rows of plaiting, and are usually made from dark brown or black vine-strip such as *Gleichenia* (*luluka*), *ongaonga*, *Cyclosorus* (*bunabuna*) or *Lygodium* (*sata*), sometimes stained black with wild banana (*sasao*) sap.

Orchid-pattern bands were still made in north Malaita and Kwaio at the end of the twentieth century. These are mostly narrow, about ten or twelve rows of plaiting wide, and have many different designs. They usually have straight or zigzag lines along the band, sometimes with zigzags across it. The north Malaita designs are often simpler and patterned only with yellow orchid, while the Kwaio ones are more elaborate and varied, usually including the red coconut cuticle.[16] Another style of wider patterned bands of thirty or more rows of plaiting, from Kwaio and also remembered in Kwara'ae, has bold right-angle lines which follow designs plaited onto the band itself.

Armbands, closely plaited of dark vine-strip with embroidered patterns in yellow and often red too, were common to various Melanesian islands from Makira to the Admiralties and beyond. Within Solomon Islands they were particularly characteristic of Malaita, but some of the finest and oldest examples, broader and with designs related to Kwara'ae and north Malaitan pattern-straps, are attributed to Makira and Savo, and in the 1880s the 'prettiest' were said to come from Savo (BM Oc,6427 and Oc,6428, as in Waite 1987: pl. 16, Guppy 1887:132).

Besides these islands of the southeast Solomons, orchid-pattern armbands were also made in the New Georgia group, western Solomons. The Shortlands, Buka and Bougainville seem to have been a major source of supply for narrow bands similar to but distinct from the Malaita line-and-zigzag designs, as well as for wider ones with right-angle lines exactly like those attributed to Malaita and Makira (Roga, Guppy 1887:133, Blackwood 1935:422, Finsch 1914:pls 499–503, Frizzi-Munchen 1914:26, Heermann and Menter 1990:84, BM Oc+3903 and Oc1929,0713.24). Such bands are said to have been 'more highly prized' than the local trochus arm-rings (Parkinson 1999:214) and, although they would not have been high-value exchange goods, they were apparently traded to New Georgia (Scales 2003:ch. 3). Orchid-pattern bands may have been traded, and their designs imitated, between islands as distant as Bougainville and Malaita, perhaps with the increased traffic of the early colonial period from which most of this information derives.

Figure 167 An orchid-pattern (*gwaroa'adi'adi*) from Lau or the north Malaita inland from the 1960s (known there as *'adi'adi*). This simple design is known also in Fataleka and east Kwara'ae. (Maranda) 100%

Figure 168 An orchid-pattern (*gwaroa'adi'adi*) from Lau or the north Malaita inland from the 1960s. (Maranda) 100%

Figure 169 An orchid-pattern (*gwaroa'adi'adi*) made in Baelelea and sold to Lau in the late 1960s. (Maranda) 100%

Figure 170 An orchid-pattern (*gwaroa'adi'adi*) from east Kwaio (known there as *tokila*), made for export under the Kwaio Cultural Centre programme in about 1983. (Burt)
100%

Figure 171 An orchid-pattern (*gwaroa'adi'adi*) made by Moruka of Ga'enāfou in east Kwaio for export under the Kwaio Cultural Centre programme in 1983. The design is called broken-orchid (*mou'adi*) for the way the yellow pattern is broken by the red. (Burt)
100%

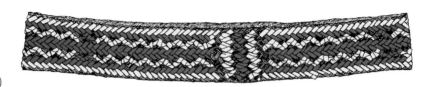

Figure 172 An orchid-pattern (*gwaroa'adi'adi*) made in 1983 by Sam Tete of Guadalcanal, who called it *bore lima*. The design, used on plaited bands and straps in Kwara'ae (see pages 8 and 151), would also have been familiar on Malaitan orchid-pattern armbands. (Burt)
100%

Figure 173 An old orchid-pattern (*gwaroa'adi'adi*) obtained from Malaita by Charles Woodford, which came to the British Museum in 1888. It resembles plaited bands from Bougainville in having the embroidered designs following changes in direction in the plaiting of red-dyed vine-shreds. (BM Oc,+93903)
100%

Figure 174 An orchid-pattern (*gwaroa'adi'adi*) from Kwaio with simple right-angular designs following the direction of the plaited band. It was too old and worn to wear in 1998, when it was sold in Honiara. (Burt)
100%

Figure 175 An orchid-pattern collected by Julius Brenchley from Makira in 1865, of a design resembling the 'arrows' on Kwara'ae pattern-straps ('abagwaro) (with another resembling north Malaita pattern-straps; BM Oc,6428). Since this design is also attributed to Savo (BM Oc,7643) it seems likely it was traded to Malaita too, if not actually made there. (BM Oc,6427) 100%

Sangisangi (also pronounced *sangesange*) is a plaited band of vine-shreds for the upper arm which has fringes of loose shreds. It might be made of coconut cuticle (*taketake niu*) or light-coloured *Anodendron* vine (*kwalo 'abe*) and was stained red with dye (*dilo*) or *Cyclosorus* (*bunabuna*), but it was not patterned with embroidery. Some use the name (or *gwarosangisangi*) for orchid-pattern (*gwaroa'adi'adi*) bands, but this is probably due to confusion among ornaments now seldom seen.

This kind of band was also made in other parts of Malaita: of pandanus cuticle in Sa'a (Ivens 1929:308) and (with the same name) in Arosi, west Makira (Scott). The Kwaio associate *sangisangi* with Kwara'ae, from where they used to buy them, but also recall Chinese traders making them for sale. Some Malaitans regard it as a western Solomons ornament, and identical bands were indeed made there, also of pandanus cuticle (e.g. BM Oc,1938,10.22, Oc,1944,02.1371 and Queensland Museum E15-572-3), as well as on Guadalcanal. In short, *sangisangi* seems to have been a general name for a widespread form of red plaited vine-strip band.

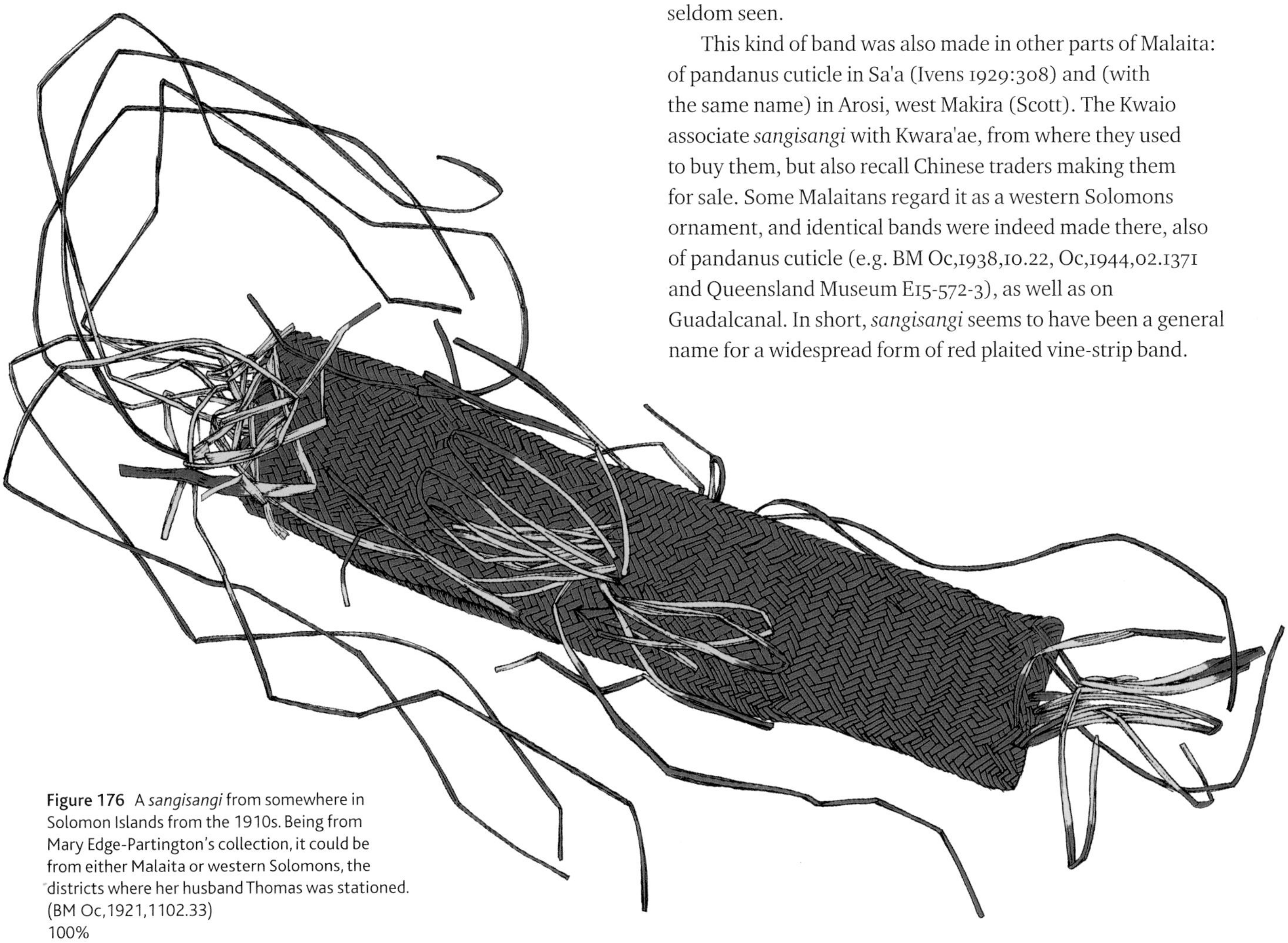

Figure 176 A *sangisangi* from somewhere in Solomon Islands from the 1910s. Being from Mary Edge-Partington's collection, it could be from either Malaita or western Solomons, the districts where her husband Thomas was stationed. (BM Oc,1921,1102.33) 100%

'**Abagwaro** or **pattern-strap** usually describes a strap woven of money-beads tied around the upper arm. This is a man's ornament, worn by women only for occasions such as their marriage. The beads are white *galu*, red *fira'i* and black *fulu*, but they are smaller and finer than those used in money, maybe re-ground from worn money-beads. The twine used to string them is strong, fine and durable, such as *Anodendron* vine (*kwlao'abe*) or *Gnetum* (*dae*) tree-bark strip, or nowadays synthetic fibres. Kwara'ae pattern-straps are narrower than most of those from other parts of Malaita, about 30 rows of beads wide, and they have a distinctive and very standard design. The strap is white with two sets of horizontal black arrows (*ma'e sima*, with barbed heads) defining a central red fish-shape (*ma'e ī'a*), which is repeated as triangles at the sides and ends. Pattern-straps of other designs, such as columns of smaller lozenges and zigzags across the strap, were made locally or obtained from elsewhere, but the great majority of Kwara'ae pattern-straps, from the earliest photographs to those still worn in the late twentieth century, have the arrows design (see Plates 12, 14 and 39, pages 17,19 and 56; Beattie photo 540, Paravicini photo 4029).

Figures 177 and 178 A pair of pattern-straps ('*abagwaro*) from east Kwara'ae, heirlooms worn by the tabu-speaker of the Atōbi clan of Latea. They were remade by the last tabu-speaker Ulungwane, who died in 1954, and in 1979 they were kept as relics with the two cowries (*buli*) on page 78 by his brother Gwa'alebe, who had joined the Jehovah's Witness church. The zigzag designs are variants of those on the wider pattern-straps of north Malaita. (Burt)
50%

Figure 179 A pattern-strap ('*abagwaro*) of the arrows design most common in Kwara'ae. This is one of a pair purchased from their maker by Riomea of Fakula'e in east Kwara'ae about 1930 and worn with the shell-disk-rattle Figure 115, page 102. (Burt)
50%

Figure 180 A pattern-strap ('*abagwaro*) from Fata'olo in Baelelea, north Malaita, from the 1960s, with the large-lozenge version of the north Malaita style. (Maranda)
50%

The arrows pattern-strap design was not common elsewhere in Malaita in recent times, although sometimes worn in northern Kwaio and in Lau (*Man* n.d.), but it is related to the design of the broader pattern-straps of Fataleka northwards, sometimes also worn in Kwara'ae. These are usually about 50 or 60 beads wide, white with black rows of frigate-birds (*tala'i gaula*) across the middle and ends, outlining five or six red fish-shapes or two or three times as many smaller nuts (*fa'i ngali*) or another row of frigate-birds. The larger fish-shapes resemble the Kwara'ae arrow design, repeated many times over without the horizontal lines of the arrow shafts. Men sometimes wore one of each design, rather than a matching pair.

All these designs use the way the beads are threaded on both warps and wefts, lying diagonally across the threads (see page 46). Diagonals and zigzags are formed by changing the direction in which the beads lie across the strap, and changing direction midway along it makes the two ends symmetrical.

Figure 181 A pattern-strap ('*abagwaro*) from Fata'olo in Baelelea, north Malaita, from the 1960s, with the small-lozenge version of the north Malaita style. As in some other examples, the maker had trouble in keeping the lines of beads regular. (Maranda)
50%

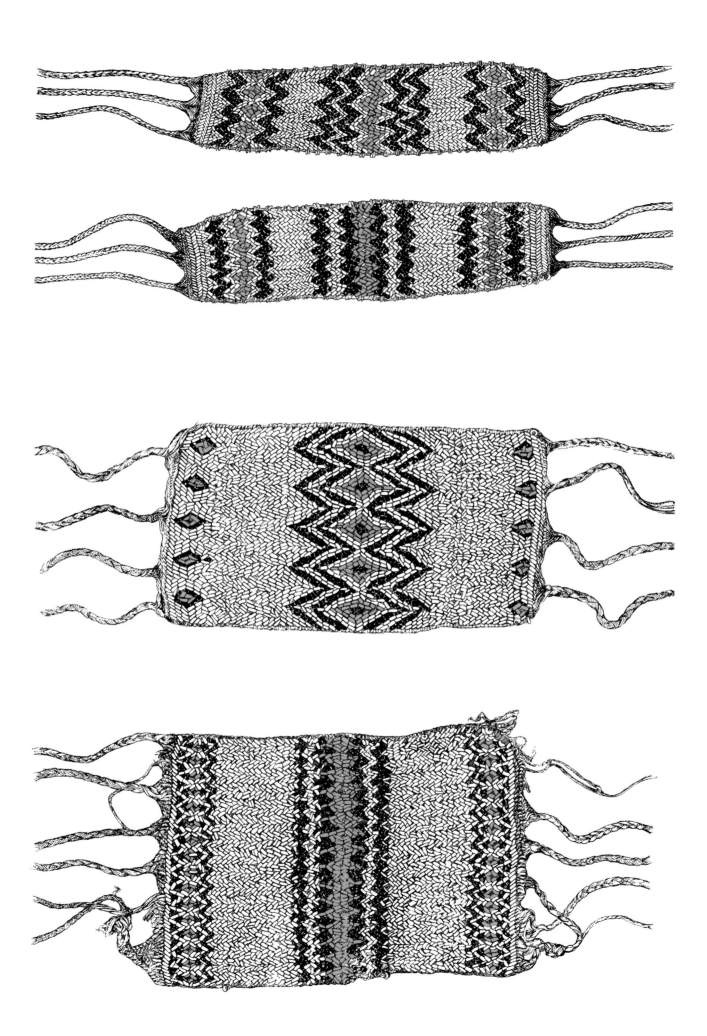

In Sa'a, south Malaita, pattern-straps were worn on the wrists and ankles rather than on the upper arms, and in this as well as in their designs they are more like those of Makira than other areas of Malaita. Most have a vertical strip across the middle between panels of parallel lines, vertical or horizontal, straight or zigzag, but other designs resemble woven money-bead belts from south Malaita and Makira (see below, page 146) or yet another variant of the Kwara'ae arrows design. (Ivens 1927:148, 316, Bernatzik 1936:pls 8, 9, 38, 43, 116, 151, Verguet 1885:201, 205). Formerly some women in Kwaio also wore pattern-straps on the wrists (called *kwaloniga'i*).

As a descriptive name, 'pattern-strap' may also be used of patterned arm ornaments, including bands rather than straps, whether of beads or vine-strip. In Kwara'ae one kind is said to have been made of black cincture (*susuru*) vine strung with white money-beads in rows of frigate-bird patterns, perhaps like a money-bead pattern-strap in reverse, made by the same technique as the woman's great-cincture belt (see page 47). In the late twentieth century the Langalanga were making money-bead armlets (*ma'elima*) in the net design used on brow-bindings (*fo'odara*) (Macintyre 1975, Guo).

The distribution of pattern-strap styles and designs illustrates the way valuable ornaments could travel by exchange over long distances by sea, bypassing the barriers to communication between inland groups imposed by the mountainous terrain. Between Kwara'ae and south Malaita pattern-straps were not worn in most of the inland, but in 1873 an example of the Kwara'ae arrows design was obtained by a British naval officer who visited Port Adam, the Lau settlement in Sa'a.[17] As mentioned above (pages 129 and 131), some old orchid-pattern (*gwaroa'adi'adi*) armbands from Makira (including Arosi) and Savo have the Kwara'ae arrows design embroidered in yellow and red, with the black lines formed by the base of dark vine-strip, and another from Arosi resembles the north Malaita pattern-strap design.[18] West of Malaita, pattern-straps of money-beads were not worn at all, making them an exclusively southeast Solomons style.

Figure 182 An unusual pattern-strap (*'abagwaro*) from Mary Edge-Partington's collection from the 1910s, with a design evidently related to both the Kwara'ae 'arrows' and the north Malaita large fish-shape designs. It has several blue glass beads among the black *fulu* beads. (Capt. T.E. Edge-Partington) 50%

Figure 183 An old pattern-strap (*'abagwaro*) which came to the British Museum in 1869, identified by elders as Kwara'ae from its similarity to the arrows design. (BM Oc,5303) 50%

Figure 184 A nineteenth-century pattern-strap (*'abagwaro*) for the wrists or ankles which came to the British Museum in 1887, with a design probably from south Malaita or Makira (see Ivens 1927:136). (BM Oc,1887,0201.36) 50%

Figure 185 A pattern-strap (*'abagwaro*) collected on the Erskine expedition of HMS *Havana*, which visited Makira and Sa'a in south Malaita in 1850. Elders identified the design as Kwara'ae, probably from former times, and it also resembles the design of some south Malaita and Makira belts (see page 146). This example is unusual in that the lines along the edges are formed by the plaiting technique (see page 46), while the diagonal patterns between are woven as normal (other examples of this design are woven throughout: BM Oc,1896,-34, BM Oc,5302). Although made so early in the colonial period, it has three blue glass beads among the black *fulu*-beads. (BM Oc,1980,Q338) 50%

Figure 186 A pattern-strap (*'abagwaro*) which the British Museum acquired in 1873, of a design associated with Sa'a in South Malaita, Ulawa and east Makira. (BM Oc,7907) 50%

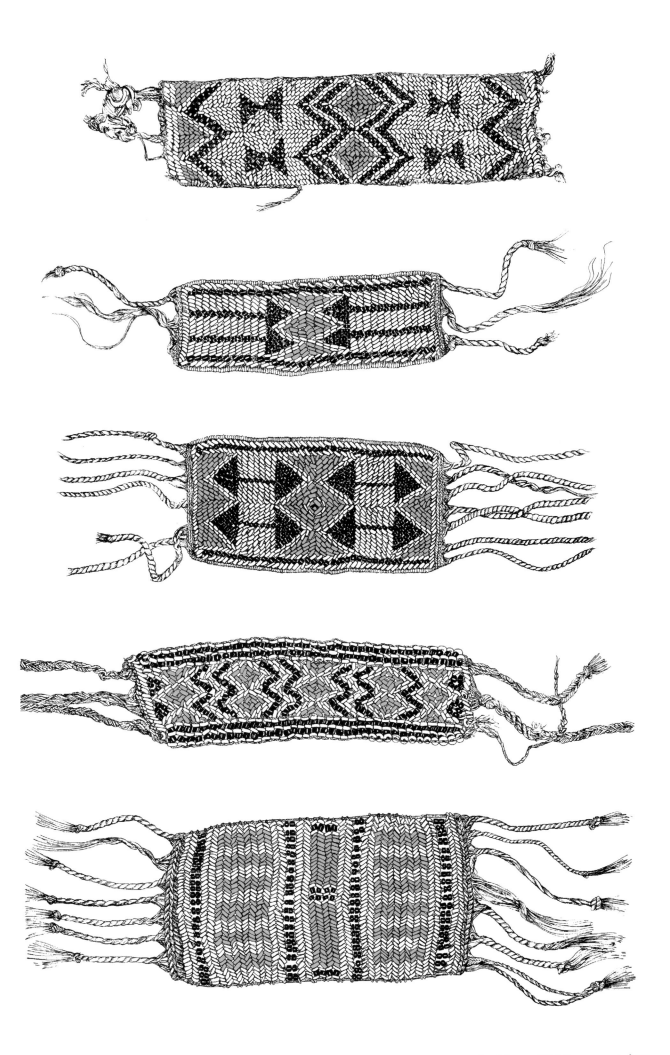

'Abagwaro kekefa or glass-bead pattern-strap

describes a kind of arm-strap made by the technique used for glass-bead belts (*fo'o'aba*, see page 47). These are shown in nineteenth-century photographs of Solomon Islanders in Fiji, often with designs derived from north Malaita money-bead pattern-straps (as in Plate 3, page 8), but they seem to have been less popular in Malaita and few survive in museums.

Figure 187 A glass-bead pattern-strap (*'abagwaro kekefa*), one of a pair in the Dublin Museum collected by Arthur Mahaffy, Assistant Resident Commissioner in Solomon Islands from 1898 to 1904. The Kwara'ae arrows design suggests they may have been among objects obtained in Kwai district, which he visited on the warship HMS *Sparrow* in 1902. (Dublin Museum 1923.234)
100%

'**Ababanibani** or **enclosed-strap** is a circular band for the upper arm (not a strap) made of glass beads (*kekefa*) that is common in photographs from the 1900s onwards. The bands are as much a colonial innovation as the beads themselves, being made by a distinctive coiling technique which may have originated in Vanuatu (see page 48;[19] although there may be other ways to make them, as with those worn by Eleson La'ake on page 32).

The designs do not have much in common with other kinds of armbands, such as orchid-patterns (*gwaro 'adi 'adi*) or pattern-straps (*'abagwaro*). Enclosed-straps were also worn in Guadalcanal, western Solomons, and as early as the 1880s in Bougainville (Hogbin photos 1965, 1945, Queensland Museum E17619, Guppy 1887:133).

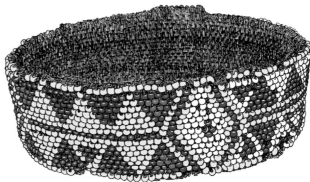

Figure 188 An enclosed-strap (*'ababanibani*), one of a pair from Fata'olo in Baelelea from the 1960s (known there as *banibani*). (Maranda) 100%

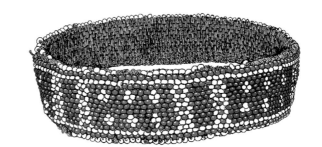

Figure 189 An enclosed-strap (*'ababanibani*), one of a pair from Fata'olo in Baelelea from the 1960s. The design is possiby inspired by a playing card suit (as recalled in Kwara'ae). (Maranda) 100%

Figure 190 An enclosed-strap (*'ababanibani*) from Lau, made by Liunasi▲ in the mid-twentieth century. (Maranda) 100%

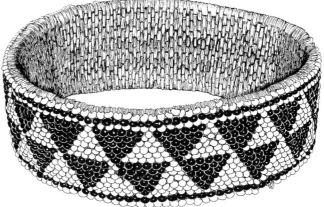

Figure 191 An enclosed-strap (*'ababanibani*) from the 1910s from Mary Edge-Partington's collection. (Capt. T.E. Edge-Partington) 100%

Fa'ikome or **conus** is an arm-ring, named from the use of conus (*kome*) shell to make rings of various kinds, even though not always made of conus. Conus arm-rings were worn above the elbow, mainly by men, but some also by women. The heavier ones in particular, made of tridacna (*'ima*) are regarded as a masculine ornament, said to have been used in fighting by grabbing an enemy around the body with both arms and then jabbing the elbows inwards so that the conus rings would break his ribs. Certain kinds of conus with projecting edges were called 'man-grabber' (*fa'ilolongwae*) or 'victim-crusher' (*igolalamua*) for this reason, while sea people also used them in turtle catching to grasp their prey (Maranda).

With hardly any conus arm-rings now in Kwara'ae possession, the best evidence for those worn in the past comes from other areas of Malaita. In the 1920s, when conus rings were still in common use, men in Sa'a were said to wear three kinds (Ivens 1927: 104, 393):

1 a deep band with concave sides, preferred by older men
2 a flat disk with a name equivalent to 'man-grabber'
3 a narrow ring of rounded square section.

Photographs and a few surviving examples show that all three kinds were also worn in Kwara'ae and other parts of Malaita, as well as many which could be either one or another, and other distinctive forms such as flat rings with one or more grooves around the edge, as in Kwaio. The first two kinds were commonly worn by men, one on each arm, but the third narrow kind was sometimes worn several on each arm, by women as well as men. The narrowest of these rings were made of the tougher conus (*kome*) shell rather than tridacna (*'ima*), and as with trochus rings (*fa'isiare*, see below), women might wear several on each arm, maybe ten or so bound together as a 'conus-fence' (*sasakome*) as in Kwaio and Sa'a (Ivens 1929:94). In perhaps the oldest photograph of Malaitans at home, probably from the 1880s, a man wears about nine conus rings on each arm, in the style of Isabel and western Solomons (Meyer & Parkinson 1894:pl. 32).

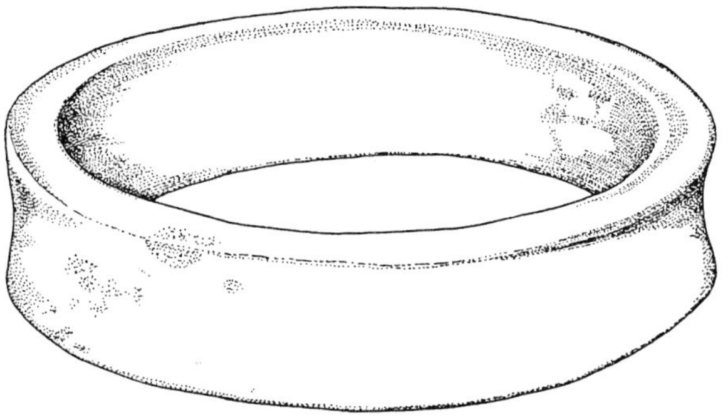

Figure 192 A conus (*fa'ikome*) ring of type 1, of tridacna (*'ima*) belonging to Arikafobaitadoe▲ of Kwakwaru, who lived four generations ago in the 1980s, when it was washed out by the sea from his grave on Ngongosila island, off the coast of east Kwara'ae. (Burt)
100%

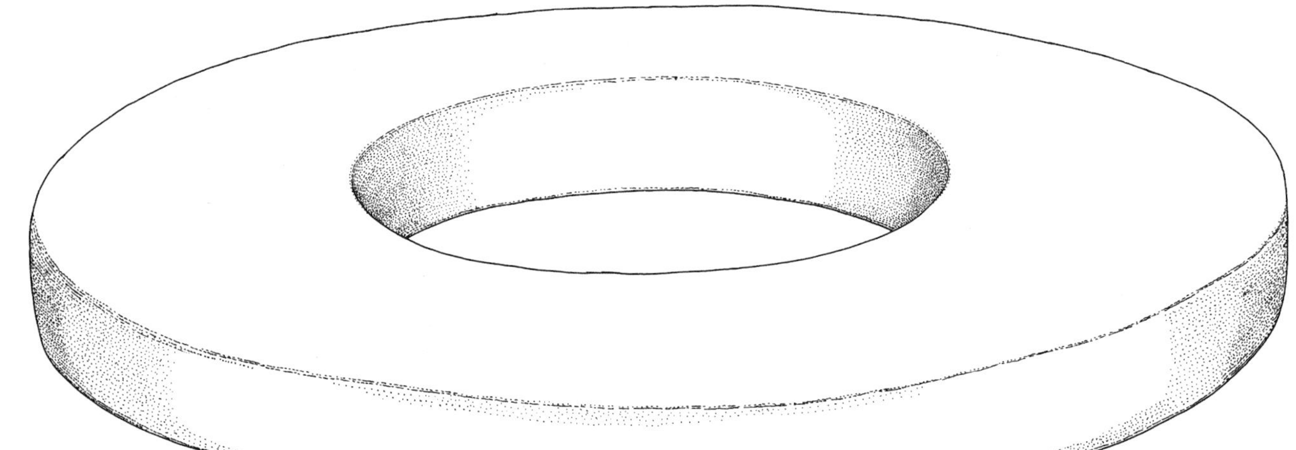

Figure 193 A conus (*fa'ikome*) ring of type 2, of tridacna (*'ima*) from Malaita, exactly like those still worn in north Malaita in the 1960s and identified as a 'man-grabber' in both south and north Malaita (Ivens 1927:104, Ross 1981:24–5, Maranda). It was given to the British Museum in 1890 by J. E. Edge-Partington, father of the first District Officer on Malaita. (BM Oc,+4646)
100%

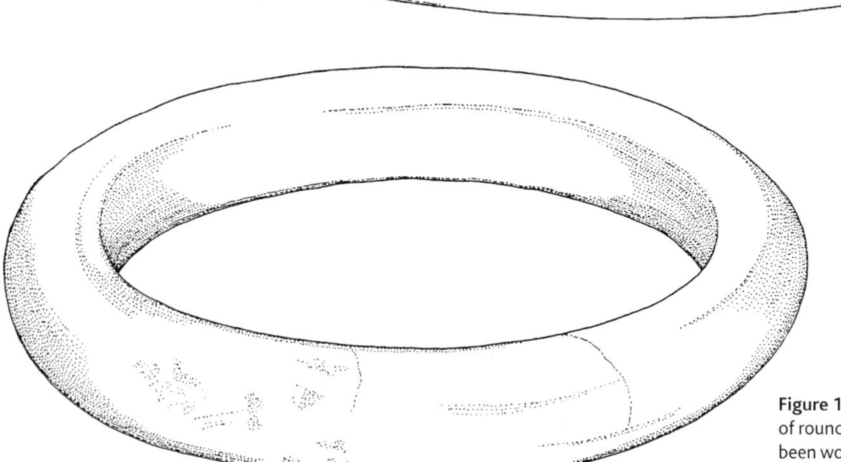

Figure 194 A conus (*fa'ikome*) ring of type 3, of tridacna (*'ima*) of round section from Baelelea in north Malaita, said to have been worn by a woman. (Maranda)
100%

Rings of tridacna and conus were worn throughout Solomon Islands, with many local variations. The three kinds worn in Sa'a are also documented for west and east Makira (Denham photo, Verguet 1885:202, Bernatzik 1936:pls 72, 74, 75, 81, 83), as well as one like the first Malaita kind but two or three times as deep, which was also worn in south Malaita (Beattie photos 480, 481, 500, 557, Mead 1973:36). In Isabel and New Georgia, and probably also Guadalcanal, men and women wore flat arm-rings more like the second Malaita type but not so wide, several or many on each arm (see Plate 38, page 55).

Rings of tridacna were made in great quantities in the western Solomons, especially in the late nineteenth century after steel tools came into use. They were used not only as arm-rings but also as money, and as prestigious neck pendants (see Hviding 1996:93–5). They were traded between islands, including eastwards to Bogotu on Isabel, from where the Langalanga would have taken them on to Malaita in exchange for money-beads.[20] In the 1890s Whitemen traders were also trading in arm-rings, buying them from New Georgia to sell in Guadalcanal and Makira, whence they would have been passed on to Malaita (Woodford 1897:15). But Malaitans, both sea and inland peoples, also made conus arm-rings themselves (see above, page 40).

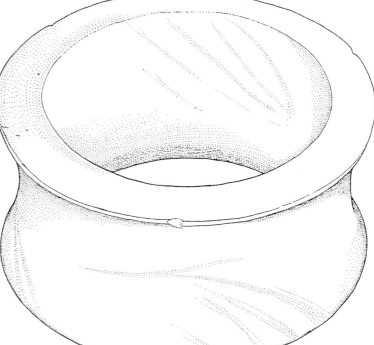

Figure 195   A conus (fa'ikome) ring from a Melanesian Mission collection, the deeper version of the first Malaita type, as worn in south Malaita and Makira. (Auckland Museum 451/180)
100%

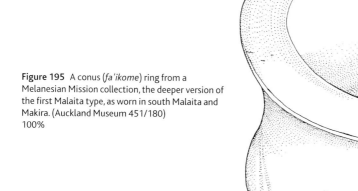

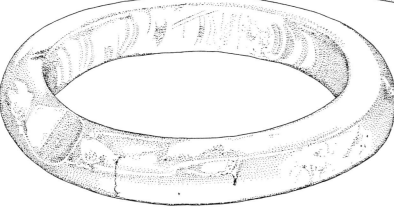

Figure 196   One of a pair of conus (fa'ikome) rings of tridacna ('ima) from east Kwara'ae which belonged to Fiu'adi Kamusudoe of Tolinga, who died in old age in about 1932. The other is slightly smaller, because he had a withered arm, and both have chipped edges, said to result from using them to fight. They were inherited and worn in turn by his son Maniramo and his grandson Samuel Alasa'a, whose son Michael Kwa'ioloa gave them to Ben Burt as a keepsake. The curved marks of the vine-strip used to cut out the centre of the ring are clearly visible. (Burt)
100%

Figure 197   A conus (fa'ikome) ring from Baelelea, one of the narrow kind worn by women. This one is actually made of conus (kome) rather than the tridacna ('ima) of the larger men's ones. (Maranda)
100%

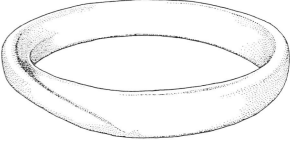

Fa'ikome faka or **foreign conus** were the most
common conus arm-rings still to be seen in Kwara'ae in the
late twentieth century. These are foreign (*faka*) imports,
triangular in section and made of glazed ceramic. The fact
that their owners usually regarded them as locally made of
tridacna shows how long it is since the Kwara'ae actually made
such things.

Whitemen were trading imitation conus rings 'of tough
white porcelain' to Solomon Islanders by about 1880 (Guppy
1887:132), although they may not have been of this particular
design. 'China bangles' were being given to both men and
women by labour recruiters in the 1910s (Herr 1978:192), by
which time the 'pot armlet from Birmingham' was already
said to be replacing local conus arm-rings in north and south
Malaita (Wilson 1895, Ivens 1897, Hopkins 1928:37).[21] Other
substitutes were probably worn too: in the 1970s a few men
in Kwara'ae wore rings of black rubber, apparently oil-drum
seals, in place of conus arm-rings.

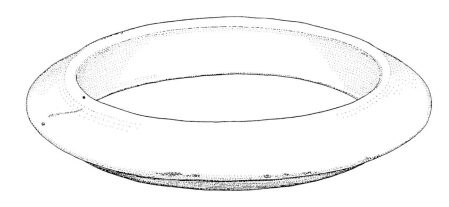

Figure 198 A foreign conus ring (*fa'ikome faka*) of
glazed white ceramic, triangular in section, of the
kind most common in Kwara'ae. (Burt)
100%

Figure 199 A foreign conus (*fa'ikome faka*) ring
of glazed white ceramic from Makira. This design
would also have been traded to Malaita, imitating as
it does the type 1 arm-ring (see previous page). The
ceramic picks up dirt where the glaze is scratched or
worn away. (Richards)
100%

Fa'isiare or **trochus** is a narrow ring for the arm made from a cross-section of a large trochus shell. Like rings of tridacna, these are sometimes known as conus (*kome*), but they are narrower than most conus rings and distinguished by the pearly inner edge. The outer edge of the ring, ground smooth to give a white finish, is usually incised with simple geometric patterns, filled with blacking. Trochus rings were worn by women, particularly by daughters of important men, several above each elbow as a conus-fence (*sasakome*), as with narrow conus rings.

Women throughout Malaita wore sets of trochus and conus rings in this way, as they did also in Makira (Ivens 1929:94, Bernatzik 1936:pls 78, 80, BM Oc,7644). In the western Solomons the rings were smooth, without the patterns, but in Bougainville and Admiralty Islands similar trochus rings were also incised with geometric patterns (Parkinson 1999:214, Heermann and Menter 1990:93).

Fa'ibibinga is a small narrow white ring for a child's arm, made from a shell of that name or from conus (*kome*) or tridacna (*'ima*).

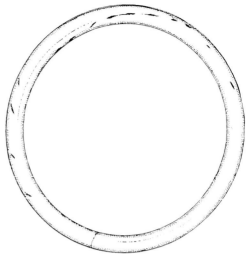

Figure 200 A particularly narrow *fa'ibibinga* of conus (*kome*) made in 1982 by Sulafanamae▲ of Tofu, southeast Kwaio (where it is known as *biibingo*). (Akin 344)
100%

Figure 201 A trochus (*fa'isiare*) ring from the British Melanesian Mission collection. (Burt)
100%

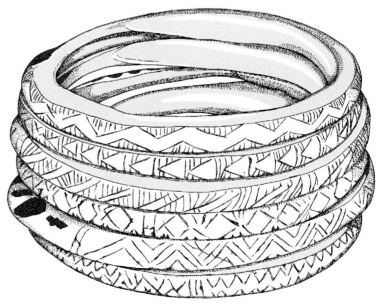

Figure 202 Six trochus (*fa'isiare*) rings from the British Melanesian Mission collection, as they would have been worn together, with a range of incised patterns as made on Malaita. (Burt, BM Oc,1991,08.53 to 55)
100%

Waist ornaments

Rū fuana laungilana alana ngwae or ornaments for the waist, of separate kinds for men and women, included girdles and bands of vine-strip and belts of strung and woven beads.

Fo'osae or girdle is a man's ornament made of four strips of the large band-rattan (*obi*), bound together with shreds of vine-strip such as Vitaceae vine (*adi'o*), *Anodendron* vine (*kwalo 'abe*), *Gnetum* (*dae*) tree-bark strip or *ongaonga* vine. The Kwara'ae kind is described as a 'strap-girdle' (*'aba 'i fo'osae*), meaning that it opens at the front, where the two ends overlap and are tied together with twine.

A girdle could be ornamented in several ways. Some or all of the band-strips might be stained with red dye (*dilo*). The bindings might have strips of contrasting colour at the ends, such as dark *ongaonga* added to light Vitaceae (*'adi'o*) bindings. Narrow rattan-strip, stained red with dye, could be laid to cover the line between the main band-strips and

fixed at the two ends of the girdle. Most ornamented was the 'patterned girdle' (*fo'osae gwaroa*), with shreds of red coconut cuticle and yellow orchid woven around each band-strip, usually before the strips were bound together but sometimes as part of the bindings.

The girdle was worn tied tightly around the waist, well above the hips and above other belts, which could be worn with it. It was intended to give a man strength, endurance and protection for fighting. It might be dedicated to an ancestral ghost with a relic such as a piece of bone tied to it, making it tabu and requiring him to pray to the ghost when putting it on. Even so, it was also worn for ornament, for visiting or for dancing. The photograph from the Kwara'ae chiefs' meeting of 1976 (Plate 10, page 16) shows a whole dance team wearing girdles, and a photo of dancers from the Kwara'ae inland performing on 'Aoke island in the 1910s (Edge-Partington BM Oc,Ca44.278) shows that this was not merely a latter-day or Christian fashion.

The Kwara'ae strap type of girdle was also used in north Malaita and by some in Kwaio (Ross 1973:21, Hogbin 1945, Maranda), but not on other islands.

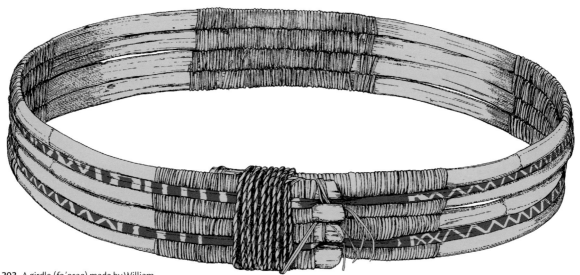

Figure 203 A girdle (*fo'osae*) made by William Kware of New Valley on the Kwaibaita river, east Kwara'ae, in 1979. It is bound with Vitaceae (*'adi'o*) strip and ornamented only with red-dyed rattan strips. (BM Oc,1979,01.20)
50%

Figure 204 A patterned girdle (*fo'osae gwaroa*) from east Kwaio made by Sulafanamae▲ of Tofu in the 1960s. The yellow orchid of the simple patterning has been woven into the bindings of black *ongaonga* vine-strip which hold the girdle together, in a design called *susudau'ai* after a kind of edible caterpillar (*dau'ai*). (Akin 155)
50%

Figure 205 A patterned girdle (*fo'osae gwaroa*) made by Balekwao▲ of Baegu and worn by Defe Dani of Foueda in Lau in the late 1960s (known there as *'ue litana nira* or patterned-waist-rattan). The black vine-strip which holds the girdle together, perhaps of *ongaonga* vine, is at the ends of the patterned sections. (Maranda)
50%

Figure 206 A patterned girdle (*fo'osae gwaroa*) from east Kwaio, made by Laete'esafi▲ of Gounaile in 1981. (They are known there as both *fo'osae* and *'ue* or rattan.) The band-rattan was smoked to darken it before adding the patterning and binding the girdle together at the ends of the patterned sections with Vitaceae (*'adi'o*) or *Gleichenia* (*luluka*) vine-strip. (Akin 154)
50%

'*Ueariari* or **coiled-rattan** is a Kwaio name for a girdle
(*fo'osae*) made of a long coil of two strips of band-rattan,
which winds around the waist two or three times. It could be
patterned (*gwaroa*) in the same way as the strap-girdle (*'aba
'i fo'osae*). This kind of girdle was worn in south Malaita (de
Coppet and Zemp 1978:117–18), by the 'Are'are Malaitans of
Marau on Guadalcanal, and as an alternative to the strap-
girdle in Kwaio and north Malaita (see Plates 4 and 5, pages 10
and 12; SSEM photo 110, Asaeda photo 3807-67).

Coiled-rattan girdles are also documented for Isabel for
about 1870 (a 'dancing girdle', BM Oc,7635), and for Ulawa
(BM Oc,+2020).

Figure 207 A coiled-rattan (*'ueariari*)
girdle in the Queensland Museum, collected
somewhere in Malaita between 1893 and
1902 by Peter Tornaros, who probably worked
in the Queensland labour trade.[22] The pair of
rattan strips are stained black, matching the
vine-shreds of the patterning. One of the red
rattan-strips laid along the join is missing.
(QM E-571-0)
50%

Figure 208 A very fine coiled-rattan (*'ueariari*)
girdle from the 'Are'are people of Marau in
Guadalcanal. It was obtained in 1865 by Julius
Brenchley on the cruise of HMS *Curacoa*.
(BM Oc,6311)
50%

'Abaobi or **band-strap** is a long vine-strip, stained red, which was worn by women around the hips. It is named for the large type of 'band' rattan (*obi*) from which it could be made. A length of rattan is flattened and split to form a broad strip, with the smooth outer surface on one side and the other shaved flat. Another name, 'hammered-vine cincture' (*susuru kwalodiu*), refers to this technique. However, band-straps were also made of coconut cuticle (*taketake niu*), as used for patterned ornaments. In both cases the strap was stained red with dye (*dilo*), sometimes with simple resist patterns made by covering small areas with stencils of leaf. The band-strap was long enough to pass several times around the hips, with the ends tied together. It was the only thing worn by maidens for everyday dress, but wives might also wear it under their great-cincture (*gwa'isusuru*) belt.

The red band-strap was worn throughout Malaita, as well as in Gela and Guadalcanal, but with some variations. In east Kwaio it is a narrower strip of split rattan, as used for plaited bands (*obi*).

Kwage'utafunu is the Kwaio name for a string of fine *'afi'afi* beads with bunches of dolphin teeth at the front, back and sides, worn by Kwaio maidens until the mid-twentieth century. Formerly in Lau maidens also sometimes wore a single strand of beads in this way (Maranda).

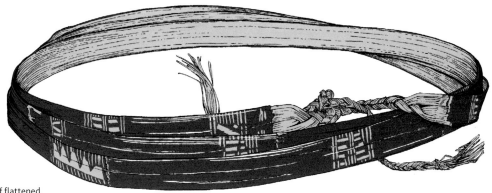

Figure 209 A band-strap (*'abaobi*) of flattened band-rattan from west-central Kwaio (known there as *lālā* and *kenekene*), made by Gala'a• of Uogwari in 1983. (Akin 159)
50%

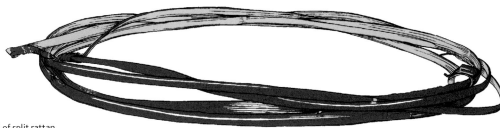

Figure 210 A band-strap (*'abaobi*) of split rattan from east Kwaio, made in the early 1980s. (Akin)
50%

Fo'o'aba or **belt** is a general name for strings and straps of money-beads (*maga mani*) or glass beads (*kekefa*) to bind (*fo'o*) around the hips. Men would wear such a belt below the girdle (*fo'osae*) and women would wear it over the band-strap (*'abaobi*) or great-cincture (*gwa'isusuru*). There seems to have been little difference between the bead belts worn by men and women, although women's had other names (see below). As valuable ornaments, the broader money-bead belts were probably worn mainly by men, but they might also be worn by maidens at marriage.

- Belts of ten or so strings of money-beads of Langalanga-type were joined by spacers like a money denomination, but shorter and with different combinations of beads.
- Belts of woven money-beads were made like pattern-straps (*'abagwaro*) for the arms, each bead threaded on the intersection of a warp and a weft to lie diagonally to the edge of the strap (see page 46). Kwara'ae ones are said to have had an 'arrows' design similar to their pattern-straps, or designs such as stars and frigate-birds, or to combine white *galu* money-beads with various coloured glass beads (*kekefa*) of the same size.
- Belts of small glass beads, as seen in the photographs from Fiji, were made by threading the beads on the wefts to lie square to the edge of the strap (see page 47). The small size of the beads allowed for more flexibility in the design, but most are based on square and diagonal lines as on money-bead straps, in the same basic colours of red, white and blue (equivalent to black). Popular motifs included the British Union Jack flag (not necessarily in its original colour arrangement) and designs said to have been taken from playing-card suits and other foreign patterns. Such belts are remembered in Kwara'ae, although no longer seen, and some there attribute them to Kwaio, where people still know how to make them.

Belts of money-bead strings were widespread in Solomon Islands, from east Makira (Bernatzik 1936:pls 8, 9, 41, 47) to Isabel and western Solomons, where the spacers were elaborately ornamented with beads, teeth and shell rings (see Plates 37 and 38, pages 54 and 55). Woven money-bead belts were worn throughout Malaita and in west Makira, but elsewhere only in Shortland Islands, western Solomons, where they were made by plaiting rather than weaving (see page 46).

Figure 211 A belt (*fo'o'aba*) of fifteen separate strings of money-beads which came to the British Museum in 1897. This kind was probably worn in Kwara'ae, although it is associated with Langalanga and north Malaita. (BM Oc,1887,0201.39) 33%

Figure 212 A belt (*fo'o'aba*) of money-beads from the British Melanesian Mission collection. The design is shared with old examples from Sa'a or Ulawa from the 1920s or earlier, Arosi in west Makira from the 1840s and 1860s, and others without provenance.[23] Although probably a south Malaita style, it is evidently related to the designs of Kwara'ae and north Malaita pattern-straps (*'abagwaro*) and north Malaita belts. (SI Museum) 33%

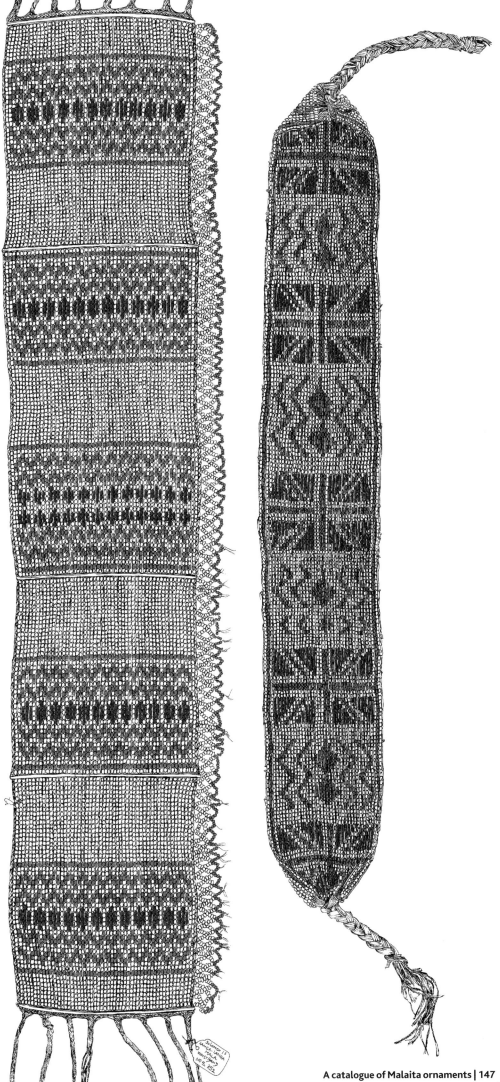

Figure 213 A belt (*foʻoʻaba*) of glass beads, with bone spacers, from Mary Edge-Partington's collection of the 1910s, labelled 'LANGA-LANGA, MALA'. (BM Oc,1921,1102.37) 33%

Figure 214 A belt (*foʻoʻaba*) of glass beads which came to the British Museum in 1931, with a variant of the Union Jack design. (BM Oc,1931,0722.81) 33%

Susuru or **cincture**,[24] also called ***gulua'afe*** or **woman's-
tie-on**, is a bead belt worn by women for special occasions.
The cincture was particularly associated with maidens since
it was not appropriate for wives to ornament themselves so
much (hence it is sometimes distinguished as a maiden's
cincture [*susuru sari'i*] from the great-cincture [*gwa'isusuru*]
worn by wives). Like men's bead belts, these included sets of
strung money-beads as well as straps of woven money-beads
and glass beads.

Examples of cincture belts from the sea and inland peoples
of north Malaita probably resemble those once worn in
Kwara'ae and Kwaio, but, as with men's belts, the woven ones
were probably not worn further abroad than Makira.

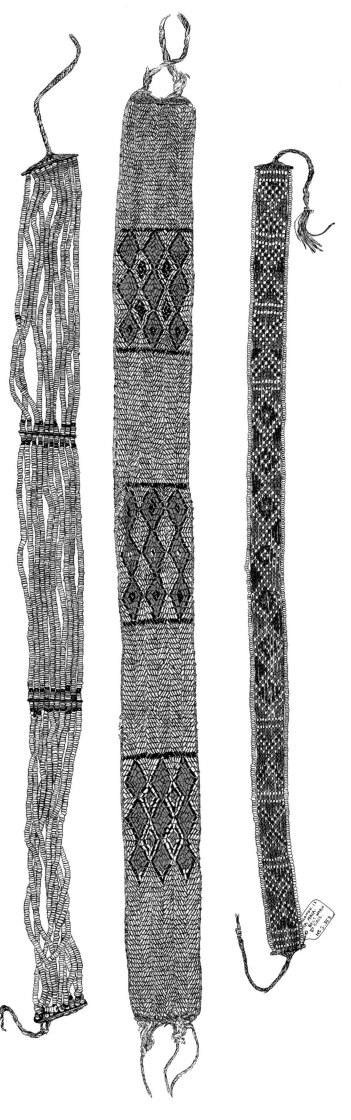

Figure 215 A cincture (*susuru*) of white *galu*
money-beads belonging to Maleke● of Ofatabu in
Baelelea in the 1960s (known there as *galua 'afe
surugalu*). (Maranda)
33%

Figure 216 A cincture (*susuru*) of money-beads
from Ofatabu in Baelelea, from the 1960s (known
there as *'aesu*). (Maranda)
33%

Figure 217 A cincture (*susuru*) of glass beads from
Ata'a, a sea community northeast of Kwara'ae,
from the 1910s. It is labelled as 'worn by girls'. This
is one of several of this design from Mary Edge-
Partington's collection, recognized as similar to
Kwara'ae. Much of the design is a half-width version
of the lozenges in Figure 223, with the diagonal
angles changed by the glass-bead technique.
(BM Oc,1921.1102.39)
33%

Gwa'isusuru or **great-cincture** is a woven strap worn by wives to support the cloth apron. It was made of the black cincture (*susuru*) stem apparently named after it, entire (not twisted into twine), or perhaps sometimes of *Gnetum* (*dae*) tree-bark twine, stained black. White beads, usually glass rather than money-beads, are strung at intervals on the warp strings of the strap between sections of wefts which are twined around the warp to keep the strap together. Both strap and apron were presented to a new wife by her husband's family.

This was a north Malaita ornament, worn as far south as north Kwaio, where since the 1980s it has been made with black nylon-strip (*'abanaelon*) deep-sea fishing line. In Lau, commoner women with no wealth might wear just a string of white *galu* beads (Maranda).

Figure 218 A great-cincture (*gwa'isusuru*) from 'Ere'ere in east Kwara'ae, from the 1970s. (Burt)
33%

Figure 219 A great-cincture (*gwa'isusuru*) from 'North Mala', collected by Revd H. Nind of the Melanesian Mission before 1912 and now in the British Museum. (BM Oc,1944,02.1338)
33%

Figure 220 A great-cincture (*gwa'isusuru*) which belonged to Sāmani● of Baelelea in the late 1960s (known there as *galu'a'afe* or woman's-tie-on). (Maranda)
33%

Figure 221 A great-cincture (*gwa'isusuru*) from north Kwaio, inland of Uru (known there as *foo'abi* or loin-tie). It was made in 1996 by Lekamae●, using black nylon-strip (*'abanaelon*) instead of cincture (*susuru*) vine. (Akin)
33%

Buru'a or **black** is the Kwaio name for a coil of black twine worn by women in Kwaio to support the apron of cloth or calico. The twine is made of *Gnetum* (Kwara'ae, *dae*) tree bark blackened with *akwasi* tree sap. This has mostly been replaced by black nylon-strip (*'abanaelon*) fishing-line, a substitute discovered in 1985 by Laete'esafi of 'Ai'eda, east Kwaio.

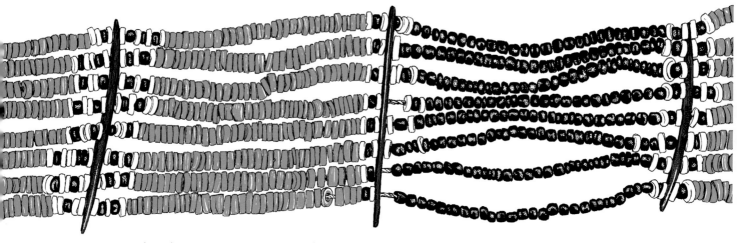

Figure 222 A cincture (*susuru*) from north Malaita from the 1960s (known there as *galu*), unusual in being of *romu* money-beads and black *fulu* seeds. (Maranda)
100%

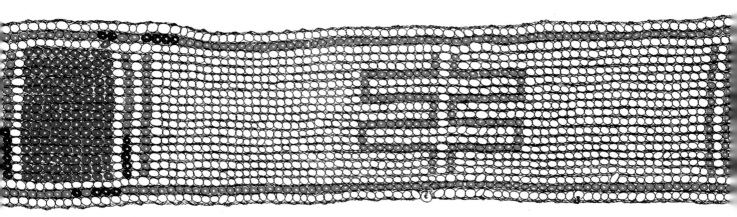

Figure 223 A cincture (*susuru*) of money-beads from Lau from the 1960s (known there as *'aesu*). (Maranda)
100%

Figure 224 A belt (*fo'o'aba*) of glass beads, presumably from Malaita, from Mary Edge-Partington's collection from the 1910s. (Capt. T.E. Edge-Partington)
100%

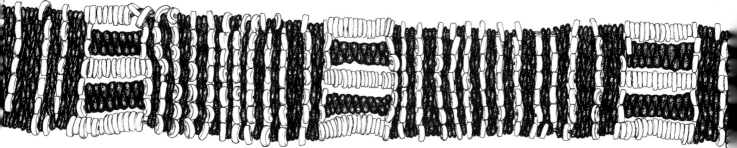

Figure 225 An old great-cincture (*gwa'isusuru*) of north Malaita style, made with *galu* money-beads, given to the Melanesian Mission in Britain, probably in the early twentieth century. (SI Museum)
100%

Obi gwaroa or **patterned-band** describes a belt of plaited dark *oko* vine-strip, patterned with yellow orchid and red coconut cuticle, like an orchid-pattern (*gwaro'adi'adi*) armband. It is said to have been worn by married women, but such belts were probably worn by both men and women throughout Malaita wherever orchid-pattern armbands were made. In Lau men wore a waist *oko* (*oko 'i litana*) belt with yellow orchid only. In Kwaio a stomach-band (*obioga*) was a red and white rattan belt worn by warriors in former times, particularly in the area of Gounakāfu.

Figure 226 A patterned-band (*obi gwaroa*) belt of uncertain origin, of a design attributed to Kwara'ae.[25] (Akin 329)
100%

'Abatarafa or **strap** is the Whiteman leather belt which long ago became a popular ornament for men. Early twentieth-century photos show straps worn to secure the lavalava, especially when a man was ornamented (see Plates 4, 20 and 21, pages 10, 26 and 27), or even worn alone with no loin covering at all (Meyer and Parkinson 1900:pl. 45). The most distinctive and popular style had a two-piece brass buckle of the kind worn by the police. Such straps were popular thoughout Malaita. In Kwaio they were sometimes treated with the same kind of fighting magic as for girdles (*fo'osae*), to suppress hunger.

Figure 227 A strap (*'abatarafa*), with an old police-style buckle on a newer leather belt, belonging to Aisah Osifera of 'Aimomoko, Kwara'ae, in 1984. (Burt)
100%

'Abala'ua or **cloth** (lit. 'flat and flexible') is a name for local cloth made from tree bark, but the name is also applied to foreign cloth, otherwise known as calico (Pijin, *kaliko*). Wives, particularly senior or older women, wore a piece of cloth as an apron, sometimes dyed black with wild banana (*sasao*) juice, held by the great-cincture (*gwa'isusuru*). Some say that only senior or post-menopausal wives wore cloth while young wives just wore leaves. When foreign cloth became available it was used instead, the preferred colour being a deep 'kingfisher' blue, and by the 1920s local cloth had gone out of use for this purpose.

Throughout Solomon Islands, before women adopted calico clothing, they wore pubic coverings only after marriage, and in most of Malaita this was a cloth apron. In Isabel women wore a skirt of local cloth made from white bark, dyed dark blue (Bogesi 1948:227, 341), and in western Solomons women wore a loincloth, in some areas with a pad or bustle behind (Williamson 1914:22, Beattie photo 705).

Sada or **skirt** is a Langalanga name for a skirt of vine-shred made from *faifai* or *fa'ola* tree bark. Such skirts became popular among Malaita sea peoples in the later twentieth century, particularly for displays of local tradition for marriage ceremonies, arts shows and performances. Formerly, however, they were more a fashion of the neighbouring islands visited by these people on their trading voyages. In the late nineteenth and early twentieth centuries women wore vine-shred skirts in Gela, Savo, Guadalcanal and Makira, described as a short fringe in Makira and the 'Are'are area of Marau on Guadalcanal, rather longer elsewhere, and of several layers on Savo (Penny 1887:45, Woodford 1890:30, Rose photo 12249, Herr 1978:39, 46, Hogbin 1945, Paravicini 1931:pls 5, 14, 27). Early references to Malaita women wearing such skirts are from the peoples most in contact with these islands. In 'Are'are and Sa'a women wore fringes of vine-shred at the front and back (Ivens 1927:91, Geerts 1970:2, 59, 102) and in Langalanga early photographs show some women wearing vine-shred skirts in the 1900s and 1910s (Edge-Partington BM Oc,Ca44.241 to 243, Johnson 1944:37).

Kabilato or **loincloth**, made of local cloth from *sala* tree bark, was formerly worn by men of the sea, and probably only by married men, in the same way that only wives wore the cloth apron. Kwara'ae inland men originally wore no loin covering except for leaves on public occasions, but photographs from the 1910s show some with loincloths of small pieces of calico, probably kerchiefs, perhaps as a concession to colonial prejudices against nakedness.

The sea men's loincloth, as shown in old photographs, appears to have been a long strip of local cloth or calico with one end wrapped tightly around the hips, turned around and over itself at the front, then passed between the legs and tucked up under the strip behind (although posed photos seldom show the back; see Paravicini 1931:pls 58, 59). An alternative was a shorter strip of calico tucked up under a belt, front and back. In the late twentieth century some Kwara'ae

adopted loincloths of this kind, but of local cloth, as traditional dress for occasions such as dances.

The man's loincloth was probably an ancient form of dress in parts of Solomon Islands, but it was adopted in Malaita only in colonial times, mainly by the sea people and not by all of them. The loincloth of pandanus leaf is said to have been introduced to Sa'a from Makira in the mid-nineteenth century, although in Arosi, west Makira, inland men also wore nothing in the early twentieth century. Sea men of Ata'a and Lau in northeast Malaita in the late nineteenth and early twentieth centuries went naked, as men following the ancestral religion continued to do in Lau in the 1960s, in the men's area of their offshore islands (Ivens 1927:91, Wilson 1932:197, Verguet 1885:206, Herr 1978:46, Rannie 1912:304, Hopkins n.d., Maranda).

Men also wore similar loincloths on Guadalcanal, Savo, Isabel and islands to the west in the nineteenth and early twentieth centuries (Brenchley 1875:287, Woodford 1890:30, Beattie photos 647, 625, Paravicini 1931:pl. 26, Hogbin 1934: photos). It seems that Malaitan men became more shy of nakedness as contact with those who wore the loincloth or Whiteman clothes increased with inter-island travel during the colonial period. While more parochial inlanders like the Kwara'ae once covered themselves only for magical protection and ornament on public occasions, the cosmopolitan sea people became shy of nakedness sooner. As even inland people came into regular contact with outsiders during the twentieth century, their nakedness would increasingly have seemed unsophisticated and even embarrassing. Elderly men in the east Kwaio inland maintained this fashion until the 1980s.

Kaliko or **calico** is a general name for foreign cloth and clothing, as introduced from overseas by migrant workers and Christian converts in the late nineteenth century and promoted by colonizing Whitemen from the early twentieth century. Although fitted clothing was popular from the first, lengths of cloth were for a long time the more usual style for reasons of practicality and cheapness.

Pagan men in Kwara'ae, when they wore calico, at first preferred to tie a strip around the waist to hang down in front, like a loincloth (*kabilato*) which has not been passed between the legs and tucked up behind (see Plate 22, page 28). A similar effect (see Plate 19, page 25) was had by hanging the calico from the front only of a girdle (*fo'osae*) or strap (*'abatarafa*). Christian men wore the wrap-around lavalava, eventually adopted also by pagans and still generally worn as casual dress around the home, and until the Second World War this was often treated as best dress. It was promoted by the colonial government, and an example was set by the Royal Solomon Islands Police (see page 13). Their uniform before the war was a plain lavalava with a coloured cummerbund waistband of 'white for Sergeants, blue for Corporals, black for Lance-Corporals, and red for ordinary Constables' (Luke 1945:89). Others wore all kinds of printed or woven patterns and stripes. Woven stripes of several colours seem to have been favoured from the 1900s into the 1920s (Beattie photos 557, 558; Young 1925:140). In the 1910s, although not later, the police had the bottom edge of their lavalava cut and hemmed into deep indents (see Plate 20, page 26 and Edge-Partington photo BM Oc,Ca44.292). This style of 'serrated-clothing' (*tagiri*), associated with Fiji, became popular in the 1930s, perhaps as a result of the introduction of sewing machines, and contrasting colours were sewn together for effect (see Hogbin 1939:40, 68).

Christian women began to wear calico first as a one-piece gathered skirt, and this was eventually adopted by pagans for visiting away from home. From the mid-twentieth century, blouses and dresses came into more common use and women became more shy about showing their breasts. In the late twentieth century, when women ornamented themselves in traditional style for their weddings and other occasions they usually wore a skirt and bra, concealing the breasts while still allowing ornaments to show against the bare body.

From the first, calico was worn for ornament according to local taste as well as Christian or Whiteman standards. In the early twentieth century men often wore pieces of calico tied at the back of the neck to hang over the chest like a kerchief (Beattie photo 528), or lengths of calico draped over one shoulder like a stole. In those days, as photographs

show, hats were also popular, probably serving as eyeshades for sea people. Shirts were worn not only in Whiteman style (with trousers by Christians), but also with lavalava and local ornaments (as in Plate 4, page 10). Shirts and trousers might be worn until reduced to rags by those who could get no better clothing.

By the late twentieth century European clothing, first introduced by returning migrant workers a century before, was the usual form of dress and ornament for almost everyone, with only a few old people wearing local styles. Even those following the ancestral religion in Kwaio and 'Are'are had clothing stored away to wear on important public occasions. Everyone dressed in the best they could afford in the way of new or second-hand clothes from Australia, Southeast Asia or beyond, men in shorts or long trousers with shirt or T-shirt, women in skirt and blouse or dress. T-shirts with printed designs were popular, including many printed in Honiara with local designs and slogans ranging from 'Nuclear Free Pacific' to 'That Betel Nut Habit', and from Christian symbols to Solomon Islands tourism motifs. By then calico had replaced local ornaments for all but a small minority, except when celebrating specifically 'traditional' (*kastom*) occasions.

Figure 228 A cloth (*'abala'ua*) made in 1984 by Christina Maenuunu at Taba'akwaru, east Kwara'ae, to demonstrate the kind of cloth formerly worn by wives as an apron (see Plate 29, page 43). The marks of the cockle-shell used to beat it can still be seen. (Burt)
33%

Leg ornaments

Rū fuana laungilana 'aena ngwae or **things to ornament the legs** were mostly tied below the knees, but included also bands around the ankles or thighs.

Siafo is the Kwaio name for a patterned band, like an orchid-pattern (*gwaro'adi'adi*) armband, which was formerly worn on the thigh by men, said to show well on strong legs. It would presumably have looked very much like a brow-band (*obidala*, see page 80), so perhaps some of the large patterned bands in museum collections were worn on the leg rather than the head.

ketekome or **conus-rattle**, sometimes called simply strung-rattle (*kete*), is a string of conus (*kome*) rings worn by men below the knee. The rings were usually graduated in size, larger to the front and smaller where the two ends were tied

at the back. Sometimes men wore two on one leg, with or without one on the other (as in Plates 4 and 5, pages 10 and 12). In recent times this ornament seems to have been replaced by the shell-rattle (*ketela'o*, see below), which is often called conus-rattle too. Although strings of beads were worn in this way elsewhere on Malaita and beyond, the conus-rattle style seems to have been characteristic of Kwara'ae, Kwaio and north Malaita.

ketela'o or **shell-rattle** is one name for a length of white *galia* beads worn by men below the knee, an old ornament which has been substituted for the conus-rattle as less valuable and more easily available. It is also called twine-rattle (*ketedadalo*), referring to the cord on which it is threaded and some use the name conus-rattle (*ketekome*) or shell-rattle (*ketela'o*) for either kind of ornament. Sometimes larger beads were worn, like a conus-rattle but all of one size, as a 'big shell-rattle' (*ketela'o doe*), and some men wore strings of seeds instead.

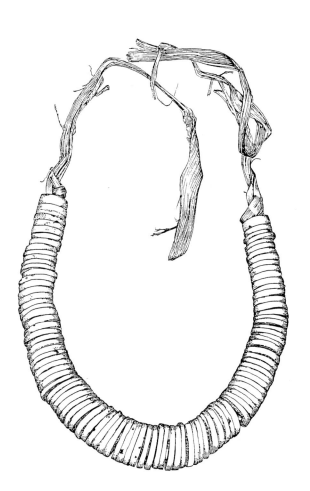

Figure 229 One of a pair of conus-rattles (*ketekome*) from north Malaita from the 1990s. (Burt)
50%

Figure 230 One of a pair of shell-rattles (*ketela'o*) of *galia* beads from east Kwara'ae from the 1980s. (Burt)
50%

Ma'e'ae or **leglet** is a Lau name for a glass-bead strap worn by men and women as an alternative to conus or *galia*-bead leg (*ketekome, ketela'o*) ornaments (Maranda). Sea people of north Malaita have worn this ornament since at least the 1910s, and in the late twentieth century the Langalanga were making similar leglets of money-beads with tight-lip (*mumu*) seed tassels (Guo).

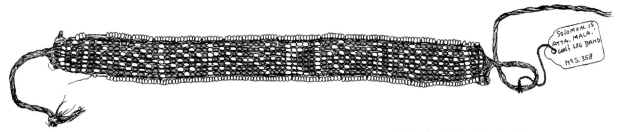

Figure 231 A leglet (*ma'e'ae*) of glass beads, one of a pair from Ata'a, a sea community northeast of Kwara'ae, from the 1910s. It is part of a set with some cinctures (*susuru*) given to the British Museum by Mary Edge-Partington in 1921 (see page 148). (BM Oc,1921,1102.43) 50%

Figure 232 A leglet (*ma'e'ae*) from Lau from the 1960s with the Union Jack design. (Maranda) 50%

'Aitomu or **tomu-tree** is a Kwaio name for the red seed from a certain tree, sometimes made into necklaces, which was threaded on twine to be worn below the knee. This is an old style in Kwaio, not worn since the mid-twentieth century. Kwara'ae and presumably other Malaitans also sometimes wore strings of seeds in this way.

Buli or **cowrie**, like those worn as head ornaments, were also worn at the knee in south Malaita and also in Lau, perhaps on a shell-rattle (*ketela'o*) of money-beads (Ivens 1927:133, 148, 1929b:6) This was also a fashion of Makira (Mead 1973:35).

Obi or **bands** of rattan-strip (*'abakalitau*), like that worn on the arms (see page 128), were also worn on the ankles by men and women. They would be plaited on the leg for special occasions such as festivals.

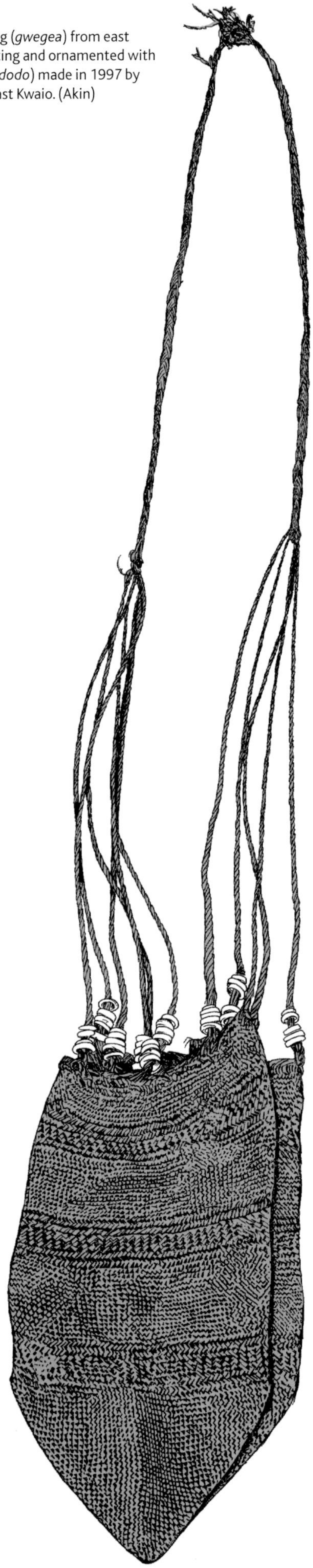

Figure 233 A fine sack-bag (*gwegea*) from east Kwaio with patterned plaiting and ornamented with small conus rings (*sona* or *dodo*) made in 1997 by Moruka● of Ga'enaafou, east Kwaio. (Akin)
33%

Figure 234 A small simple satchel-bag (*gwanagwana*) made by Adriel Rofate'e of Gwauna'ongi, east Kwara'ae, in 1979. (Burt)
33%

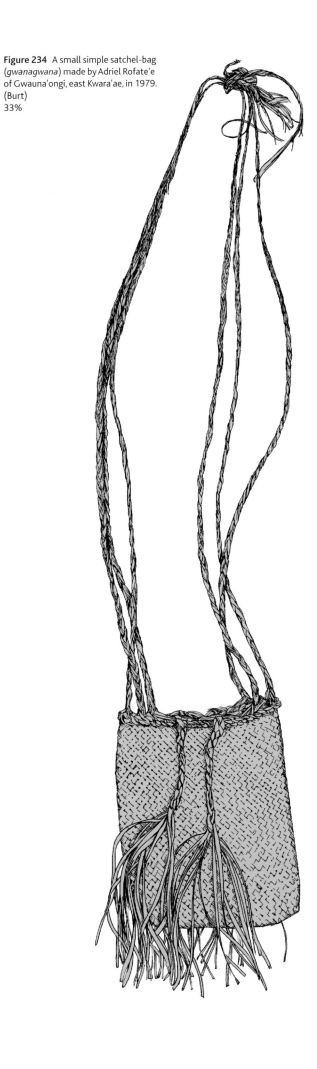

Bags

Ngwa'i or **bags**, which men and women wear to carry personal possessions, were also part of everyday dress. Inland people usually wear smaller bags around the neck at the back or side, sea people usually over one shoulder. Some bags were made to be ornamental, and people also ornamented them when they ornamented their bodies.

Bags are made from vine-strip from the bark of certain trees, often from *sula* or *malao* (both *Trichospermum*), sometimes from *Abroma* (*kwasikwasi*), which gives a decorative white vine-strip, or from mallow (*fa'ola / Hibiscus*), which can be cooked to make it more flexible. Two broad strips are split into shreds and plaited together from the bottom of the bag, with more added as the work moves up towards the rim. In the late twentieth century Kwara'ae bags were usually of plain weave, but in Kwaio and elsewhere the finest are still plaited in twilled patterns which show as the light catches the grain of the vine-strips. At the top of the bag the shreds are braided into the rim and then plaited or twined into carrying cords, which are tied together at the ends.

Bags are sometimes ornamented with rattle or tight-lip seeds (*fa'i kete, mumu*) or a row of conus rings hanging from the fringes of a satchel or the top of a sack (Paravicini photo 3900). Some men used their bags to proclaim daring secret offences committed successfully by themselves and their clan, displaying prowess and the power of their ancestral ghosts. A pig thief, once retired, would hang a chain of small plaited bands (*tala obi*) from his bag, one for each pig. Clement O'ogau of Manādedo, east Kwara'ae, who had stolen 190 pigs in his youth in the early twentieth century, compared this to wearing war medals. Sometimes pig-tusks were hung from the bag (Beattie photo 237x). In Kwaio, and no doubt in Kwara'ae, men also displayed conus rings for secret killings, miniature bags or rings of money-beads for stolen money and sometimes small orchid-pattern armbands or red bands for sexual exploits.

Gwegea or **sack** is a bag with a flat four-cornered bottom and rounded body.

Gwanagwana or **satchel** is a flat bag, usually with several groups of shreds left to hang down each side as a decorative fringe.

Ngwa'ifirua or **tangled-bag** has a fringe of hanging shreds far longer than the bag itself, which has to be untangled to look good. White *Abroma* (*kwasikwasi*) vine-strip is particularly good for this effect. A tangled bag might be worn hanging down the back of the neck (see Plate 2, page 6).

Baosi or **pouch**, of Whiteman make, was a popular addition to the man's strap (*'abatarafa*) from the early days of labour migration, useful for keeping small possessions, like a bag. Accounts from those times suggest that it also served as an ornament (see page 15 and Plate 20, page 26).

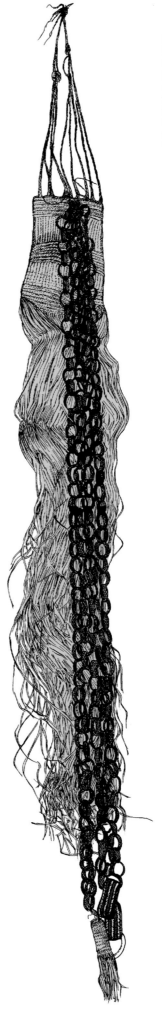

Figure 235 A tangled-bag (*ngwa'ifirua*) made by Moruka● of Ga'enāfou, east Kwaio, in 1983 (known there as *wa'ifirua*). It has many plaited bands for pig thefts, two orchid-pattern bands for sexual trespass, a conus ring for a secret killing and a bag for shell-money theft. (Akin)
17%

Fou'atolēleo or **stone-and-pearl** is a Kwaio name for a small baton which was worn hanging from the back of the neck or on a tangled-bag (*ngwa'i firua*) by a man who had killed. It would be brandished during the ceremony when he collected a reward for a killing, the stone grasped in the right hand if more killing was to follow (as re-enacted by an 'Are'are elder in de Coppet and Zemp 1978:117–18).

The name stone-and-pearl comes from the 'Are'are practice of using a pyrite nodule for the head, encased in woven vine-strip and attached to a handle covered with pearly nautilus shell (*lēleo*) stuck on with putty. Most Kwaio and northern 'Are'are examples have a carved wooden knob instead of the stone. Some from Kwaio have a foot carved at the other end and those from Kwarekwareo (between west Kwaio and 'Are'are) often have a carved hand instead (Akin 1982).

The stone-and-pearl was only used by the Kwaio and peoples to the south, and in Kwara'ae few elders had seen or heard of it. However, it became well known overseas because the first Spanish visitors to south Malaita mistook the iron pyrite nodules for gold and acquired as many as they could (Amherst and Thompson 1901:343). People of south Malaita and Kwaio have been making stone-and-pearls as attractive curios for visiting Whitemen since the beginning of the twentieth century (Woodford 1908b, Paravicini 1931:162). They ceased to be used for reward ceremonies after the colonial government abolished reward-killing from the 1920s, but for a time some continued to use them in similar human-life exchanges when claiming children for adoption.

Ra'irū kī or **leaves** were used to ornament the body, with ornaments or on their own, depending on the occasion.

When men ornamented themselves for an event such as a festival or dance they would stick leaves or sprigs in their armbands, girdles or belts, and hang them from their bags. Some of these leaves were chosen for appearance, some for their pleasant smell or to repel biting insects, and some because of particular symbolic meanings or magical properties. Cordyline (*sango, dili*) and croton (*'ala'ala*) were the most used, for their colour, and *Euodia* (*ri'i, Euodia aff. anisodora*) for its scent. These and other decorative leaves also had other virtues, whether as charms (*'oto'a*) planted around homes and sanctums to ward off sorcery, wild ghosts and enemies, or as magic to protect the body or attract the opposite sex. Hence youths wore *Euodia* (*ri'i*) or *Hedyotis* (*bulu*) leaves to attract maidens, and *Premna* (*kwa'u*) leaf was worn in the armband to cool the power of hostile ghosts and sorcery. Men who wore no calico sometimes wore two or three *sarufi* (*Cryptocaria / Litsea*) leaves in front of the genitals or in armbands to cool damaging-magic (*'ainifalia*) and encourage goodwill (*ngwanaogale'a*). Wives wore 'shut' leaves (*bono*, a kind of wild taro) when they needed to avoid spoiling or defiling their cloth aprons. A man might show he had just killed someone or stolen a pig by wearing *'ama'ama* fern sprigs in his hair. (For a fuller list of such leaves, see Kwa'ioloa and Burt 2001:92–3).

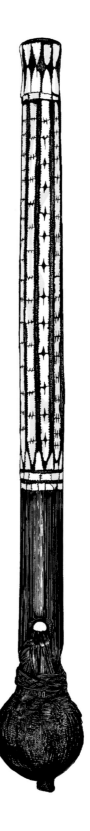

Figure 236 An early twentieth-century stone-and-pearl (*fou'atolēleo*) with a stone head in the British Museum, probably from south Malaita (where it is known as *hau āno rereo*). (BM Oc,1929,071.3.87) 100%

Preparing the body

Fala'a or **piercing** was necessary for wearing most ear and nose ornaments. This could be done fairly painlessly by wearing a turtleshell earring (*tege*) with a break which allowed it to pinch into the flesh and gradually work its way through. Alternatives were piercing with a rattan thorn, a tool such as a sharpened frog bone (as in Kwaio) or a fish-hook or pig's tusk (as in Sa'a, Ivens 1927:82). Holes around the ears and through the septum of the nose would be stretched and enlarged by the ornaments inserted in them. In the late twentieth century a few of the oldest men also had a hole in the tip of the nose for inserting ornaments, probably also made with the frog bone.

Oko is a kind of pyrite stone used to blacken the teeth. It is pounded to a paste with the leaf-shoot of the with-ease tree (*akwasi, Rhus taitensis*). In Kwaio, where the practice continues, the paste must first be held in the mouth for several hours, then later applied regularly after chewing betelnut. Besides making the teeth look good, shiny and black, this helps to strengthen them and protect teeth and gums from disease.

Onga or **tattoos** are more a fashion of the sea people of Lau, Langalanga and south Malaita than of inland people like the Kwara'ae, although some adopted it from the early twentieth century. The designs, on face and upper body, are linear and geometric (see Plate 35, page 53 and Ivens 1927:83–6) and in Lau they vary according to clan. Designs incised onto the face as shallow scars are also a sea people's fashion, sometimes adopted by the Kwara'ae and Kwaio.

The most common tattoo in Kwara'ae is a 'mangrove flower' (*takako'a*) high on each cheek, made up of a central dot surrounded by four dots. This design is said to have originated during labour migration to Fiji and Queensland in the late nineteenth century, and is hence 'new' to Kwara'ae. Other designs on men's arms and chest are also of colonial origin, including patterns from printed calico and written names. During the invasion of Solomon Islands by American troops during the Second World War some men gained tattoos of American designs such as stars.

Formerly tattooing was done with three rattan thorns tied in a bundle, with blacking made from burning resin from the nut tree (*ngali, Canarium*). In recent times three metal sewing needles were dipped in water, poked into a Chinese ink block and then stabbed several times into the skin, and the Kwaio also use wood ash and burnt rubber (see Akin 1995–7:videotape 4). Tattooing deserves a chapter in itself, but lack of information puts it beyond the scope of this book.

Ngwaingwai or **oil** for anointing the body was made by cooking coconut milk in a bamboo flask, with yellow (*sa'osa'o, Cananga odorata*) flowers to perfume it. Men and women would 'bathe' (*siu*) in oil to make their skin gleam when ornamenting the body. The grease from a sprouting coconut could also be used, without preparation.

Totoniramo or **warrior-marks** are red lines of betelnut juice smeared on the cheeks with the stick used for dipping in the lime eaten with the betelnut. They are said to be the mark of a thief boasting of having stolen something such as a pig and getting away with it, but generally show happiness.

Sufi'a or **barbering** was basic to the presentation of the body. Formerly men kept their hair fairly short and combed it, while long hair and a full or unkempt growth of beard was regarded as uncouth, the style of an 'eater' or cannibal (*fafanga*). Women and children kept their hair short and had their heads shaved with a flint (*naki*). Both men and women sometimes shaved their hair in patterns, as the Kwaio still do, especially for children. One Kwara'ae women's style was to cut the hair into a round shape and then cut out strips across the head from side to side, leaving the hair in three or four parallel blocks.

Men's hairdressing was described by Filiga Takangwane of Latea, an old-fashioned elder in the 1980s, in the story of a youth about to go courting:

> he reached for a bowl on the rack, put it on the ground, poured a bamboo [of water] into the bowl, it settled and cleared, he went behind the sanctum and broke a piece of flint, then he came back and squatted by the bowl of water and trimmed the ends of his hair, set tree bark alight to singe his hair, he trimmed and then singed and rounded his hair. Then he came back and reached for his girdle, he put it on and reached for his bag and his angle-club. Then he went.

Not everyone followed this method: for the Ubasi clan of east Kwara'ae trimming the hair by burning was tabu for fear of death or baldness, because the smell reminded the ghosts of the singeing bristles of sacrificial pigs.

Men shaved or trimmed their beards by plucking the hairs with a pair of small clam-shells (*dora*) as tweezers, a practice continued by older men long after razor blades came into use. In the late twentieth century the old-fashioned style for the most conservative old men was to pluck the beard from the face while allowing it to grow below the jaw, while younger men were usually clean-shaven. Photos from the early twentieth century also show men clean-shaven or with moustaches, said to have been introduced by migrant workers returning from Queensland.

Barbering, like wearing ornaments, was given up during mourning. When an important member of the community died, people would let their hair and beards grow long during the tabu period until they were normalized (*mola*) again, or if the person had been killed, until his death had been avenged. This period might last for many months or even years.

Many Malaitans, especially children and sea people, have blond or reddish hair, partly bleached by sea and sun. In Sa'a youths and maidens once bleached their hair with lime, covering it during the process with a bast sheath, as shown in the carved figures from the area (Ivens 1927:83). This is reminiscent of the founding ancestor of Kwara'ae, who covered his red hair with a hat because it was tabu for anyone to see.

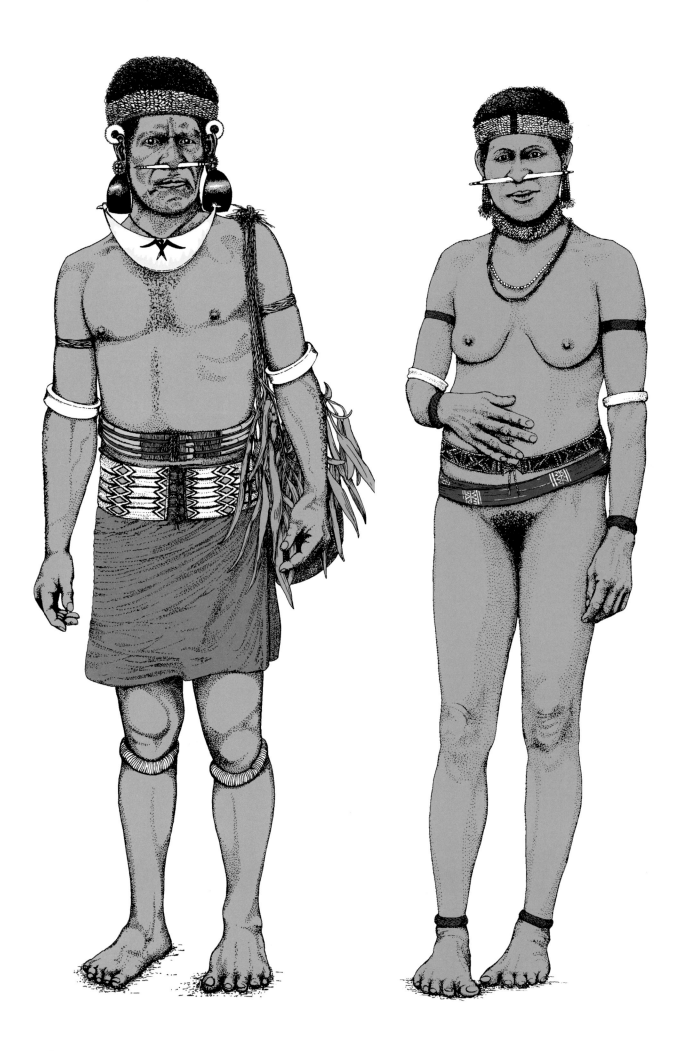

Recollections of former times

In the 1990s some Kwara'ae elders recalled how they and their relatives ornamented themselves for important occasions in former times.

Figure 237 Ornaments worn by Ma'usae of Latea, as described by his son Marcus Bualimae in 1991. Ma'usae was from the Tolinga clan of Latea. He and one of his brothers died in the 1930s, leading the rest of their family to join the SSEM church.

fish teeth (*lifa ï'a*) strap of 600 teeth as a brow-binding
fafangalalo conus rings at the top of the ears
bamboo-trees (*'ai'au*) with bat teeth at the bottom of the ears
turtle-skin (*ulifunu*) ear ornaments, worn with the bamboo-trees
pin (*usuusu*) through the nose
crescent (*dafe*) with birds' heads on the ends and a turtleshell frigate-bird in the middle, at the neck.
conus (*fa'ikome*) or victim-crusher (*igolalamua*) rings above the elbows
girdle (*fo'osae*)
belt (*fo'o'aba*) of money-beads, an heirloom, about 6 inches wide with a design like the 'arrows' on pattern-straps (*'abagwaro*), worn below the girdle
short lavalava
shell-rattles (*ketela'o*) below the knees, of graduated size conus rings (i.e. conus-rattles, *ketekome*)

Figure 238 Ornaments worn by Maefatafata of Latea, as described by herself in 1991. Maefatafata was the daughter of Ramo'itolo, the last tabu-speaker of Latea, and married Kirifo'oa Lō. She joined the Jehovah's Witness church after both her husband and father died in the 1960s. This is how she dressed for festivals as a maiden under the traditional religion.

two fish-teeth-cluster (*barulifaï'a*) straps, one as a brow-binding, one around the neck
pin (*usuusu*), a long one, through the nose
fish-tassels (*ora ï 'a*) with four strings of money-beads and dolphin teeth in the ear lobes
conus (*fa'ikome*) rings, like men's ones, above the elbows
bands (*obi*) of coconut cuticle (*taketake niu*) on the wrists and ankles
band-strap (*'abaobi*) made of rattan at the waist
cincture (*susuru*) of glass beads at the waist

Ornaments worn by Kirifo'oa Lō of Latea, as described by his wife Maefatafata in 1991. Lō was a son of Ulungwane of the Atōbi clan of Latea and he took over as tabu-speaker after his father died and his brothers later joined the church in the 1950s. Lō used to make patterned ornaments himself, including big patterned combs. This is how he would have dressed up to his death in 1965:
patterned comb (*kafa gwaroa*), a small one, in the hair
four cowrie winkles (*karango buli*) strung as a browband
pin (*usuusu*) through the nose
patterned-bamboos (*fa'i'au gwaroa*) in the earlobes
crescent (*dafe*) at the neck (recalled by an acquaintance)
circle-fence (*barafa*) of four coils around the neck
bandoliers (*'abararao*) of red *safi* and white *galu* money-beads, two strings to each side joined in a net pattern front and back
patterned girdle (*fo'osae gwaroa*)
enclosed-straps (*'abebanibani*) of red and white glass beads on upper arms
big shell-rattles (*ketela'o doe*) of very large shell beads below the knees

Ornaments worn by Ulungwane of Latea, as described by his son Malakai Kailiu in 1991. Ulungwane was tabu-speaker of the Atōbi clan of Latea. When Ulungwane died in 1954 his ornaments were buried with him and his sons became Christians a few years later.
patterned comb (*kafa gwaroa*) in the hair, with one hornbill tail feather fitted into a bamboo socket fixed into the comb, so that the feather revolved in the wind
two cowries (*buli*), one each side of the forehead
patterned-bamboos (*fa'i'au gwaroa*) in the ears
stopper stud (*afu du'udu'u*) at end of the nose, because he was a warrior who had killed
pin (*usuusu*), quite a long one, through the nose
crescent (*dafe*) with a turtleshell bird but plain tips, at the neck
pattern-straps (*'abagwaro*) with the arrows pattern on the upper arms
conus (*fa'ikome*) rings above the elbows
girdle (*fo'osae*), plain, not patterned
rattles (*kete*) of white *galu* beads below the knees
bands (*obi*) of rattan on the ankles

Ornaments worn by Marcus Mua of Lidia, as described by his son Japhlet Iana in 1993. Mua was tabu-speaker of Lidia in 'Ere'ere, and this is what he wore until he joined the church shortly before the Second World War:
patterned comb (*kafa gwaroa*) in the hair, with a bunch of *Euodia* (*ri'i*) leaves in it
three cowries (*buli*) in the hair
turtle-skin (*ulifunu*) ear ornaments
pin (*usuusu*), a long one, through the nose
crescent (*dafe*) with a turtleshell frigate-bird and birds' heads on the ends, at the neck
pattern-straps (*'abagwaro*) on the upper arms
conus (*fa'ikome*) rings above the elbows

bands (*obi*) on the wrists and ankles
girdle (*fo'osae*)
a strip of cloth hanging down from the front of the girdle
strung-rattles (*ketedadalo*) of white *galu* beads below the
knees (i.e. *ketela'o*)

Ornaments worn by Kolodia Kwako of 'Ere'ere, as
described by her son Iana in 1993.
Kwako was the wife of Marcus Mua. This is what she wore for
festivals when she acted as the woman tabu-speaker before
the Second World War:
hair cut to a round shape and shaved crosswise to form several
blocks of hair
fish teeth (*lifa ī'a*) strap of 500 teeth as a browband
rolls of cordyline (*sango*) leaf in the ears
bands (*gwa'iobi*), stained red, on upper arms, wrists and
ankles
trochus (*fa'isiare*) rings, two above the elbow, one on the wrist
great-susuru (*gwa'isusuru*) strap
worship (*folota*) leaf to cover her front, for festivals only. She
normally wore an apron of local cloth (*laua*)
ring-strap (*'abaobi*) of band-rattan (*obi*) dyed red with resist
patterns, for festivals only

Ornaments worn by Nakisi of 'Ualakwai, as described
by his 'son' James Abera'u (his father's true brother's son).
Nakisi died in 1984, probably well over 100 years of age. This is
how he would have dressed probably before the 1930s, when
his family joined the SSEM church.
big patterned comb (*kafa gwaroa*) in the hair
two cowries (*buli*) in hair, one on each side of the forehead
turtleshell (*ta'uta'u*) in earlobes
patterned-bamboos (*fa'i'au gwaroa*) also in the earlobes
pin (*usuusu*), about 6 inches long, through the nose
crescent (*dafe*) with plain ends and turtleshell frigate-bird in
the middle, at the neck
stud (*otu*) in end of the nose, showing he had killed
pattern-straps (*'abagwaro*) with the arrows design on the
upper arms
conus (*fa'ikome*) rings above the elbows
patterned girdle (*fo'osae gwaroa*)
he wore no lavalava and no leaf, except when visiting his in-
laws, then wore any kind of leaf
shell-rattles (*ketela'o*) of white *galu* beads below the knees

Ornaments worn by O'iramo'a of Lidia, as described
by his brother's son Japhlet Iana in 1993. O'iramo'a was a true
brother of Marcus Mua and also a tabu-speaker. He would
have appeared like this before the Second World War.
big patterned comb (*kafa gwaroa doe*) on top of the head,
coloured side forward
cowrie-row (*talabuli*) browband
turtle-skins (*ulifunu*) in the earlobes
pin (*usuusu*), a long one, through the nose
necklace (*'alu'alu*) around the neck of three strings of red *safi*
money-beads with dolphin teeth at intervals

crescent (*dafe*) with birds' heads on ends and a turtleshell bird
in the middle, at the neck
pattern-straps (*'abagwaro*) on the upper arms
bands (*obi*), plain and not dyed, on the wrists and ankles
strap (*'abatarafa*) of leather with a plain buckle
lavalava of calico brought from Queensland
twine-rattle (*ketedadalo*) below the knees, of big conus rings
(i.e. *ketekome*)
bag (*ngwa'i*), a big one with a smaller one inside it for his
betelnut equipment
he carried an angle-club (*subi*)

**Ornaments worn by Moses Gwagwa'ufilu of
'Ere'ere**, as described by Japhlet Iana in 1993. Gwagwa'ufilu
was a Queensland migrant worker who returned home as
a Christian and then rejoined his pagan relatives in 'Ere'ere
and became both a warrior and a tabu-speaker (see Burt and
Kwa'ioloa 2001:101). His mother Takamanu was the sister of
Iana's father Marcus Mua. Gwagwa'ufilu was very tall and
wore a beard and a long twisted moustache. This is how he
dressed for festivals:
big patterned comb (*kafa gwaroa doe*) in the hair
fish teeth (*lifa ī'a*) strap as a browband
stud (*otu*) in end of his nose as the sign he had killed
pin (*usuusu*) through the nose
shell-disk-rattle (*ketesa'ela'o*) around the neck
turtle-skins (*ulifunu*) in the earlobes (probably those inherited
by Timi Ko'oliu, see page 89)
pattern-straps (*'abagwaro*) on the upper arms
conus (*fa'ikome*) rings above the elbows
big bag (*ngwa'i*) hanging from neck in front
patterned girdle (*fo'osae gwaroa*)
calico tied at the waist and hanging down in front, or
cordyline (*sango*) leaves stuck under the girdle instead
twine-rattle (*ketedadalo*) below the knees, of big conus rings
(i.e. *ketekome*)
angle-club (*subi*) carried in the crook of his left arm, cradled
with the butt in his right hand

Ornaments worn by Bitana of Mānadodo, as described
by Brian Billy Kaluae in 1991. Bitana was the last tabu-speaker
of the Mānadodo-Fiu clan; he remained pagan until about
1965 and died in 1984.
two or three cowries (*buli*) as a browband
patterned-bamboos (*fa'i'augwaroa*) in the earlobes
pin (*usuusu*) through the nose
something like a rolled leaf in the hole in end of the nose
crescent (*dafe*) at the neck
pattern-straps (*'abagwaro*) on the upper arms
conus (*fa'ikome*) rings above the elbows
girdle (*fo'osae*)
no calico at all
strings of black seeds below the knees

Notes

1   For video recordings of formal presentations of shell money of the southern type at a 1996 east Kwaio mortuary feast, see Akin 1995–7: videotapes 12 and 14.

2   Ivens illustrates a protruding-comb, apparently the same one shown here, in a plate captioned 'Ulawa Hair-combs' (1918:pl. 6B). While two others in the plate are characteristic of Ulawa and Makira, patterned combs were not, so this may be an example of the vague attributions of many artefacts illustrated in his books. Whether this comb once belonged to him or to the Melanesian Mission, it is more likely to have originated in Malaita.

3   The origin and significance of the Solomon Islands 'kapkap' (a name from the islands of Papua New Guinea) has been the subject of much futile speculation by ethnographers over many years, based on no more local information than is offered below. Schuster (1964) reviews this literature and documents more than thirty designs to demonstrate the derivation of certain elements from the human figure, but without explaining much else about them.

4   The following observations are based on thirty-eight old turtle-designs from Solomon Islands (excluding Bougainville). Of these fourteen are clearly identified with Malaita: BM Oc,RHC33, BM Oc,RHC44, BM Oc,1944,02.1341, Hogbin 1939:frontispiece, Irobaoa photos as below, Ross 1981:21, Woodhead and Maranda 1987, Auckland Museum AM19401, Cambridge University Museum Z.10859, Australian Museum E.26505, and those illustrated here. Twenty-four turtle-designs are attributed to other islands including one from Makira (Pitt-Rivers Museum 1912.60.1), and Brenchley remarked on them on Ulawa (1873:253).

5   There seem to be very few of these simple ear ornaments attributed to Malaita in museums. From the way this pair have been linked and tied together, it is unclear exactly how each was worn, and there are three earrings (tege) and one soela ring in the set.

6   For example, BM Oc,1944,02.1303 from Makira, BM Oc,1944,02.1355 and BM Oc,1944,02.1356 from Savo, BM Oc,1947,01.4 and BM Oc,1947,01.5 from New Georgia or Guadalcanal.

7   The name could also mean 'sewn-bamboo', referring to the way vine-strip is poked (susu'ia) through with a pin or needle to embroider or plait the patterned designs.

8   Moruka is a daughter of 'Elota, a local leader whose autobiography was published by Roger Keesing (1983; Moruka's photo appears on p. 17).

9   The similarity with Irobaoa's ornament can be seen in a close-up photograph in the same series (BM Oc,Ca46.120).

10 Other examples of this style attributed to south Malaita include Christie's 1982, de Coppet and Zemp 1978 dustjacket, and an Akin fieldnote.

11 Julius Brenchley obtained nine such pendants in 1865 between Makira and Isabel, of which two are attributed to Makira and one to Gela; see Waite 1987:68 (who misses the Makira attribution of BM Oc,6369).

12 For instance, an old crescent in the British Museum was newly drilled to take a hanging money-bead panel and presented to the Duke of Gloucester at Independence in 1979 (BM Oc,1978,07.3).

13 The similar names for goldlip pearlshell and the crescents made from it in the languages of Malaita and neighbouring islands has also been taken as confirmation of this recent introduction (Ivens 1927:393–4). The Kwara'ae dafe is a variant of the names used in Lau (dafe), Kwaio (dafi, dami), 'Are'are (tahi), Sa'a (dähi) Gela (davi), Kia in Isabel and Ranonga in western Solomons (davi) and Makira (tahi, tafi) (Ivens 1921:33, 1927:393–4, Belshaw 1950:178, Mead 1973:36, Maranda, Tetehu, Roga). However dafe does not only mean pearlshell, which is 'umari in Kwara'ae and north Malaita, where dafe describes crescent phases of the moon.

14 There seems no evidence for Ivens' suggestion (1927:394–5) that Solomon Islanders adopted the style from Polynesians crewing mid-nineteenth-century whaling ships.

15 The name is also given to the beads themselves elsewhere in Malaita, so may have other meanings.

16 These observations are based on the collections of David Akin and Pierre Maranda; a limited sample, but the only documented sources available.

17 The pattern-strap can be attributed to Port Adam because his other stops in Solomon Islands were Makira and Gela. Another in the same collection is similar to the last of those illustrated below (Christies 1-12-82, Renard Log).

18 BM Oc,6427 and BM Oc,6428 are from the Brenchley collection of 1865 (illustrated in Waite 1987:pl. 16), BM Oc,7643 from Savo was donated in 1875, and BM Oc,1921,1025.33 is identified as 'S. Cristoval'.

19 The only information on the sole example in the British Museum – 'Solomon Islands, made in the mission schools' (BM Oc,1949,05.28) – could be a clue to where this type of ornament originated.

20 An old ring which is evidently a bakiha from New Georgia is kept as an heirloom in Kwaio.

21 Ongoing research into imported ceramic arm-rings in Solomon Islands is summarized in Richards 2003.

22 According to the recruiter John Cromar, there were two brothers named Turnaros working as ship's captains in the labour trade in the 1880s, one of whom Anglicized his name to Turner (Cromar 1935:ch.8).

23 Another seven of these belts have been published, as follows: Verguet 1885:204; Waite 1987:pl. 16 (Maidstone Museum 260, Brenchley collection); Dufty photo Stone 484/19; Ivens 1927: facing p. 316 (Otago Museum D.26.603); Sotheby's 1978:62; Phelps 1976:pl. 5 (Hooper collection 1162); Neich and Pereira 2004:111 (Auckland Museum 12908).

24 This obscure translation has been chosen only because the number of Kwara'ae names for different kinds of belts exceeds common English ones.

25 One of this same design in the Solomon Islands National Museum (SI74.73) is labelled 'Kwara'ae, obi gwaroa for married women. Worn on special occasions. Design represents snake.'

References

Akin, D., n.d., 'Malaitan use of porpoise teeth'. Unpublished MS.

Akin, D., 1981, 'Porpoise teeth in East Kwaio artwork', *Journal of the Traditional Money Association* 2:4–7.

Akin, D., 1982, 'Kwaio fou'atoleeleo', *Pacific Arts* 14:6–8.

Akin, D., 1987, 'The commoditization of Solomon Islands art'. Paper presented at the University of Hawai'i Center for Pacific Islands Studies Symposium 'Contemporary Pacific Arts: Culture Versus Commodity', Honolulu Academy of Arts.

Akin, D., 1988–9, 'World War II and the evolution of Pacific art', *Pacific Arts* 27:5–11, 28:11–12.

Akin, D., 1993, *Negotiating Culture in East Kwaio, Solomon Islands*. Ph.D. dissertation, University of Hawai'i.

Akin, D., 1994, 'Cultural education at the Kwaio Cultural Centre'. In L. Lindstrom and G. White (eds), *Culture, Kastom, Tradition: Developing Cultural Policy in Melanesia*. 161–72. Institute of Pacific Studies, University of the South Pacific, Suva.

Akin, D., 1995–7, Video recordings from Kwaio. Geisel Library Special Collections. University of California, San Diego.

Akin, D., 1999, 'Cash and shell money in Kwaio, Solomon Islands'. In D. Akin and J. Robbins (eds), *Money and Modernity: State and Local Currencies in Melanesia*: 103–30. University of Pittsburgh Press, Pittsburgh.

Akin, D., 2002, *Plaited East Kwaio Combs*. Information leaflet.

Amherst, W.A. and Thompson, B. (eds), 1901, *The Discovery of the Solomon Islands by Alvaro de Mendaña in 1568*. Hakluyt Society, London.

Austin, R., 1986, *Handcrafts of the Solomon Islands*. Ministry of Trade, Honiara.

Bartle, J.F., 1952, 'The shell money of Auki Island', *Corona* 4:379–83.

Beattie, J.W., n.d., *Catalogue of a Series of Photographs Illustrating the Scenery and Peoples of the Islands in the South and Western Pacific*. Hobart.

Beattie, J.W., 1906, 'Journal of a Voyage to the Western Pacific in the Melanesian Mission Yacht Southern Cross'. Royal Society of Tasmania, Hobart, Mss. RS.29/3.

Belshaw, C.S., 1950, 'Changes in heirloom jewellery in the central Solomons', *Oceania* 20:169–84.

Bennett, J., 1987, *Wealth of the Solomons: A History of a Pacific Archipelago, 1800–1978*. Pacific Islands Studies Program and University of Hawai'i Press, Honolulu.

Bernatzik, H.A., 1935, *Südsee: Travels in the South Seas*. Constable, London.

Bernatzik, H.A., 1936, *Owaraha*. Bernina-Verlag, Wein-Leipzig-Olten.

Blackwood, B., 1935, *Both Sides of Buka Passage: An Ethnographic Study of Social, Sexual, and Economic Questions in the North-Western Solomon Islands*. Clarendon Press, Oxford.

Bogesi, G., 1948, 'Santa Isabel, Solomon Islands', *Oceania* 18:208–32, 327–57.

Bolton, L., 2001, 'What makes Singo different: North Vanuatu textiles and the theory of captivation'. In C. Pinney and N. Thomas (eds) *Beyond Aesthetics: Art and the Technologies of Enchantment*. 97–116. Berg, Oxford and New York.

Bolton, L., 2003, *Unfolding the Moon: Enacting Women's Kastom in Vanuatu*. University of Hawai'i Press, Honolulu.

Brenchley, J.L., 1873, *Jottings during the Cruise of H.M.S. Curacoa among the South Sea Islands in 1865*. Longman, Green and Co., London.

Brown, G., 1910, *Melanesians and Polynesians: Their Life-Histories Described and Compared*. Macmillan, London.

BSIP, n.d., *Manufacture of Money on Malaita*. Government report, probably 1950s. Solomon Islands National Archives, file 8/II/F3/15/2.

Burnett, F., 1911, *Through Polynesia and Papua: Wanderings with a Camera in Southern Seas*. Francis Griffiths, London.

Burt, B., 1994a, *Tradition and Christianity: The Colonial Transformation of a Solomon Islands Society*. Harwood Academic Publishers, Chur, Switzerland.

Burt, B., 1994b, 'Land in Kwara'ae and development in Solomon Islands', *Oceania* 64:317–35.

Burt, B. and Kwa'ioloa, M. (eds), 2001, *A Solomon Islands Chronicle, as Told by Samuel Alasa'a*. British Museum Press, London.

Carlier, J-E., 2002, *Regard sur les îles Salomon*. Voyageurs et Curieux, Paris.

Christie's, 1982, *Auction Catalogue, 1 Dec.*, London.

Clark, M. and Kelesi, M., 1982, *Solomon Islands Art and Artefacts*. Honiara Coin Centre, Honiara.

Collinson, C.W., 1926, *Life and Laughter 'midst the Cannibals*. Hurst & Blackett, London.

Connell, J., 1977, 'The Bougainville connection: changes in the economic context of shell money production in Malaita', *Oceania* 48:81–101.

Conru, K., 2002, *Bernatzik: South Pacific*. 5 Continents Editions, Milan.

Cooper, M., 1971, 'Economic context of shell money production in Malaita', *Oceania* 41:266–76.

Coppet, D. de, 1995, '"Are'are society: a Melanesian socio-cosmic point of view. How are bigmen the servants of society and the cosmos?' In D. de Coppet and A. Iteanu (eds), *Cosmos and Society in Oceania*: 235–74. Berg Publishers, Oxford.

Coppet, D. de and Zemp, H., 1978, *'Are'are: Un Peuple Melanesien et sa Musique*. Seuil, Paris.

Cromar, J., 1935, *Jock of the Islands: Early Days in the South Seas*. Faber & Faber, London.

Davenport, W.H., 1968, 'Sculpture of the Eastern Solomons', *Expedition* 10:4–25.

Dawbin, W.H., 1966, 'Porpoises and porpoise hunting in Malaita', *Australian Natural History* 15:207–11.

Dickinson, J., 1927, *A Trader in the Savage Solomons*. Witherby, London.

D.O. Malaita, 1935, District Officer's Annual Report. Solomon Islands National Archives, file BSIP 1/III/F14/7.

Duff, R., 1947, 'The Solomon Islands' Ndala', *Australian Museum Magazine* 9:120.

Edmundson, A. and Boylan, C., 1999, *Adorned: Traditional Jewellery and Body Decoration from Australia and the Pacific*. Macleay Museum, University of Sydney.

Errington, S., 1998, *The Death of Authentic Primitive Art and other Tales of Progress*. University of California Press, Berkeley, Los Angeles, and London.

Festetics de Tolna, R., 1903, *Chez les Cannibales: Huit Ans de Croisiere dans l'Ocean Pacifique a Bord du Yacht "Le Tolna"*. Librairie Plon, Paris.

Finsch, O., 1914, *Südseearbeiten*. Friederichsen & Co., Hamburg.

Firth, R., 1992, 'Art and anthropology'. In J. Coote and A. Shelton (eds), *Anthropology, Art and Aesthetics*: 15–39. Clarendon Press, Oxford.

Forge, A., 1973, 'Style and meaning in Sepik art'. In A. Forge (ed.), *Primitive Art and Society*: 169–92. Oxford University Press, London and New York.

Fox, C.E., 1924, *The Threshold of the Pacific: An Account of the Social Organisation, Magic and Religion of the People of San Cristoval in the Solomon Islands*. Kegan Paul, London.

Frizzi, E. (ed.), 1914, 'Ein beitrag sur ethnologie von Bougainvilleund Buka mit spezieller berücksichtigung der Nasoi', *Baessler-Archiv: Beiträge zur Völkurunde* 6.

Geerts, P., 1970, *'Are'Are Dictionary*, Pacific Linguistics Series C, No. 14. Australian National University, Canberra.

Gell, A., 1998, *Art and Agency: An Anthropological Theory*. Oxford University Press, Oxford.

Graeber, D., 1996, 'Beads and money: notes toward a theory of wealth and power', *American Ethnologist* 23:4–14.

Guppy, H.B., 1887, *The Solomon Islands and Their Natives*. Swan Sonnenschein, Lowey, London.

Hammerton, J.A., 1934, *Peoples of All Nations*. The Amalgamated Press, London.

Heermann, I. and Menter U., 1990, *Schmuck der Südsee, Ornament und Symbol: Objekte aus dem Linden-Museum, Stuttgart*. Prestel-Verlag, München.

Henderson, C.P. and Hancock, I.R., 1988, *A Guide to the Useful Plants of Solomon Islands*. Ministry of Agriculture and Lands, Honiara.

Herr, R.A. (ed.), 1978, *A Solomons Sojourn: J.E. Philp's Log of the Makira 1912–1913*. Tasmanian Historical Association, Hobart.

Hill, L., 1989, Traditional Porpoise Harvest in the Solomon Islands. A preliminary report from the University of Papua New Guinea, Port Moresby.

HMS *Renard* Log, 1873, Public Record Office, London. File Adm 53/10450.

Hogbin, H.I., 1937, 'The hill people of northeastern Guadalcanal', *Oceania* 8:62–89.

Hogbin, H.I., 1938, 'Social advancement in Guadalcanal, Solomon Islands', *Oceania* 8:289–305.

Hogbin, H.I., 1939, *Experiments in Civilization: The Effects of European Culture on a Native Community of the Solomon Islands*. Routledge, London.

Hogbin, H.I., 1945, *Peoples of the Southwest Pacific: A Book of Photographs and Introductory Text*. Asia Press, New York. (Photographs lack page or plate numbers.)

Hogbin, H.I., 1964, *A Guadalcanal Society: The Kaoka Speakers*. Holt, Rinehart and Winston, New York.

Holdsworth, D., 1977, *The Solomon Islands*. Land and People Series 5, Robert Brown and Associates, Port Moresby.

Hopkins, A.I., n.d., Autobiography of Fr. Arthur Hopkins. Transcription of typescript from Church of Melanesia Archives in Solomon Islands National Archives, Honiara (pagination altered by electronic transmission).

Hopkins, A.I., 1928, *In the Isles of King Solomon: An Account of Twenty-Five Years Spent amongst the Primitive Solomon Islanders*. Seeley, Service, London.

Hopkins, A.I., 1930, *From Heathen Boy to Christian Priest*. St Christopher Books, no. 33, Talbot Press (Society for Promoting Christian Knowledge), London.

Hviding, E., 1996, *Guardians of Marovo Lagoon: Practice, Place and Politics in Maritime Melanesia*. Pacific Islands Monographs Series, 14, University of Hawai'i Press, Honolulu.

Ivens, W.G., 1897, 'First experiences', *Southern Cross Log*, March: 4–7.

Ivens, W.G., 1902, 'Porpoise hunting', *Southern Cross Log,* July :22–3.

Ivens, W.G., 1918, *Dictionary and Grammar of the Languages of Sa'a and Ulawa, Solomon Islands*. Carnegie Institute, Washington, D.C.

Ivens, W.G., 1921, *Grammar and Vocabulary of the Lau Language, Solomon Islands*. Carnegie Institute, Washington, DC.

Ivens, W.G., 1927, *Melanesians of the South-east Solomon Islands*. Kegan Paul, London.

Ivens, W.G., 1929, *A Dictionary of the Language of Sa'a (Mala) and Ulawa, South-east Solomon Islands*. Oxford University Press and Melbourne University Press.

Ivens, W.G., 1930, *The Island Builders of the Pacific*. Seeley, Service, London.

Johnson, O., 1944, *Bride in the Solomons*. Houghton Mifflin, Boston.

Joyce, T.A., 1910, *Handbook to the Ethnographical Collections*. British Museum, London.

Keesing, R.M., 1983 [1978], *'Elota's Story: The Life and Times of a Solomon Islands Big Man*. Holt, Rinehart and Winston, New York and London.

Keesing, R.M., 1985, 'Killers, big men, and priests on Malaita: reflections on a Melanesian troika system', *Ethnology* 24:237–52.

Kupiainen, J., 2000, *Tradition, Trade and Woodcarving in Solomon Islands.* Transactions of the Finnish Anthropological Society 45, Finnish Anthropological Society, Helsinki, and Intervention Press, Højberg, Denmark.

Kwa'ioloa, M. and Burt, B., 1997, *Living Tradition: A Changing Life in Solomon Islands*. British Museum Press, London, and University of Hawai'i Press, Honolulu.

Kwa'ioloa, M. and Burt, B., 2001, *Na Masu'u kia 'i Kwara'ae: Tualaka 'i Solomon Islands fa'inia logo na Rū ne'e Bulao saena Fanoa kia kī.* *Our Forest of Kwara'ae: Our Life in Solomon Islands and the Things which Grow in our Home*. British Museum Press, London.

London, J., 1971, *The Cruise of the Snark*. Seafarer Books, London.

Luke, H., 1945, *From a South Seas Diary 1938–1942*. Nicholson & Watson, London.

Malaita Council, 1955, Council Minutes for 16–17 May. Solomon Islands National Archives, Honiara, file BSIP 12/I/34.

Man: The Solomon Islanders, n.d. Film, made probably in the 1970s, Japan.

Macintyre, M. (director), 1975, *Man Blong Custom*. Film, Tribal Eye series, BBC, London (in collaboration with David Attenborough).

Mead, S.M., 1973, *Material Culture and Art in the Star Harbour Region, Eastern Solomon Islands*. Ethnography Monograph 1, Royal Ontario Museum.

Melvin, J.D., 1977, *The Cruise of the Helena: A Labour-Recruiting Voyage to the Solomon Islands* (ed., P. Corris). The Hawthorn Press, Melbourne.

Meyer, A.B. and Parkinson, R., 1894, *Album von Papua-Typen: Neu Guinea und Bismark Archipel*. Stengel & Co., Dresden.

Meyer, A.B. and Parkinson, R., 1900, *Album von Papua-Typen: Neu Guinea und Bismark Archipel*, vol. 2. Stengel & Co., Dresden.

Montgomery, H.H., 1896, *The Light of Melanesia*. Society for Promoting Christian Knowledge, London.

Mytinger, C., 1943, *Headhunting in the Solomon Islands*. Macmillan, London.

Naitoro, J., 1993, The Politics of Development in 'Are'are, Malaita. M.A. thesis, University of Otago.

Naramana, R.B., 1987, 'Elements of culture in Hograno / Maringe, Santa Isabel', *'O'o, A Journal of Solomon Islands Studies* 1(3):41–57.

Neich, R. and Pereira, F., 2004, *Pacific Jewelry and Adornment*. University of Hawai'i Press, Honolulu.

Norden, H., 1927, *Byways of the Tropic Seas*. Macrae Smith, Philadelphia.

Not In Vain (*NIV*). Newsletter of the South Sea Evangelical Mission, from 1887. Gordon, NSW.

O'Hanlon, M., 1989, *Reading the Skin: Adornment, Display and Society among the Wahgi*. British Museum Publications, London.

O'Hanlon, M. and Welsch, R.L. (eds), 2000, *Hunting the Gatherers: Ethnographic Collectors, Agents and Agency in Melanesia, 1870s–1930s*. Berghahn Books, New York and Oxford.

Paravicini, E., 1931, *Reisen in den britischen Salomonen*. Verlag Huber, Frauenfeld and Leipzig.

Paravicini, E., 1940, 'Uber Kapkap und Kapkapahnlichen Schmuck von den Britischen Salomoninseln', *Ethnos* 5:148–64.

Parkinson, R., 1999, *Thirty Years in the South Seas: Land and People, Customs and Traditions in the Bismark Archipelago and on the German Solomon Islands.* Crawford House Publishing, Bathurst, and University of Sydney.

Penny, A., 1887, *Ten Years in Melanesia*. Wells, Gardner, Darton, London.

Phelps, S., 1976, *Art and Artefacts of the Pacific, Africa and the Americas: The James Hooper Collection*. Hutchinson, London.

Piko, G., 1976, 'Choiseul currency', *Journal of the Cultural Association of the Solomon Islands* 4:96–110.

Raucaz, S.M., 1928, *In the Savage Solomons: The Story of a Mission*. Society for the Propagation of the Faith [no place of publication].

Richards, R., 2003, 'Artefacts Copied for Indigenous Trade: Thoughts on Two Ceramic "Tridacna" Shell Rings from Solomon Islands'. Unpublished MS.

Robbins, J. and Akin, D., 1999, 'An introduction to Melanesian currencies'. In D. Akin and J. Robbins (eds), *Money and Modernity: State and Local Currencies in Melanesia*: 1–40. University of Pittsburgh Press, Pittsburgh.

Ross, H.M., 1973, *Baegu: Social and Ecological Organisation in Malaita, Solomon Islands*. Illinois Studies in Anthropology 8, University of Illinois Press, Urbana, Chicago and London.

Ross, K., 1981, 'Shell ornaments of Malaita: currency and ritual valuables in the central Solomons', *Expedition* 23:20–6.

Russell, T., 1972, 'A note on clamshell money of Simbo and Roviana from an unpublished manuscript of Professor A.M. Hocart', *Journal of the Solomon Islands Museum Association* 1:21–30.

Russell, T., 2003, *I Have the Honour to Be*. Memoir Club, Spennymore, Co. Durham.

Salisbury, E. A., 1922, 'A Napoleon of the Solomons', *Asia: The American magazine on the Orient* 22(9): 707–20.

Salisbury, E. A., 1928, *Gow the Killer* (film, 2006 DVD edition), Alpha Home Entertainment, Narberth, PA.

Scales, I., 2003, 'The Social Forest: Landowners, Development Conflict and the State in Solomon Islands'. Ph.D. thesis, Australian National University.

Schuster, C., 1974, 'Kapkaps with human figures from the Solomon Islands', *Acta Ethnographica* 13: 213–79.

Simons, G., 1977, 'A Kwara'ae spelling list'. Working paper for the Language Variation and Limits to Communication project, No.6. Summer Institute of Linguistics.

Somerville, B.T., 1897, 'Ethnographical notes in New Georgia, Solomon Islands, *Journal of the Royal Anthropological Institute* 25:357–453.

Sotheby's, 1978, *Auction catalogue, 29 June*. London.

Southern Cross Log (*SCL*). Newsletter of the Melanesian Mission, from 1901. London.

Takekawa, D., 'The method of dolphin hunting and the distribution of teeth and meat: dolphin hunting in the Solomon Islands 2'. In T. Akimichi (ed.), *Coastal Foragers in Transition*. Senri Ethnological Studies 42:67–80, National Museum of Ethnology, Osaka.

Tetehu, E., 2006, 'Some family treasures of Santa Isabel'. Conference paper for 'Art and History in the Solomon Islands: collections, owners, and narratives'. British Museum, London.

Vandercook, J.W., 1937, *Dark Islands*. Harper, New York and London.

Verguet, L., 1885, 'Arossi ou San-Cristoval et ses habitants', *Revue d'Ethnographie* 4:193–232.

Vigors, P.D., 1850, 'Private Journal of a Four Month's Cruise through some of the South Sea Islands, and New Zealand in HMS "Havannah"'. MS, University of Hawai'i Hamilton Library, Honolulu, microfilm 788.

Waite, D.B., 1987, *Artefacts from the Solomon Islands in the Julius L. Brenchley Collection*. British Museum Publications, London.

Waite, D.B., 1990, 'Mon canoes of the Western Solomon Islands'. In A. Hanson and L. Hanson (eds), *Art and Identity in Oceania*: 44–66. Crawford House Press, Bathurst.

Wawn, W.T., 1893, *The South Sea Islanders and the Queensland Labour Trade*. Swan, Sonnenschein, London.

Welsch, R.L. (ed.), 1998, *An American Anthropologist in Melanesia: A.B. Lewis and the Joseph N. Field South Pacific Expedition 1909–1913*. University of Hawai'i Press, Honolulu.

Welsch, R.L., 2002, 'Changing themes in the study of Pacific art. Introduction'. In A. Herle, N. Stanley, K. Stevenson and R. Welsch (eds), *Pacific Art: Persistence, Change and Meaning*: 1–12. Crawford House, Adelaide.

White, G., 1991, *Identity Through History: Living Stories in a Solomon Islands Society*. Cambridge University Press.

Williamson, R.W., 1914, *The Ways of the South Sea Savage: A Record of Travel and Observation amongst the Savages of the Solomon Islands & Primitive Coast & Mountain Peoples of New Guinea*. Seely, Service, London.

Wilson, C., 1895, 'Old scenes viewed through new glasses: Bishop Wilson's journal of his first voyage in the Melanesian islands, 1894'. Serialised in *Southern Cross Log* 1894–6.

Wilson, C., 1932, *The Wake of the Southern Cross: Work and Adventures in the South Seas*. John Murray, London.

Wolf, E.R., *Europe and the People without History*. University of California Press, Berkeley.

Wood, C.F., 1875, *A Yachting Cruise in the South Seas*. Henry S. King, London.

Woodford, C.M., 1890, *A Naturalist Among the Head-hunters: Being an Account of Three Visits to the Solomon Islands in the Years 1886, 1887, and 1888*. George Philip & Sons, London.

Woodford, C.M., 1897, *Report on the British Solomon Islands*. HMSO, London.

Woodford, C.M., 1905, 'Further note on funerary ornaments from the Solomon Islands'. *Man* 5:38–9.

Woodford, C.M., 1908a, 'Notes on the manufacture of Malaita shell bead money of the Solomon Group', *Man* 43:81–4.

Woodford, C.M., 1908b, 'Note on stone-headed clubs from Malaita, Solomon Islands', *Man* 91:165–6.

Woodford, C.M., 1922, 'The Solomon Islands'. In W.H.R. Rivers (ed.), *Essays on the Depopulation of Melanesia*: 69–77. Cambridge University Press, Cambridge.

Woodford, C.M., 1926, 'Notes on the Solomon Islands', *Geographical Journal* (NS) 68(1):481–7.

Woodhead, L. and Maranda, P., 1987, *The Lau of Malaita*. Film, Disappearing World series, Granada Television, London.

Young, F.H., 1925, *Pearls from the Pacific*. Marshall Bros., London.

Zemp, H., 1995, *Écoute le Bambou qui Pleure: Récits de Quatre Musiciens 'Are'are, Îles Salomon*. Éditions Gallimard, Paris.

Photographic sources

Akin, David. Photographs taken during his research in Malaita, in his possession. Videos from the 1990s showing the making, wearing and presentation of ornaments and money are held by the Geisel Library Special Collections, at the University of California at San Diego (Akin 1995–7).

Asaeda, Toshio. Photographs taken on the 1933 Templeton Crocker Scientific Expedition to the South Pacific, for the American Museum of Natural History, New York, on the yacht *Zaca*. Includes Langalanga and Tae on Malaita. Original prints in the National Museum of Ethnology, Osaka.

Attenborough, David. Photographs taken in 1973 during filming of *Man Blong Custom* (McIntyre 1975) on Guadalcanal and Langalanga. Photographs in his possession.

Beattie, John Watt. Photographs taken in 1906 on a tour of the Melanesian Mission ship *Southern Cross* from Norfolk Island to Vanuatu and the Solomon Islands. A collection of about 600 original prints (formerly belonging to the Melanesian Mission in Britain) and copies of many more (from the Edge-Partington collection) in the British Museum Africa, Oceania and Americas Dept. pictorial collection. Original negatives are in the Auckland Institute and Museum. The whole collection is listed in Beattie's (undated) catalogue.

Brown, Terry (Bishop of Malaita until retirement in 2008). Photographs taken in the course of his work, in his possession.

Burt, Ben. Photographs taken during research in Malaita and Honiara from 1979 onwards. In his possession, with copies in the British Museum Africa, Oceania and Americas Dept. pictorial collection.

Brodziak, Adolphus Meyer. Trader and publisher of postcards in Suva, Fiji from about 1900, using photographs from various unacknowledged sources.

Dufty, F. A. Owner of a photographic studio in Fiji from the 1870s. Some of their prints of Solomon Islanders in Fiji, dated 1879, are in the Sir Benjamin Stone collection, Birmingham City Library.

Denham collection. Paintings by J. Glen Wilson at Makira Bay, 1854. Copy photos are in the British Museum Africa, Oceania and Americas Dept. pictorial collection.

Edge-Partington, Thomas. More than 700 photographs, mainly of western Solomons and Malaita, in six albums plus loose prints and stereos, dating to the 1910s and before. They include photographs by himself, Beattie, Rose and others. Digital copies are in the British Museum Africa, Oceania and Americas Dept. pictorial collection, originals are in possession of his heirs.

Francis, Revd David Lloyd. Over 400 photographs taken between 1926 and 1937 during service with the Melanesian Mission in Santa Cruz, Ugi, Malaita, New Britain and Vanuatu. Original prints are in British Museum Africa, Oceania and Americas Dept. pictorial collection.

Fulbright, Tim. Photographs taken in Baelelea in 1987, in his possession.

Hogbin, Ian. Photographs of To'abaita in Mitchell Library (State Library of New South Wales) Sydney.

Johnson, Martin. Photographs taken in 1917 on a tour of the Pacific Islands, including Malaita and other islands in the Solomons. Some are published by Osa Johnson (1944); a set of prints are held by the Martin and Osa Johnson Safari Museum, Chanute, Kansas.

Laka, Levi. Photographs taken for UNESCO at the Kwara'ae Chiefs' meeting of 1976. Negatives are in the National Museum of Solomon Islands (UNESCO 25/L. Laka/Aimela/11 Feb. 1976).

Moore, Clive. Photographs taken in 2008 during Independence celebrations in Honiara.

Paravicini, Eugen. Photographs taken on a visit to Solomon Islands in 1928–29, including Malaita. Held by the Museum der Kulture, Basel.

Rose, George. A set of photographs taken in 1907 on a tour of Solomon Islands on the ship *Makambo*, including a visit to the northwest coast of Malaita apparently on a recruiting voyage, which he published in his series *The Rose Stereographs*. Copies (from the Edge-Partington collection) are in the British Museum Africa, Oceania and Americas Dept. pictorial collection (Oc,CA47.1 to 128).

Royalist, HMS. Photographs taken during a cruise in Solomon Islands in the early 1890s. From an album in the Fiji Museum . Copy photos are in the British Museum Africa, Oceania and Americas Dept. pictorial collection.

Russell, Thomas. Twenty photographs taken by himself and others during service with the BSIP administration on Malaita, mainly 1949–50. Copies are in the British Museum Africa, Oceania and Americas Dept. pictorial collection.

Salisbury, Edward. Photographs and film made on a cruise through Polynesia and Melanesia in 1921, published in Salisbury 1922 and 1928. Some photos are held (unattributed) by the Corbis photo agency.

South Sea Evangelical Mission (SSEM). Photographs taken from the 1900s onwards by members of the mission, in early years particularly by Northcote Deck, on Malaita and other islands of the Solomons. Copies of 116 photos in the British Museum Africa, Oceania and Americas Dept. pictorial collection.

Wilson, Alexander 'Spearline'. Thirty-six photographs from various sources acquired while BSIP Commissioner of Lands, from about 1927 to 1946, mostly Tulagi and Guadalcanal. Copies in the British Museum Africa, Oceania and Americas Dept. pictorial collection, from prints in possession of his daughter Andrea Bannatyne.

Index